# FOUR SCORES AND SEVEN REELS AGO

## The U.S. Presidency through Hollywood Films

### Dale Sherman

APPLAUSE
THEATRE & CINEMA BOOKS
Essex, Connecticut

Published by Applause Theatre & Cinema Books
An imprint of Globe Pequot, the trade division of
The Rowman & Littlefield Publishing Group, Inc.
4501 Forbes Boulevard, Suite 200, Lanham, Maryland 20706
www.rowman.com

Distributed by NATIONAL BOOK NETWORK

British Library Cataloguing in Publication Information Available

**Library of Congress Cataloging-in-Publication Data Available**

ISBN 978-1-4930-6393-2 (cloth: alk. paper)
ISBN 978-1-4930-6394-9 (electronic)

♾™ The paper used in this publication meets the minimum requirements
of American National Standard for Information Sciences—Permanence of
Paper for Printed Library Materials, ANSI/NISO Z39.48-1992.

To Jill Sherman, who is always pushing me forward

I'd like to thank Ashleigh Cooke, Chris Chappell, Laurel Meyers,
and Niki Guinan for the help given me here,
as well as two individuals who helped with early editing,
Brian Schnau and Mike DeGeorge.

# CONTENTS

# INTRODUCTION

Arthur Bryon, who played the President, as we'd like to believe all our Presidents play their role—with dignity, and force, and charm of personality.

—Mayme Ober Peak, review of *The President Vanishes*,
*Boston Globe*, November 16, 1934

**G**od, we need Henry Fonda to guide us.

Maybe not the man as he was in real life. No, we need the Henry Fonda whom we saw on the silver screen. The one who stands tall against the bureaucratic captain in *Mister Roberts* (1955) to help those under him, who defiantly votes against the other jurors in *Twelve Angry Men* (1957) for the sake of justice, and who soliloquizes the common man in *The Grapes of Wrath* (1940). Of course, as an actor, he didn't always play that type; he is sinister in one of his few villainous roles as Frank in *Once upon a Time in the West* (1968), confused and lost in *The Wrong Man* (1956), and charmingly innocent and goofy in the 1941 comedy *The Lady Eve*. Nevertheless, when you saw Fonda in a role, he often played someone you want in your corner to defend your life and liberties, someone who seems to listen before speaking and then converses in a quiet, forceful manner, always thinking, with little patience for fools.

Henry Fonda's presidential image was solidified early on with his star role as Abraham Lincoln in the 1939 John Ford film *Young Mr. Lincoln*. Portraying Lincoln in his lawyer days, Fonda manages to display the winning nature of the man who would eventually become the sixteenth president of the United States. In portraying those years in Lincoln's life, *Young Mr. Lincoln* tells somewhat exaggerated stories about Lincoln's life based on events that have been common parts of his biography, such as a supposed romance with a woman named Ann Rutledge in New Salem, Illinois, when Lincoln was a young man and the *Farmer's Almanac* trial from his law days. There are nuggets of truth in those tales, albeit stretched by Hollywood for better storytelling, as with *Young Mr. Lincoln*, explained in chapter 4, and with other films dealing with other presidents described in the pages ahead.

Fonda would build on our trust in his leadership in *Fail Safe* (1964), where he plays a president who hopes to prevent World War III through desperate measures after Moscow is accidentally bombed by American planes. It's an astonishing gambit supported through the guidance of strong dialogue by Walter Bernstein (based on the novel of the same name by Eugene Burdick and Harvey Wheeler) and direction by Sidney Lumet, but it is through the care that Fonda conveys that dialogue that convinces the viewers of his actions. Fonda's role as president in *Fail Safe* is quite constrained; he spends nearly the whole movie sitting in a bare room with a Russian interpreter (played by Larry Hagman in an early role) and talking on phones. Yet, in close-up and hearing only his end of a conversation, we get a president who is personable, calm even when frustrated, and able to think on his feet. By the time Fonda commits to dropping a bomb on New York City, as insane as that resolution is, we believe him to be presidential, and we believe him to be right—at least for the two hours we're in the darkened theater.

Fonda didn't play many other presidents in his career, but he would have additional run-ins with them in other films. The same year as *Fail Safe* saw him as a candidate running for the office in the drama *The Best Man*, where his character deals with the ugly side of campaigning and with an unscrupulous former president who is determined to treat those running as chess pieces. Two years earlier, he had played a man under scrutiny after the president nominates him to be secretary of state in the film *Advise and Consent*. In both films, Fonda's character may have skeletons in his closet, but we believe he has integrity and really does want to do what is best for the country, even if things don't work out as planned. Both films also give us hints of presidents using their powers for their own goals—this is especially true in *The Best Man*, as is shown later—rather than what is best for the country, a somewhat rare theme in Hollywood movies but one that becomes more common as we move into the later twentieth century.

By the time of one of his last film roles, again as the president in the disaster film *Meteor* (1979), Fonda appears not only because producers of disaster movies used popular stars in small roles to help bring in moviegoers but also because he's cinematic shorthand. If you want a president we'll believe when he says that a meteor is coming and we're going to have to trust the Russians to destroy it with nuclear warheads, then get Fonda. He was Abe Lincoln, after all, and negotiates with the Russians in *Fail Safe*. The audience will accept the cornball premise from him because he conveys what we expect from a president, even a fictional one.

Though Fonda's approach to the presidency is common in movie-making, he was certainly not the first. In nearly 250 years of American history, the country has seen a wide variety of presidents in office, from those remembered around the world as excellent leaders to those examples of what can go wrong in such a role. Further, with shifting worldviews, it isn't unusual to find that our expectations of what a president should be or do has evolved, with some once-glorified presidents now seen as detrimental to our country's growth and others who were once pigeonholed as not very good being given better evaluations in the years since. This change in our perspective of presidents can be seen in the movies as well as in how we expect a president to behave in office.

With the arrival of cinema in the United States, there was an immediate and natural interest in showing presidents in movies, starting with staged footage of William McKinley in September 1896 being told of his nomination for the presidency. Documentary film of presidents was soon overtaken by narrative depictions of them, particularly George Washington and Abraham Lincoln, who sometimes were repeatedly played by the same actors across different films. Hollywood then branched out from Washington and Lincoln, depicting other presidents in their most colorful moments, such as Teddy Roosevelt in Cuba with

Henry Fonda, one of the Founding Fathers of Film Presidents, shown keeping the country at ease in the 1979 disaster film *Meteor*. *Original press photo by James Globus, author's collection, © 1979 by American International Pictures.*

the Rough Riders and Andrew Jackson during the War of 1812. The year 1942 would see the first well-known fictional depiction of a president still in office, with Captain Jack Young as President Franklin D. Roosevelt in *Yankee Doodle Dandy*. It was a feat some deemed vulgar for such an important role in the government. Nevertheless, it would lead to many other such interpretations in the years following, with some more flattering than others.

But Hollywood is a dream machine, and with that comes the need to create presidents out of whole cloth. One of the first fictional presidents in movie history came in 1913's *The Sons of a Soldier* (covered in chapter 10), but the journey truly began in the early 1930s, with stories of fictional presidents dealing with situations that no sitting president has faced—or at least as far as we know. Since then, we've seen alien invasions, kidnapped presidents, presidents in action sequences, kidnapped vice presidents, conspiracy theories, kidnapped presidential families, supernatural events, and at least one kidnapped presidential analyst (see chapter 5), among the many comedies and dramas that put a president in difficult situations for our amusement and sometimes reflection. How presidents follow the better angels or their own demons, as well as society's perceptions of the presidency and perhaps even ourselves, are built into the plots of these films.

In the following pages, my focus is on our film presidents—historical and fictional, good and bad—and the many ways Hollywood has portrayed the office over the years. Surprisingly, nearly every president has been depicted on film in some form and in many cases as a prominent character. True, we're never going to see a marathon of Grover Cleveland pictures, but films featuring such presidents as Lincoln and Kennedy, to name two, are easily recalled by many. I delve into the biographies of real historical leaders, the various genres that have featured fictional presidents, and how and why portrayals have changed over time.

Although there are occasional glimpses into pivotal television productions that shaped our expectations for future movies—such as *Eleanor and Franklin* (1976) and *The Missiles of October* (1974)—the focus of *Four Scores and Seven Reels Ago* is theatrical films. While readers hoping for a discussion about Space-Lincoln from "The Savage Curtain" episode of *Star Trek* will be disappointed, this avoids long discussions about a series like *The West Wing*, which has already produced various books about its role in politics and television in the years since it aired and does not need to be revisited here.

I also examine "fly on the wall" docudramas, such as *The Missiles of October* and its theatrical equivalent, *Thirteen Days* (2000), as they are a variation on the age-old historical film. However, I do not cover conventional documentaries—those featuring a variety of experts describing actions and motives to an off-screen interviewer. This includes those documentaries that try to have it both ways by breaking up such "talking head" segments with reenactments by actors trying to look serious while prancing around in cheap fancy dress in old buildings or a forest in order to excite viewers with the prospect of actual drama unfolding.

**Jane Alexander as Eleanor and Edward Herrmann as Franklin in the TV mini-series *Eleanor and Franklin* (1976). It would be the start of many appearances by Herrmann as FDR over the years. *Official press still, author's collection, © 1976 by American Broadcasting Company.***

Where do we draw the line on including presidential appearances? Should movies be considered where a president appears only briefly, or should the list be limited to those where the president propels the plot in some fashion? For example, lists of filmic depictions of Franklin Delano Roosevelt sometimes include *This Is the Army*, a 1943 movie that features future president Ronald Reagan but in which Jack Young as FDR appears for only a few seconds, about fifty feet away from the camera, waving high up on a balcony. While it may be of interest for completists, Young's appearance has no ramifications for the plot and therefore warrants only a brief mention in the chapter on FDR. Conversely, John Carradine's one scene as Abe Lincoln in the 1938 film *Of Human Heart*, with Henry Fonda's old roommate Jimmy Stewart, may be brief, but his performance as Lincoln is pivotal to the plot. Thus, I discuss it in more detail in chapter 4.

At the beginning of this introduction is a quote from Mayme Ober Peak's review of Arthur Bryon's performance as one of the first fictional American presidents in movie history, in *The President Vanishes* (1934). Peak speaks of Bryon handling the role perfectly, with "[d]ignity, and force, and charm of personality," and it seems a natural description of the president of the United States or any country's leader. We want someone who can calm us through the bad times and convince us of our path toward the future—like how Henry Fonda does so many times in the movies.

Yet before the journey to fictional accounts of presidents, we must first turn our attention to where it all began: in 1788 with the election of George Washington as the first president of the United States. His legacy would set up all the presidencies to follow, including, oddly enough, our perception that such a role requires "dignity, and force, and charm of personality."

# 1

# THE FOUNDING FATHERS AND THE BIRTH OF THE MACGUFFIN PRESIDENT

And when you're gone, who remembers your name?
Who keeps your flame? Who tells your story?

—"Who Lives, Who Dies, Who Tells Your Story"
from the musical *Hamilton*

One of the most recent and popular depictions of the first president of the United States, George Washington, came not in the movie theaters but from the stage in the Broadway musical *Hamilton*, created by Lin-Manuel Miranda. Premiering in 2015, *Hamilton* depicts the life of Alexander Hamilton, a Founding Father of America who helped form the US government and create the economic structure of the country, on which it still relies. In revisualizing the history through the lens of modern music, alongside more traditional musical numbers, and using people of color for the roles to convey the complex diversity of America, *Hamilton* rekindled interest in the Founding Fathers of the country for another generation.

The musical was professionally filmed in 2016, and while a theatrical release of that footage was planned for October 2021, the movie was released through the streaming channel Disney+ on July 3, 2020, after the start of the COVID-19 pandemic that year. Christopher Jackson originated the role of George Washington in *Hamilton* on Broadway and appears as such in the film, while two other Founding Fathers are also represented: Thomas Jefferson (Daveed Diggs) and James Madison (Okieriete Onaodowan). In keeping with the reinterpretation, all three are played by people of color rather than the traditional White faces we commonly see. Miranda and company go a step further with the interpretation of Jefferson and Madison: Jefferson is portrayed as flashy in both clothing and personality as well as flippant with others to the point of rudeness; Madison, who rarely speaks on his own, is portrayed as a manservant to Jefferson. At the time, it was noted that Jefferson and Madison are based on the personas established for Morris Day and Jerome Benton in *Purple Rain* (1984), who spend that film being antagonistic to "The Kid" (Prince) until the end, when they realize he is the better man, which also is reflected in *Hamilton*.

Even with these changes, we are never far from our preconceived notions of these men. Jefferson really was considered a man of style and certainly an extraordinary speaker and writer—maybe not to the point of being able to spout rapid-fire dialogue like in *Hamilton*, but you believe he could be the one to write the Declaration of Independence and become president. Madison is referenced in act 1 for his work on the

**Christopher Jackson as fatherly figure and first US president George Washington, with Lin-Manuel Miranda as Alexander Hamilton looking on, from the filmed version of the Broadway musical *Hamilton* (2016). *Courtesy of PhotoFest.***

Federalist Papers, writing a third of the essays supporting the Constitution, and even his eventual repositioning as a minion for Jefferson has its roots in historical popular opinion. Most importantly is Washington, whom Miranda writes as how he will be eternally depicted: tall and wise. He listens, guides, and tempers all those around him, especially our hero. He appears as a father figure to Hamilton, even calling him "son," and as Hamilton is the audience surrogate, we are Washington's family, as well. Once Washington disappears from the story, Hamilton and the others are set adrift, with scandal and political pressure pulling Hamilton toward his ultimate demise. Further, most of the historical facts about the agreements and disagreements between these men presented in the musical are accurate for two reasons: because one cannot stray too far from the history and because their majestic story is intertwined with the birth of a nation.

It is that very topic that sets these individuals apart. There were many "founding fathers," but the prime founders remembered today are those who not only appear on our money but also who became presidents. Beyond Hamilton, on the ten-dollar bill, and Benjamin Franklin, on the one-hundred-dollar bill, our first five presidents, George Washington, John Adams, Thomas Jefferson, James Madison, and James Monroe, are all named as the Founding Fathers of the United States. Their placement isn't simply because they happened to be "in the room where it happened" (to paraphrase from the musical) but because they created work that guided the country during its birth and for several years after. Because of this, we tend to know more about these presidents than many who came after, except for those who were in office in the last few years or at times of great conflict, such as Abraham Lincoln, Franklin Delano Roosevelt, John F. Kennedy, and Richard Nixon; most likely because that's what is emphasized in school: the founding, the Civil War, World War II, and then whatever is happening in our current culture. It's what resonates with us as a nation and people.

Thus, we know George Washington as the first commander in chief, the first president of the United States, and the man who helped steer us toward the Constitution and the Bill of Rights. Beyond these tidbits, there are the famous images of the man: cloaked in his uniform, leading his men as he stands in the boat while crossing the Delaware River, striding by on horseback in full uniform with his men in the cold at

Valley Forge, and patiently sitting for the unfinished portrait by Gilbert Stuart (which would become the image used on the one-dollar bill—again, money leads to history). He's not alone; it is the same with all the Founding Fathers. And when we "tell your stories," as *Hamilton* would put it, Hollywood is going to concentrate on what we already know. But sometimes to understand their stories, there is more that can be told.

George Washington was born in Westmoreland County, Virginia, on February 22, 1732. He had a limited education, and by the age of fifteen, he began a career as a surveyor, scouting out land in the wilderness of western Virginia. Wishing to follow the path of his stepbrother Lawrence and because he wanted to see more of the frontier along the Ohio Valley, he joined the Virginia militia and was soon fighting alongside the British against the French in the French and Indian War (1754–1763). His early military career was not completely prosperous; he tended to dismiss his soldiers as inept and lazy (emphasized in the correspondences heard in the musical *1776*) and to blame them for mistakes that he should have acknowledged as of his own making. His early campaigns were known for either weak victories or retreats, such as a 1754 campaign at Fort Necessity, a small fort Washington had built, that ended in surrender and with Washington signing a document in French (which he couldn't read) acknowledging the "assassination" of a French officer. However, experience guided his hand, and by the time of the Battle of Monongahela in 1755, he was commended for his composure even while suffering from dysentery in staging a retreat that saved many lives after the commanding officer, General Edward Braddock, was killed trying to reach and capture Fort Duquesne. Washington had two horses shot out from under him in the battle, with multiple bullet holes in his clothing, but managed to escape without injury.

Soon after, Washington returned to Virginia, married widow Martha Dandridge Custis, and became a planter and a purchaser of land as well as a delegate in the First Continental Congress. He quickly gained a reputation as a man who didn't say much (it's been hinted in more than one biography that this tendency came more out of growing issues with his dentures than with wishing to stay silent), but when he did speak, he demonstrated his knowledge, experience, and cooperative spirit. Joining the consensus that the colonists needed to break away from Britain over their trampling of rights, Washington found himself elected commander in chief of the newborn country's defenses in 1775. He was a perfect fit: a southerner who held northern political values and a politician with military experience.

Building the military was not easy, and the first couple years of the Revolutionary War were depressing for the struggling new country. Contrary to most recollections and rarely mentioned in the movies, Washington was seen by some as an inept leader, and there were talks and schemes to replace him in the early years of the war. Yet time was of importance, and Washington's attitude with his men slowly evolved after months of being in the fields with them; he gained their confidence, and they, his. Support within and outside the army continued to grow, and many saw (and still see) the tides of war turning with Washington's capture of Hessian troops (German soldiers hired by the British to fight the Americans) during Christmas 1776 and additional wins the following week in New Jersey. After the French agreed to join in the fight on the side of the Americans, the war increasingly weighed in the colonists' favor, and in October 1781, the British surrendered, with Washington a national hero.

As it took time for the British to leave, it would be another two years before Washington would attempt to return to his planter life. That didn't last long; the newfound government was quickly divided by two factions: those who wanted an indivisible nation under a strong central government, supported by such men as Alexander Hamilton and John Adams of the Federalist Party, and those who saw it as a confederacy of states held together by a common-cause government, like Thomas Jefferson and James Madison, two prominent creators of the Democratic-Republican Party. (As one can see, we hardly have moved far from the argument over state and federal rights 250 years later.) The one thread that held those two separate viewpoints together, and perhaps still to this day, was the president's ability to unite people from the various sides of politics. No doubt, Washington's experience in leading the country in the war transcended his military ability to one of political wisdom, at least in the eyes of the public (and hence Congress). His reluctance for the role of president further endeared him as a safe choice, as fears of setting up a monarchy were very real and eventually, if briefly, touched upon in a few feature films listed here, such as *Alexander Hamilton* (1931). He was elected on February 4, 1789, and served two terms until March 1797, when John Adams, Washington's vice president, was elected the second president of the United States.

George Washington died two years after leaving office, on December 14, 1799. There have been dozens of presidents since then, but Washington defined our core concepts of the role. His stance as the commander in chief of the military has been carried over to the presidents who have come after him. His definition of the three branches of the government, with set walls between them, may at times face shaky moments, but they continue to be a political bedrock for the United States. Having suffered from smallpox while younger (in his only trip overseas), Washington also promoted smallpox inoculations in 1777, going against the concerns of the Continental Congress and some of the public who feared the spread of the disease and creating the first mass military inoculation in American history. Of course, not all his hopes for the nation have come true: For example, in his farewell speech, he urged the country to avoid a two-party system, as it tends to turn politics into an "us versus them" dynamic that harms the people's progress. He also felt that the role of president was one that may be needed only for a time but eventually could be dismissed when the people as a collective begin ruling, which certainly hasn't been the case. His freeing of those enslaved on his plantation after his death to entice others to do the same was also dismissed as the quirks of an old man.

Yet if we want to learn these things about Washington or more, we won't find it at the movie theater. The closest we've ever come to a full filmic narrative that concentrates solely on Washington is in television, most notably the two CBS miniseries about the first president done between 1984 and 1986 and starring Barry Bostwick (who would go on to play a parody of Franklin D. Roosevelt in a movie covered in chapter 7) as Washington and Patty Duke Astin as Martha Washington. The original three-part miniseries, simply titled *George Washington* and based on a book by James Thomas Flexner, covers Washington's life, from his beginnings as a surveyor up through the end of the Revolutionary War and his return to Mount Vernon. The second miniseries, *George Washington II: The Forging of a Nation*, ran for two episodes and covers his presidential life. With those episodes came the narratives listed previously as well as depictions of his personal life that typically get glossed over, including his illnesses that set him back, such as a recurring tumor on his left thigh that had to be excised twice while he was in office. Of course, some scenes were obviously done to add Washington to the narrative of some events—there is no doubt Washington did not get Jefferson and Hamilton into a boat to convince them to agree to the location of the new capital, for example. Even so, the two series cover his life and career with a good amount of accuracy.

The same can nearly be said for the second president of the United States, John Adams (1735–1826). While there is very little in theatrical films about Adams, there are two television miniseries with plenty of personal history about the man: the 1976 PBS thirteen-part miniseries *The Adams Chronicles*, with George Grizzard as John Adams and Mark Winkworth as John Quincy Adams, and the HBO seven-part miniseries *John Adams*, with Paul Giamatti (who won an Emmy Award for Outstanding Lead Actor in a Miniseries or Movie) as John Adams, Laura Linney (who later appears in the FDR film *Hyde Park on Hudson*; see chapter 7 for details) as Abigail Adams, and Ebon Moss-Bachrach as John Quincy Adams. But besides the film *1776*, when Adams does appear, it's to stand around looking a bit cross.

Adams was born in Braintree, Massachusetts, on October 30, 1735. He began Harvard at the age of sixteen and was a practicing attorney by the age of twenty-three. In 1764, he married Abigail Smith, and they had five children. Their oldest, John Quincy Adams, would become the sixth president of the United States (covered more in chapter 3). John and his older cousin Samuel Adams opposed the oppressive British taxation acts at the time. Of the two, Samuel Adams had the more exciting history—and thus more films, such as *Johnny Tremain* (1957) and the three-part miniseries *Sons of Liberty* that aired in 2015 on the History Channel. Meanwhile, John Adams opposed the tyranny of the king through the political process, which makes for solid government but less-than-thrilling cinema.

Adams believed strongly in a sense of justice that sometimes put him at odds with his fellow colonists, including defending a British captain and eight of his men who shot and killed five civilians during the Boston Massacre of 1770. His defense would acquit the officer and six soldiers, while the other two were convicted of the lower charge of manslaughter. The results would also rub some of his fellow Americans the wrong way, including Samuel Adams, who would campaign against his cousin when

John was nominated for the presidency. Many others, however, respected his ability to fight for the soldiers' rights, and he was eventually selected as a delegate for Massachusetts to the Continental Congress in 1774. That would lead directly to his involvement in breaking away from Britain and helping to create the Declaration of Independence as part of the Committee of Five, which included Thomas Jefferson, Benjamin Franklin, Roger Sherman, and Robert Livingston.

Adams was well known for being forthright and sincere in his quest to better what became the United States, although historians are quick to point out that he was not as disliked at the time as he would reflect on later in life and as is commonly portrayed in the media. He could be impatient watching the slow wheels of Congress move and was vocal about it, which didn't help his push for certain aspirations. The bigger problem, reported in all biographies about Adams, was that he appeared to be one step behind those around him, and he knew it. His frustration we see in the *John Adams* miniseries and *1776* are very much spot on; certainly, he knew that for the better of the country he loved, others had to be pushed in front of him. It was Adams who nominated Washington to be commander in chief of the Colonial Army because he knew Washington would be the perfect choice. He recommended Jefferson to be the writer of the Declaration of Independence because he knew Jefferson was a better writer and had a calmer relationship with his fellow delegates than he did. He went to France to set up a treaty for support of America in the battle against Britain and later to Britain for a peace treaty after the war but was seen as secondary to Benjamin Franklin's success there.

This tendency to let these men have the glory worked against him, as others felt he could be pushed aside or ignored. When the time came to select the first president, there were no concerns of anyone winning but Washington; yet when it came to vice president, Adams barely squeaked by with less than half the votes cast. Washington rarely spoke with Adams while he was vice president, and when President Adams tried to entice Washington back into commanding the military in preparation against a possible war with France, Washington demanded Hamilton be his second, even though Adams saw Hamilton as thirsty for war for personal glory.

Adams served only one term, from 1797 through 1801, noting in a letter to his wife, Abigail, that Washington handed the office to him with the thought, "I am fairly out, and you fairly in! See which of us will be the happiest!" Forced to keep Washington's cabinet, Adams found himself at odds with their desires and treachery. The risk of France going to war against the country split Congress, with Jefferson seeing Adams as looking for war against the country he loved and Hamilton seeing Adams willing to weaken the country to avoid conflict. Adams also signed the Alien and Sedition Acts, which introduced the ability to screen immigrants from entering the country, and targeted the press if they wrote something malicious or false about the government. Jefferson saw this as sidestepping the Bill of Rights, even though Adams was not enthusiastic to sign the Alien and Sedition Acts but eventually agreed to. Adams, always the second in line, would find himself frequently tested and undermined by Hamilton, Jefferson, and members of the cabinet in private and in public while president. It had been enough. After being voted out by eight votes in the next election, Adams retired to his farm life and seldom spoke about political events occurring after his time in office. A disruption of his friendship with Jefferson was eventually healed several years later (the one-time friendship between Abigail and Jefferson never truly rekindled, however), and the two communicated by mail until their mutual passing on the same day, July 4, 1826.

Adams found himself stuck between two powerhouses when it came to the presidency: Washington and Jefferson. Oddly perhaps, Adams may have ended up being more fairly represented in the movies, even if Jefferson had the more well-documented life. Jefferson is remembered for writing the Declaration of Independence, being vice president to John Adams, his famed plantation Monticello, working to establish a separation between religion and state, founding the University of Virginia, and helping to establish a new national library when the Library of Congress was burned down during the War of 1812. Jefferson is also remembered for his ties to slavery and in particular Sally Hemings, but more on her in a bit.

Born April 13, 1743, Thomas Jefferson quickly embraced learning. He knew Latin and Greek by the age of fourteen and was an attorney at the age of twenty-four. In 1769, he was elected to the Virginia legislature, and in 1772, he married Martha Wayles Skelton, who would die ten years later. Known for his writing skills and (much like Washington) as a southerner who tended to side with northerners on certain political aspects, he was a natural to write the Declaration of Independence. However, soon after, he returned to Virginia to be closer to his ill wife and help stabilize the state legislature, feeling much more affiliation to Virginia than to the new country's government. He served as governor of Virginia between 1779 and 1781, before returning to Congress in 1783, and traveled to Europe in 1784 to help with trade treaties and later as a minister (ambassador) for the country in France. He returned to America in 1789 to become the secretary of state to Washington just as the French Revolution began.

Back in the United States, Jefferson soon butted heads with Alexander Hamilton, fearing Hamilton's methods would lead to a people dependent on a chosen few instead of the independence Jefferson had envisioned for the country. He also was disappointed with the refusal of America to help a fellow country in revolution when France found itself facing war with various other countries, especially as France had supported the colonists in the Revolutionary War. (Washington was convinced that because the treaty with France was with the monarchy, which no longer existed, America was not obligated to help when they were still struggling to establish their own footing in the world.) Jefferson left for a time but returned upon the announcement of the Jay Treaty in 1794, which stopped a pending war with Britain in exchange for a written contract with Britain that put the United States in opposition to France. The ultimate results of the Jay Treaty were positive for the United States, but at the time, it was heavily disliked by many and tarnished Washington's reputation. When Washington stepped down as president, there was an attempt to vote in Jefferson as the second president of the United States. As in the first election with Washington and Adams, when Jefferson came in second, he became vice president. He would go on to become the third president of the United States in 1801.

As president, Jefferson helped negotiate the Louisiana Purchase from France, effectively ending both Spanish and French expansion in the land that eventually became the United States. His time in office was relatively peaceful, leading to many wanting him for a third term. Instead, he supported James Madison in the next election and went back to Virginia and his beloved Monticello. A year later, the University of Virginia, which he founded, was opened. He passed away on July 4, 1826.

James Madison followed in Jefferson's footsteps, but his time in the Hollywood limelight is even less than Adams's and Jefferson's. Born in Port Conway, Virginia, on March 16, 1751, Madison was a tad younger than the other Founding Fathers and thus missed out on the Declaration of Independence, as he was working in the Virginia House of Delegates, where he got to know Thomas Jefferson. As a delegate, Madison sensed that the Articles of Confederation had weakened the federal government, creating havoc between the states and pulling the new country apart. Madison pursued a new convention to create a revised document, known as the Constitution, that he would help write and that gave a better balance of power between the states and the federal government. Madison would also write a third of the essays in the Federalist Papers in 1787 (the rest were written by Alexander Hamilton and John Jay), which helped promote the new Constitution. In 1789, he also proposed the Bill of Rights as amendments to the Constitution, which were quickly agreed upon with some changes in 1791.

Washington was taken by Madison and turned to his advice while president, including the suggestion of Thomas Jefferson for the role of secretary of state. When Jefferson took over as president, Madison became secretary of state and helped push for the Louisiana Purchase. In 1809, Madison became the fourth president of the United States just as attacks by both the British and the French on American commercial ships were increasing, leading to the War of 1812 with Britain. A hoped-for short-lived series of confrontations, with the British far too busy fighting the French, eventually led to the burning of Washington, DC, in 1814, including attempts to burn down the White House. In 1815, just as General Andrew Jackson defeated the British at the Battle of New Orleans, Madison negotiated an end to the war with the British.

Madison retired after his second term. Before doing so, he found himself ushering in the Second Bank of the United States, fulfilling the continuation of Hamilton's financial structure for the country after the First Bank had lapsed in 1811. He died June 28, 1836. Amazingly, for a man whom many consider an important member of the Founding Fathers, his wife, Dolley Madison, is probably better remembered today for her historical importance as a hostess of parties during the

Jefferson-Madison era of the White House (and being the name of a certain snack cakes company doesn't hurt, either).

After James Madison was James Monroe, a pick of both Jefferson and Madison to become the fifth president and carry on their ideals. Monroe was president from 1817 to 1825, doing so well in the Era of Good Feelings that he ran unopposed in the 1820 election. Born in 1758, he actively served in the Continental Army and thus was the only other Founding Father besides Washington to participate in fighting during the Revolutionary War. He would spend time as a Virginian delegate before eventually being sent to France in 1794 as an ambassador. He was relieved of that duty in 1796 after making promises to the revolutionists that Washington and others saw as divisive in the United States. Then, Jefferson sent him back in 1803, where he chanced upon the opportunity for the United States to buy the Louisiana Territory, allowing for Jefferson and Madison to work on the purchase.

During the War of 1812, Monroe became both the secretary of state and the secretary of war to Madison, helping to turn the country's early failures into promising victories before the war ended. This led to his popular stance with the public that transitioned to his winning the 1816 election for the presidency. He was the first president to actively campaign with the public, helping him win his second term, and he would negotiate the purchase of Florida from Spain in 1719. One of his most important actions, whether good or bad, occurred in his State of the Union speech on December 2, 1823, when Monroe put forth the warning that any attempts by European powers to interfere with the governments formed in the Americas (both North and South America) would be considered an act against the United States itself. This was put forth in a document cowritten by Monroe's secretary of state, John Quincy Adams, and became known as the Monroe Doctrine. By claiming this defense for all the Americas, the Monroe Doctrine hoped to steer other countries from any claim in the United States itself. In essence, protection of the area around the United States was protection for the United States proper.

The Monroe Doctrine has a convoluted history. With a tendency to cherry-pick when it is used, such as ignoring British colonization in the Falkland Islands and Honduras, many in Latin America were suspicious of its meaning. Later, Teddy Roosevelt and others adapted the policy from avoiding colonization to imposing US policy on governments in Latin America, which further eroded trust in the doctrine. The Monroe Doctrine has been interpreted in many ways by administrations over the years, but one of its goals did prove true: It made the United States a world power not to be ignored.

James Monroe died on July 4, 1831, the third president out of the first five to die on Independence Day. He may have been highly sought after at the time of his presidency and historically renowned, but on the silver screen he is little represented. Even the one film made about his time in office, 1939's *The Monroe Doctrine*, is simply a fifteen-minute short subject, with Monroe (Charles Waldron) and John Quincy Adams (Grant Mitchell) seen for only a third of its run time. The short deals with the creation of the doctrine and its subsequent use up through Theodore Roosevelt (Sidney Blackmer). In all, besides Roosevelt, Adams, and Monroe, there are five other presidents seen, including Washington (uncredited), James K. Polk (Edwin Stanley), Millard Fillmore (Millard Vincent), and Grover Cleveland (Stuart Holmes), while Thomas Jefferson gets a brief mention. With so much to cover, including a fictional romantic subplot featuring George Reeves (TV's Superman) and Nanette Fabray, the short zips through with no one character making much of an impression, certainly not Monroe.

James Monroe pops up in the 1936 film *Hearts Divided*, starring Marion Davies (*Janice Meredith*, mentioned later this chapter) as Elizabeth Patterson, the short-term wife of Jérôme Bonaparte (Dick Powell), brother of Napoleon Bonaparte (Claude Rains). Monroe (John Elliott) appears briefly with Thomas Jefferson (played by George Irving, who would later play Robert E. Lee in *Abe Lincoln in Illinois*), thanks to the story being set during the Louisiana Purchase, but because the film is about Bonaparte's romance with Patterson, it is easy to understand why Jefferson and Monroe are merely window dressing in the film.

Monroe and Jefferson get a bit more to do in *Alexander Hamilton* (1931), which stars George Arliss in the role he created in 1917 for the Broadway play, also written by him (shades of Lin-Manuel Miranda) with Mary P. Hamlin. Although the film kicks off with General George Washington's farewell speech to the troops in November 1783, most of the film takes place after Washington (Alan Mowbray) has become president in 1789. The film's main plot deals with Hamilton working to get the Funding Act of 1790 passed, which would have the federal government assume the debts of the states and create the Department of the Treasury. Mowbray as Washington, who reappears at the end of the film to announce the passing of the bill, acts well in the role but is heavily made up to appear older, possibly to compensate for the clear age of George Arliss, who was sixty-two at the time. While Washington appears fleetingly, more is seen of Jefferson (Montagu Love, who would go on to play Washington a few years later, as mentioned elsewhere in this book) and James Monroe (Morgan Wallace). As can be expected by anyone who followed the *Hamilton* musical nearly eighty-five years later, the main plot thread for Jefferson and Monroe is their somewhat devious blockage of Hamilton's assumption bill and securing the location of the nation's capital, which is resolved in the popular "The Room Where It Happens" of the musical and in a similar moment in the 1931 film.

James Madison makes his presence known, albeit as a secondary character, in one feature film: 1946's *Magnificent Doll*, starring Ginger Rogers as Dolley Madison, Burgess Meredith as James Madison, Grandon Rhodes as Thomas Jefferson, and David Niven as the most charmingly villainous Aaron Burr you'll ever see. As previously mentioned, Dolley was a famed First Lady and long remembered as a hostess for social functions at the White House. That may sound trivial on the face of it, but Dolley had a keen ability to bring opposing political sides together in a friendly atmosphere outside of Congress, allowing for greater bipartisanship to occur. Dolley performed the same function for the widowed Thomas Jefferson when he was president and James was his secretary of state, so for nearly sixteen years, Dolley was considered the great hostess of the nation's capital. She also was the first president's wife to sponsor charities publicly while her husband was in office and to choose the look of the White House, thus setting up an important ongoing role for the president's significant other to this day. She is probably best remembered for her actions during the War of 1812: As the British approached Washington, DC, with plans to burn down the White House and with the president out of the area, Dolley organized the removal of many valuable artifacts from the White House, including a portrait of George Washington by Gilbert Stuart and a copy of the Declaration of Independence.

This daring rescue of the painting opens *Magnificent Doll* and immediately falls into historical fantasy, with Dolley taking a pair of scissors in hand and climbing up to rescue the painting herself when it is well known that she left the work for others to do. Yet the film is a showcase for Ginger Rogers, so although Dolley's life story is full of amazing incidents that could make up a film, the Hollywood script exaggerates aspects of her life that were not entirely true. Most importantly, the film suggests a long-term affair between Aaron Burr and Dolley. Near the end of the movie, Burr blurts out to her his plans to destroy the government, leading to her emotional turmoil, but their real-life relationship was one of friendship and nothing more. Further, although Burr did have disagreements with the evolving American government and Jefferson and would eventually be tried for treason, there was no evidence that he wished to destroy the government and certainly nothing to suggest that Dolley saved him from a lynch mob, as seen in the final scene of the film.

It is nearly a third into *Magnificent Doll* before James Madison appears, but even so, it is one of the few films to feature the fourth president for any real length of time. Madison is presented as quiet and somewhat innocent in nature, waiting things out until he can win Dolley as well as become president. He is given only one showcase in the movie, where Dolley asks him his opinions on freedom, leading to a slightly awkward speech from Madison that is resolved with a proposal to Dolley for marriage. The diminutive Meredith has the proper look for a youngish Madison, and his calm performance is good and perhaps a bit startling to viewers used to the gruff Burgess Meredith of *Rocky* (1976) and many later slightly villainous roles. The only off-putting element is that Rogers and Meredith were similar in age, while there was a noticeable seventeen-year difference between Dolley and James.

Burgess Meredith as Madison is at least given a platform to express some ideals about America, which is not afforded Grandon Rhodes as Thomas Jefferson in the movie. While Jefferson is mentioned many, many times, he makes only three appearances in *Magnificent Doll*, and one, his tour of the White House after becoming president, has Rogers doing a voice-over throughout the scene. Besides, in the end, it's really more David Niven's movie, with Aaron Burr as a type of debonair antihero, than a movie about Jefferson, Madison, or even Dolley. That's more than can be said for the 1938 film *The Buccaneer*, which dramatizes part of the War of 1812 and begins in a similar fashion as *Magnificent*

**Burgess Meredith as President James Madison, stuck between Ginger Rogers as Dolley Madison and David Niven as the most charmingly villain- ous Aaron Burr you've ever seen, in *Magnificent Doll* (1946). *Courtesy of PhotoFest.***

*Doll*, with Dolley (Spring Byington) rescuing the painting and the Dec- laration of Independence, but Dolley quickly disappears from the plot soon after, and James Madison only gets a name-check in the film.

Depictions of the first three presidents in the movies are more plen- tiful than the fourth and fifth presidents, although Washington is the obvious and early favorite of filmmakers, as they were sure that audi- ences would recognize his image. One of the earliest-known depictions of Washington is *Washington at Valley Forge*, released in March 1908 by the Kalem Company, with Gene Gauntier, a female writer/director/ actor, directing the ten-minute film. Considered lost, there is little known about the film (and in 1908, a movie running ten minutes would have been considered the main attraction for theaters to run), although advertising sometimes listed it as being "beautifully colored" (probably a frame-by-frame coloring of the film used in some theaters), and the *Star-Gazette* in Elmira, New York, advertised the film as having "about ten great scenes, closing with the Battle of Trenton." William Wright, who was working for Kalem at the time, remembered the film a bit more realistically in *The Moving Picture World* in 1917 as being "eight soldiers in the army" sloshing around in the cold by a creek, but there was enough accuracy to persuade audiences at the time. A review in the *Times-Tribune* from Scranton, Pennsylvania, gives us more details about the story: Washington is seen giving his mantle to a freezing soldier at Valley Forge and endearing himself to the troops, while German soldiers help the British kidnap a young woman who overhears their plans against Washington. An American spy witnesses her capture and trades places with her so she can escape and give vital information to Washington before the Battle of Trenton. This implies that Washington's troops moved from Valley Forge to the Battle of Trenton, but the Battle of Trenton and the famous Crossing of the Delaware occurred during Christmas 1776, while winter quarters at Valley Forge happened in the winter of 1777–1778. To be fair, the film is not alone in getting these two events chronologically mixed up; even Bugs Bunny got the order wrong in the 1954 *Looney Tunes* cartoon "Yankee Doodle Bugs."

The film's plot of the girl spy who saves Washington's life appears to be a variation of a popular story about an assassination attempt against Washington. The typical story is that Samuel Fraunces, a tavern owner in New York City (sometimes referred to as a spy for the Americans and who later would become a steward for Washington when he was president), overheard a plot by one of Washington's guards, Thomas Hickey, to assassinate him with poisoned food. Although there has never been anything stated explicitly about attempts to assassinate Washington, there were rumors, and there really was a tavern owner named Samuel Fraunces and a guard named Thomas Hickey who was executed by the Continental Army but for mutiny and sedition. Over time, the story was transformed to Fraunces's daughter Phoebe saving Washington while at the inn by discarding poisoned peas he was to eat. This makes for a nice legend, even though Fraunces had no daughter by that name, and her story was changed to her sacrificing her life for the future president in a variety of fashions, depending on who told the story.

The legend of Phoebe Fraunces would be the basis of two other early films about Washington besides 1908's *Washington at Valley Forge*: *A Heroine of '76* (1911, with Gordon Sackville as Washington) and

*Washington at Valley Forge* (1914, with Francis Ford as Washington). In both, an innkeeper's daughter overhears men strategizing the death of Washington while he sleeps in his room at the inn, with her father the assassin in the 1911 feature and a boyfriend the killer in the 1914 one. The daughter trades rooms with Washington, allowing herself to die in his place when the assassin attacks, before dramatically "dragging herself downstairs" and dying in her father's arms. Ironically, in all three films, Washington does very little beyond being present to move the plot along. At least in *Washington at Valley Forge* (1914), Washington discovers the plot afterward, allowing him to be involved in the resolution to the plot, but otherwise, as the *Moving Picture World* describes it, Washington has "little he has to do" in the features, even those using his name in the titles.

Things looked up in more two one-reelers from 1909 that bookend a biography with Joseph Kilgour as Washington: *Washington under the British Flag* and *Washington under the American Flag*. Kilgour began a long career portraying Washington in both films and onstage starting in 1903, when he appeared as the first president in Boston for the play *Captain Barrington*. The play, written by Victor Mapes, once again deals with a character stopping an attempt against Washington, in this case a kidnapping. The review of the play for the *Boston Globe* notes that "whereas in other countries the national heroes have often been presented on the stage, this has seldom been the case in the United States." It certainly would be a more frequent occurrence in the years to come.

Although the two films are only twenty minutes combined, they do focus on Washington's life and career, which make them a rarity for presidential plots in Hollywood. The first, *Washington under the British Flag*, begins with Washington as a sixteen-year-old surveyor, followed by his fight at Fort Necessity; the death of General Edward Braddock; and his subsequent return to Fort Duquesne in 1758, where the British advancement scared off the French who were occupying the land. The film spices up this final military action by placing Washington as the head of the forces, when in reality he objected to the mission and tagged along only under orders by General John Forbes. The film, though, does accurately show the French burning down the fort as they left. The final scene is of Washington marrying Martha.

The second film, *Washington under the American Flag*, came out a week after the first film and mainly reviews Washington's entry into the Revolutionary War. This includes the crossing of the Delaware and Valley Forge (in their proper order), before we see General Cornwallis surrender for the British. The last five minutes then focus on Washington's presidential years before ending with Washington at Mount Vernon in retirement and the closing statement "The fame of Washington stands apart from every other in history. His name by all revered forms a universal tie of brotherhood."

Joseph Kilgour continued his acting career as Washington with the 1915 film *The Battle Cry of Peace*, which also features Paul Scardon as Ulysses S. Grant and William Ferguson as Abraham Lincoln. (Ferguson was in the performance at Ford's Theatre the night Lincoln was assassinated, and *Battle Cry of Peace* made that coincidence part of their advertising for the movie.) Only a few snippets of battle scenes from *The Battle Cry of Peace* still exist today. It was labeled a propaganda film by many critics, although Franklin D. Roosevelt, who was assistant secretary of the navy at the time, and Theodore Roosevelt endorsed it. The film, also called *A Call to Arms, An American Home*, and *The Battle Cry of War*, is a futuristic tale based on the book *Defenseless America* by Hudson Maxim. As one can expect from all these titles, the film is a cautionary tale of European forces convincing pacifists in America to not fight in the upcoming war, leading to an unnamed country (heavily suggested to be Germany) bombing New York and conquering America. Washington, Lincoln, and Grant appear only briefly early on to demonstrate the needed power of the American military to fight others that would oppress the country. With that in mind, one suspects that Kilgour as Washington has very little to do in the film except to stand proud over his troops, but because that footage is now lost, this is just a guess.

Kilgour made one final cinematic appearance as Washington in *Janice Meredith* (1924, also known as *The Beautiful Rebel*), directed by E. Mason Hopper and starring Marion Davies as the title character. The film, at more than two hours long, is based on an 1899 novel (in two volumes) written by Paul Leicester Ford, who also helped write the script with Edward Evertt Rose. Ford had written biographical works on Washington, Thomas Jefferson, and Benjamin Franklin, so his novel about a young aristocratic woman who, as a spy (they always end up as spies in these films, it appears), contributes to defeating the British would have a sense of accuracy to it. The novel was soon turned into a play and then the film, which gives Washington a handful of pivotal scenes. Most of the second half of the film cuts back and forth between him gathering the troops to cross the Delaware and Janice fighting off the sadistic British. The movie ends with Washington, as well—announcing the engagement of the heroine and her hero boyfriend in the finale at Mount Vernon. During the movie we get a quick glimpse of Benjamin Franklin (Lee Beggs) negotiating France's involvement in the war, while Thomas Jefferson (Lionel Adams) and Alexander Hamilton (Burton McEvilly) also appear. Even so, and naturally enough for a Marion Davies vehicle by her boyfriend, William Randolph Hearst, the emphasis is on Janice Meredith and her escapades. Kilgour is given little to do besides looking tall and serious during the Revolutionary War, which is the most common thread of nearly all the subsequent films featuring Washington.

*America* (1924) was directed by D. W. Griffith and, as with *Janice Meredith* that same year, intertwines the fictional characters of the plot with many familiar names from the Revolution: Samuel Adams; John Hancock; Thomas Jefferson (Frank Walsh, briefly in a Declaration of Independence scene); Patrick Henry; Paul Revere; and, of course, George Washington (Arthur Dewey). The plot deals with an evil British captain (played by Lionel Barrymore) enticing Native American tribes to fight against the colonists during the Revolutionary War, while the daughter (Carol Dempster) of a rich family known as the Montagues falls in love with a commoner (Neil Hamilton, much later the commissioner on the 1960s *Batman* television series). Washington here is a friend to the Montagues and is peppered throughout much of the proceedings, with the typical detour through Valley Forge, the British surrendering, and finally Washington's inauguration. Oddly, Washington's first scene is shot with him sitting with his face away from the camera, and while this would become a norm for some presentations of presidents in films starting in the late 1930s, once Franklin Delano Roosevelt took office (for more details, see chapter 7), it was commonly reserved only for those presidents still in office and not a common practice for representing earlier presidents and certainly not Washington. Yet soon after this early scene, we see Dewey as Washington with his face revealed, so it is curious that the first scene was shot as it was (perhaps a case of the actor not being available for the first scene and thus shot with a double from behind). Beyond this curio, though, there is little substance to Washington's role in the film that makes it stand out; he is simply a character called on to remedy a crisis for the main characters before the end of the movie.

In 1927 came a short film, this time in early two-color Technicolor, called *The Flag: A Story Inspired by the Tradition of Betsy Ross*. Francis X. Bushman, famed silent movie actor who had been in the 1925 version of *Ben-Hur*, played Washington, with Enid Bennett as Betsy Ross. The film, directed by Arthur Maude, who also cowrote the script with L. V. Jefferson, puts Washington front and center for the duration (figuratively and physically—Washington is center stage in nearly all shots in the film). As one might suspect, the plot of the twenty-minute short deals with the creation of the American flag. And as can be expected from previous examples, the film diverts from that story to tell a fictional one about a British soldier who crosses enemy lines to visit his wife, a friend of Betsy. When Washington discovers the soldier, he is determined to have him executed as a spy until Betsy convinces him to pardon the soldier and send him back to his troops unharmed. The soldier thanks Washington, shaking hands with him in front of the new American flag and stating that someday the two warring countries will unite. The scene then dissolves to show the flags together with the French flag during a battle scene in World War I. Even with the action staged around Washington, however, it is still the action of others that directs the story.

Alan Mowbray returned to the role of Washington twice more and both in musical moments. The first was in 1932, where he appears as Washington within a painting at the White House that joins paintings of Lincoln (Charles Middleton, better remembered as Ming from the *Flash Gordon* serials); Thomas Jefferson (uncredited); and Teddy Roosevelt (uncredited) singing about the film's fictional president in *The Phantom President* (1932). The second is in the 1945 musical *Where Do We Go from Here?* where he interacts with the hero (Fred MacMurray), who wishes himself, by way of a genie, into the military to fight in World War II, only to end up in the Colonial Army at Valley Forge. Another magical musical Washington role is Alan Dinehart as Washington in *The Road Is Open Again*, with Charles Middleton once again as Lincoln and Samuel S. Hinds as Woodrow Wilson. They pop up to help a young songwriter, played by Dick Powell, come up with a song to help support FDR's National Recovery Act in the 1933 featurette.

The short-subject *Give Me Liberty* (1935) is about Patrick Henry (John Litel, perhaps best remembered as the father in the Henry Aldrich movie series), with Robert Warwick as Washington and George Irving as Thomas Jefferson. John Adams gets a name-check, as well, although the short is mostly a retelling of Henry's 1775 famous speech at the Second Virginia Convention. *Sons of Liberty* (1939), meanwhile, is a short film with Montagu Love as Washington, who is seen briefly in this story about Haym Salomon (Claude Rains), a spy and financier for the Revolutionary War. *Sons of Liberty* went on to win the Academy Award for Best Short Subject (Two-Reel) that year.

Montagu Love returned to the role in 1942 as a ghost in *The Remarkable Andrew*, alongside Thomas Jefferson (Gilbert Emery), Benjamin Franklin (George Watts), Chief Justice John Marshall (Brandon Hurst), Jessie James (Rod Cameron), and Henry Smith (who isn't of any consequence to history and just tagging along, played by Jimmy Conlin). The film's focus (and main ghost) is Andrew Jackson, so there are more details about the comedy in chapter 3. Washington is given a few lines to say, including a brief show of humor when suggesting the protagonist tell a white lie to get him out of trouble while laughing off the whole "chopping down the cherry tree" myth of his youth. Even so, it is interesting that Washington is not "President Washington" but rather "General Washington," suggesting that his prepresidential days were more significant, as is common in most of his film appearances. Washington's turn may be minimal, but it is better than what occurs with Jefferson, who stays rigid, with little to add to the proceedings, save for the handful of scenes featuring the ghosts. Gilbert Emery nevertheless must have made an impression in the role, as he appeared as Jefferson again the same year in *The Loves of Edgar Allan Poe* and had a larger speaking role. The B movie, running just over an hour, from Twentieth Century-Fox stars Shepperd Strudwick (also known as John Shepperd) as Poe, who meets with Jefferson at the University of Virginia, which Jefferson founded. The scene has Jefferson encouraging Poe in his career and gives Emery a chance to play Jefferson as fatherly to the young writer, but it's a scene made from whole cloth and not based on reality, as there are no records of Poe meeting Jefferson in such a manner. As for

Washington, he next appeared in the 1946 Bob Hope movie *Monsieur Beaucaire*, played by Douglass Dumbrille and only for a quick visual gag at the very end of the movie. The scene erroneously makes it appear that Washington was in Philadelphia around the time of the signing of the Declaration of Independence, but he was actually in New York with the army. (Why spoil a joke with the facts?)

Jefferson finally gets a shot at the limelight with *The Howards of Virginia* (1940), directed by Frank Lloyd and based on the novel *The Tree of Liberty* by Elizabeth Page. The movie heads down the familiar road of D. W. Griffith's *America* (which itself was based on Robert W. Chamber's 1905 novel *The Reckoning*), with a fictional family being connected in some fashion to one of the Founding Fathers, who then find themselves intertwined with the war. In this case, it's Matt Howard (Cary Grant) and his family, including his young sons, Peyton (Phil Taylor) and James (Tom Drake), who end up fighting for the Continental Army. (The 2000 film *The Patriot*, with Mel Gibson and Health Ledger, and the 1985 movie *Revolution*, with Al Pacino and Dexter Fletcher, also deal with father-son combinations who end up fighting in the Revolutionary War, although only *The Patriot* even fleetingly shows us a Founding Father.) Grant's character is boyhood friends with Thomas Jefferson, played by Richard Carlson, who is largely remembered these days for his roles in several science fiction films, including *The Creature from the Black Lagoon*. Washington (George Houston) and Patrick Henry (Richard Gaines) make appearances, but it's Jefferson who gets a chance to shine in the film, with Carlson playing a strong, charismatic Jefferson, which is different from the older, stodgy, aristocratic Jefferson commonly portrayed in many of these features.

Richard Gaines returns to the eighteenth century in the 1947 Gary Cooper film *Unconquered*, directed by Cecil B. DeMille and costarring Paulette Goddard. This time, however, Gaines plays Washington rather than Patrick Henry. As the film takes place near the end of Pontiac's War between Native American tribes and the British (1763–1764), Washington's involvement is fleeting, and Gaines has only a handful of lines in a scene with many other individuals, thus he gets a bit lost in the mix. Even so, reviewer Roderick Heath is correct in his review for the film on his blog *This Island Rod* that Washington is "portrayed with a refreshing effect of professional good-humor," a stance rarely seen in cinematic Washingtons.

Warfare between the colonists and several Native American tribes did occur before, during, and after the Revolutionary War. Unfortunately, Hollywood tends to visualize such conflicts as stereotypical "cowboys and Indians" nonsense, and *Unconquered* is a good example. It even stars Gary Cooper, who made more than his share of westerns, and the film ends with both the "calvary arriving" and a "fast on the draw" show-down. The previously mentioned *America* is darker with stereotyping, although its worst atrocities are by British soldiers disguising themselves as part of the tribes. *When the Redskins Rode* (1951) is no different, starting out as more of the same, and even though it is set during the French and Indian War, the Native Americans attacking and killing settlers in the first two minutes of the film are played out as expected in any standard western set decades later. The twist here, however, is that the protagonist is Hannoc (John Hall), the son of the Delawarean tribe's chief, whom the British hope to convince to organize the tribe against the French in the upcoming war. In the process, Hannoc defeats a couple nasty French spies trying to stop him, sees his childhood love fight off the traitorous femme fatale, and ends up saving Washington at Fort Necessity. The film is a rarity, as George Washington (James Seay) has more to do than sit on a horse or in a chair until "saving the day" in the final reel, though Seay is visually much older than the twenty-one-year-old Washington was at the time of the events depicted. It also takes an event where Washington clearly faced defeat in surrendering Fort Necessity and gives it what we call today a Tarantino twist by having the fictional Hannoc turn the defeat into a victory for Washington instead because Hollywood can do that kind of thing. Beyond that uniqueness, it's a standard 1950s western dressed in colonial garb.

*John Paul Jones* (1959), which features Robert Stack (*Written on the Wind, Unsolved Mysteries*) as the title character, is best remembered for helping create the American Navy and his famous quote, "I have not yet begun to fight" during the Battle of Flamborough Head. Washing-ton makes his first appearance nearly halfway through the film in the traditional movie location of Valley Forge. Interestingly, Washington, played by John Crawford, is seen only from behind, with Jones lower-ing his head in seeming reverence to Washington as he dictates the dangerous conditions of his troops in a letter. While such positioning of a president was somewhat traditional in films by this point, after so many years of seeing Washington full face in the movies, the filmmakers apparently thought of him as more of a holy figure than a military one. John Adams (Robert Ayres) does not get off as well, however, as he is seen briefly and is dismissive of Jones's plans, thus coming off as boorish and too short-sighted. We do at least get to see his face on camera.

Washington is brought back to Earth in the French-Italian movie *La Fayette* (1961), about the young French aristocrat who became a general in the Continental Army and helped secure French backing for the war. He would fight for the army between 1777 and 1781, including meeting with Washington at Valley Forge and helping secure the defeat of the British at Yorktown, leading to the end of the war. While a major selling point to the film was Orson Welles as a rather large Benjamin Franklin, Howard St. John portrays George Washington and shows him in fine humor, usually not associated with the general in movies. (La Fayette and Washington became close friends and corresponded after the war until Washington's death.) The movie is hard to find, having yet to be released on DVD, and was considered a commercial failure at the time, but it is worth searching for an "outsider's view" of the war that is still very much a patriotic film and more realistic than others before it.

One of the last movies to feature Washington as anything other than a passerby is *An American Carol* (2008), written and directed by David Zucker (*Airplane!*, *Top Secret!*, and the *Naked Gun* trilogy). Jon Voight (who plays FDR in the 2001 film *Pearl Harbor*) looks somewhat like Washington and functions as a type of Ghost of Christmas Present in this parody of *A Christmas Carol*, but even here, the part is fleeting. Voight has little to do in the two-minute scene, with a speech that sounds very unlike Washington, but the cameo of a caliber like Voight as the father of the country is what matters to the film more than the meaning behind it.

Thomas Jefferson finally got a movie to himself in the Merchant Ivory (produced by Ismail Merchant and directed by James Ivory) production *Jefferson in Paris* (1995), only for the film to face dismal ticket sales and very frail critical praise for a James Ivory–directed movie. The film stars Nick Nolte as Jefferson as the US minister to France from 1784 to 1789 and focuses on Jefferson's romantic interest in the married

Maria Cosway (Greta Scacchi) two years after the death of Jefferson's beloved wife, Martha. There is also a secondary plot about Jefferson's strained parenting of his daughter Patsy (Gwyneth Paltrow), besides some attention made to how the French saw the Declaration of the Independence and the developing French Revolution. The final third of the movie then pushes most of these storylines aside to periodically focus on Sally Hemings (Thandiwe Newton), an enslaved person sent as a nurse for Jefferson's daughter Polly, and her brother James Hemings (Seth Gilliam), a chef for Jefferson. The film heavily implies that Jefferson begins a sexual relationship with the sixteen-year-old Sally, leading to her pregnancy just as Jefferson receives word that Washington wishes him to return to America for the post of secretary of state. With the National Assembly taken hold in France at the start of the French Revolution, enslaved people had the opportunity to be free, and the film ends with both James and the pregnant Sally contemplating staying before negotiating with Jefferson the eventual freedom of James and of Sally's children if they return to America with him. Ending title cards

**Thomas Jefferson (Nick Nolte) and Sally Hemings (Thandiwe Newton) in** *Jefferson in Paris* **(1995). Although advertising and reviews at the time suggested otherwise, their controversial relationship is only a subplot in the film.** *Courtesy of PhotoFest.*

mention that Jefferson freed her children when they turned twenty-one, but this was not strictly the case: Two essentially escaped without pursuit (one with money given to them before they left), and the others were released as part of Jefferson's will, while Sally would eventually be freed by Jefferson's daughter after his death. But in a movie where a twenty-something-year-old woman plays the twelve-year-old daughter Patsy, certain truths are easily stretched.

The movie has typical Merchant-Ivory flair, as in *A Room with a View*, *Howards End*, and *The Remains of the Day*: full of fabulously dressed aristocrats politely dissing each other in stunning locations while forbidden or unrequited love simmers underneath all the flourishes. To be fair, the movie tries to cover a lot of details about Jefferson's stay in Paris, and Merchant Ivory Productions tend to drift in and out of multiple stories toward an emotional arc that pulls the threads together into a common filmic quilt. Yet *Jefferson in Paris* doesn't carry enough weight to tell any of those stories to a satisfactory conclusion, and even reviews at the time questioned what the point was. Jack Garner of the Gannet News Service called it a "dull, lifeless film. If *Jefferson in Paris* was any slower, it'd be a still photograph." Robert W. Butler of the *Kansas City Star* called the film "pretty, but empty, without a real center," while Eve Zibart of the *Washington Post* called it a "disaster, intellectually infuriating and thoughtlessly racist."

It doesn't help that because most of his dialogue is based on his letters, Nick Nolte as Jefferson is confined to narrating the actions of everyone around him as he vacantly stares at them. Nor that the promise of forbidden romance suggested by at least two of the movie posters finds little sexual tension between Jefferson and either Maria or Sally. Perhaps the worse offense is that the movie wore the Sally Hemings story as a badge of honor in its promotion, "daring" to tell this story about Jefferson and Hemings, only for the filmmakers to buckle by suggesting Sally was an initiator and willing participant at times while at other points painting Jefferson as an aggressor. In trying to have it both ways, it ends up saying little.

Which is a shame, as Sally Hemings's life story is important to discuss as a part of American heritage. Here is someone who briefly had the opportunity to remain in Paris as a free person but chose (of her own free will, as far as we know) to return to America and stay enslaved to

Jefferson. Her return may have been based on multiple reasons, and two have been suggested: (1) She had family she didn't want to leave behind if she stayed in France, and (2) Jefferson supposedly promised to free her children once they reached the age of twenty-one. Upon returning, Jefferson and Hemings found themselves the subject of gossip, as well, when in 1802 the rumor had been published in a Virginian newspaper. Jefferson never spoke of the matter publicly or privately, but he never stated in his records who was the father of any of her children, which he commonly did for other births of those he enslaved, and the Hemings children were the only ones Jefferson allowed to be freed.

And how does this color our view of Thomas Jefferson when this side of his story is told? Here is one of the Founding Fathers of the country, the man whom we proudly remember telling us that "all men are created equal," yet not only are we reminded he was an enslaver of hundreds, but also there is evidence that he used this young, enslaved girl as a concubine at best. Yes, he paid James while in France, and we can stretch to imagine, as does the film, that there is some mutual consent between him and Sally, but it doesn't excuse the fact that James and Sally were enslaved to him and remained that way for some time (in Sally's case, until after Jefferson's death). We know Jefferson attempted to ban slavery in parts of the country, but he was a willing practitioner at the same time and had written that he did not conceive of freed people of color and a White society being able to successfully live together (he wasn't alone there; it was a popular stance at the time to deport former enslaved people rather than simply free them into society). Why wasn't this or the liaison investigated in the movie? Was it a mutual affection, or was Hemings pushed into the relationship because it was commonly expected of young, enslaved women to do so with their enslaver? Is it possible that the rumors were true, and Sally looked enough like her supposed half-sister, Jefferson's deceased wife Martha, that Jefferson was attracted to her for that reason? As a young woman who was written as being a tad naïve, did she simply not know what would occur, or were further rumors true that she was a bit shrewd in negotiating the freedom of her children in exchange for returning to a country she planned to go back to anyway?

Thus, *Jefferson in Paris* hedges, and with all its pageantry it cannot hide that there's very little it wants to say. Part of that may be due to historians at the time the film was made (and still today) arguing whether Jefferson fathered some or all of Sally Hemings's children, even after the Thomas Jefferson Foundation agreed with 1998 DNA testing that proved Hemings's male descendants were from the Jefferson line. (Some have taken that to mean someone else in Jefferson's family fathered the children, but that hardly makes Jefferson's place in history better; instead of him being the father without comment, he becomes an accessory who turned away as others in the family took advantage of those enslaved under him.) With no records to demonstrate the relationship Jefferson had with Hemings beyond the physical, the film breaks down because it cannot capture how they were brought together in a realistic manner; it just happens.

There's a mixed-up attitude about slavery in the film beyond this, as well. Sally may be young, but she's given dialogue that is barely the level of Butterfly McQueen in *Gone with the Wind*, which explains some of the charges of racism in the film, as she appears not simply young but it is suggested that women of color were not very bright. Even discussion of slavery in the movie is a tad suspect, as Jefferson is at one point scolded for the practice in America; meanwhile, France saw only a brief respite from slavery just before Jefferson left in 1789, which it returned to in 1802 and had not ended in their colonies. (France would not completely abolish slavery until 1848, less than a generation before America did.) Heavy restrictions and racism also existed for people of color in France, even with other freedoms available, so it was hardly the utopian society that the film attempts to depict.

And yet *Jefferson in Paris* can be credited for at least touching on slavery, which so rarely was covered in the stories about the Founding Fathers, with the exception of one movie made in 1972, *1776*. Oddly enough, for a musical, it is also a rare effort where the Founding Fathers are seen as realistic human beings rather than the mythical figures found in so many other movies. The movie *1776* began as a musical created by Sherman Edwards, with a book by Peter Stone (*Charade*, *The Taking of Pelham One Two Three*). Edwards, a lyricist and amateur historian, had spent many years on the idea of a musical-comedy for the stage that dealt with the men who signed the Declaration of Independence. After repeated attempts to get producers interested in the project, which many felt was not in sync with the late 1960s' government protests, Broadway producer Stuart Ostrow put Edwards with Stone to work on the production together.

The musical features John Adams (William Daniels) as the main protagonist of the story and several members of the Continental Congress as they discuss independence from Britain. Washington is not in the play, per history, as he was already on the battlefields trying to hold back the British with the soldiers he could round up, but periodic letters by Washington are read throughout, giving the audience a chance to hear his voice (albeit in grave despair over the lack of funds, training, and weapons given to the soldiers to fight the battle). Congress is split on how to act, with John Dickinson (Paul Hecht onstage and Donald Madden in the film) leading the opposition to Adams. To delay a vote that readily could go against Adams's efforts, Adams; Benjamin Franklin (Howard Da Silva, who would go on to play FDR in *The Private Files of J. Edgar Hoover*); Roger Sherman (David Vosburgh onstage, Rex

**John Adams (William Daniels) confronts Thomas Jefferson (Ken Howard) on the slow goings in writing the Declaration of Independence in the 1972 film adaptation of the musical *1776*. Lobby card, *author's collection*, © 1972 by Columbia Pictures Industries.**

Robbins in the film); Robert Livingston (Henry Le Clair onstage, John Myhers in the film); and Thomas Jefferson (Ken Howard) are assigned the task of creating the Declaration of Independence. The musical then follows the path of the document from the writing to the debates in Congress and finally the vote that led to its signing.

Opening on March 16, 1969, the musical would be a success, winning three Tony Awards, including Best Musical and Best Direction of a Musical (for Peter Hunt). Its success led to Warner Brothers buying the rights to the show and beginning production of a film version in 1972. While studios tend to make major changes to Broadway musicals when reinterpreting them for the screen, Warner Brothers agreed to using many of the same cast members from the Broadway production for the film, with only some minor changes in order to open the film a bit, as naturally would be the case for a film over a stage production. Studio head and conservative-leaning Jack Warner did have two edits he wanted made to the material, however: the deletion of the songs "Momma Look Sharp," with its despairing and brutal depiction of warfare at a time of heated arguments over the ongoing Vietnam War, and "Cool, Cool Considerate Men." Warner was willing to let the first slide a bit, but he was more adamant about deleting "Cool, Cool Considerate Men" completely from the feature. The song, sung by Dickinson and several other members of Congress, is an indictment of conservative political values, seemingly more concerned about wealth and power for those in control than the health of the country and its people, including such obvious lines as "To the right, ever to the right, never to the left, forever to the right." It was quite well-known that before a private performance of the musical for Nixon and invited guests at the White House in February 1970, the administration asked that the "Cool, Cool Considerate Men" number be cut. The producers refused to do so, saying that it could be seen as censorship, and the administration backed down. Jack Warner, however, felt it needed to be cut when filmed and edited the number out for its original theatrical release in late 1972. Fortunately, although Warner demanded that the film created for the number be destroyed, it was kept in the vaults but can now be seen as most versions of the film are available on disc or streaming for all to see.

The film's several musical numbers and the dialogue between them were based on narratives written by those involved in the years after the declaration was signed, and thus there's a certain air of authenticity in the dialogue spoken. Of course, not everything in the film or the original Broadway musical is accurate. Adams never sent for Jefferson's wife to help him concentrate on writing the declaration, for example. While Jefferson was peeved over having to write the document when he'd rather have been home with Martha, the reasoning because of her illness at the time, which would have made her arrival in Philadelphia impossible. Her appearance does at least allow for a female voice to be heard in a musical full of men, which is also why Abigail Adams appears, albeit in a rather clever manner of her "talking" with John Adams via their numerous letters back and forth. Several members of Congress are also combined into single characters, reducing a room of fifty-seven to twenty so as to not confuse the audience, including giving some aspects of Samuel Adams to John Adams in the play and film.

Perhaps the most injured for narrative sake is John Dickinson, the delegate from Pennsylvania, who in the film sabotages the attempts to declare independence for the colonists. It is fair to say that Dickinson tried to avoid war with Britain through reconciliation, such as with the Olive Branch Petition of 1775, written with Benjamin Franklin and Thomas Jefferson, among others. However, Dickinson the same year would help write with Jefferson *The Declaration of the Causes and Necessity of Taking up Arms* to explain why the colonists felt they needed to protect themselves against the British, and he would write the first draft of the Articles of Confederation, which would be the basis of the government until the Constitution replaced it in 1789. All this is hardly the work of a man who refused to seek independence from Britain, but the play and film needed a heavy, and the fictional composite of Dickinson, who took on traits of others in the Congress who disagreed with Adams's plans, became the villain of the piece. His fellow delegate James Wilson was also not the milquetoast presented in *1776* (it's difficult to watch Wilson and Dickinson in *1776* and not compare them to Jefferson and Madison in *Hamilton*). Wilson strongly supported independence but only delayed his vote because he wanted to convey the consensus of his constituents. His turnabout to vote for independence in the film, just like the walk-out of delegates in the eleventh hour, are there due to dramatic license rather than accuracy.

Yet from what we know, many aspects of the process seen in the film were much as they occurred. There were delays; Congress could be sluggish; and there were many changes made to what Jefferson and party had written before it was agreed to be ready to sign. What is perhaps most important is that *1776* doesn't dodge the topic of slavery. It may not have been 100 percent accurate in how it was handled in Congress, but at least the play and film tried to give the audience some insight into how the Founding Fathers viewed slavery. Perhaps it was because the musical was created when the civil rights movement of the 1960s and 1970s was going strong, or perhaps it was intended to try to convey the humanity of these men, but it was a rare effort to do so among the movies discussed here.

The topic comes through loud and clear with Edward Rutledge (John Cullum) and his late number from the musical, "Molasses to Rum." The number comes when Rutledge motions to discuss a paragraph in the text dealing with slavery. The play presents the text as if it was to abolish slavery in the states under the document, but this was not the case. The paragraph dealt with denouncing the king in the international trading of enslaved individuals, and, while critical of slavery, it did not claim to end slavery in the new country (the banning of the international slave trade for the United States finally came in 1808, by way of negotiations that occurred when creating the Constitution). The musical has Jefferson admitting that he was an enslaver but then fantasizes by having him announce that he plans to free those whom he enslaved. As previously discussed, Jefferson did no such thing, and there are no records that he offered this up in conversation in Congress at the time.

The song "Molasses to Rum," however, makes the point of contention many of the delegates had with the wording Jefferson added, which strongly suggested slavery was wrong. That in and of itself is rather progressive for such a document at the time. Abolition of slavery was not a popular topic, and many delegates were enslavers. Twelve of the first eighteen presidents of the country had enslaved individuals working for them at one time or another. Benjamin Franklin had a handful of enslaved people until 1781 and was hesitant to discuss the matter in Congress, although he would become an abolitionist later in life. Of the five members who collaborated on the Declaration of Independence, only two did not have people enslaved under them—John Adams and Roger Sherman—and both were willing to compromise personal opinions about the topic in order to preserve the unity of the states to achieve consensus on independence.

There were areas in the North that did not have slavery, but the South—in particular the colonies of Georgia and South Carolina—had 90 percent of the slave population. More important to the delegates, there was no denying that the country's economy was driven by goods born out of that slavery, and as mentioned previously, there was little conception of what to do with those formerly enslaved individuals if they were freed. To disdain the practice while profiting from it was seen as hypocritical, and the possible ramifications of eliminating it in the future made it simply unfeasible to many there. The song makes that point, with Rutledge as a spokesperson, although there is no evidence he played that part in actuality; he was just one of many expressing those views. Adams, within the play, film, and his letters, voiced the thought that to not deal with slavery in the document was only delaying the inevitable bloodshed when the country finally did face the reality of the practice, but as the musical makes clear, those who were in favor of adding the paragraph knew that it would split the states apart. As Benjamin Franklin puts it in the film, "First things first, John. Independence. If we don't secure that, what difference will the rest make?"

The musical makes the elimination of this text on slavery out to be a last-minute do-or-die moment in getting the declaration signed, which wasn't the case, as it was easily agreed to in the convention, although there were delays in tackling it until near the end of negotiations. Nevertheless, the film at least addresses the issue and makes clear that someone such as Jefferson was not quite the squeaky-clean superhero we were brought with in school because it is made clear he was an enslaver. Washington, who in his will did eventually release his enslaved individuals upon his death, was hardly better, and neither were other Founding Fathers, even Alexander Hamilton. Further, while making that point, it illustrates, as well, that the dismissal of slavery was not something that could have easily come to fruition at the time.

Most of this ignorance in the movies about such topics as slavery and how our forefathers dealt with them comes not from arrogance but because it disrupts the narrative flow of a story about a new nation that was supposed to be fostering new ideals and promoting freedom for its people. The Founding Fathers strove to create a new country and new government in the middle of a growing battle with its mother country and side skirmishes with others like the French. What they achieved was incredible, and their work was the building blocks upon which the country has thrived for nearly 250 years, even with mistakes made along the way.

The fallacy of our tendency to elevate our heroes, such as Jefferson, Washington, and Adams, is that we put them on a higher level than ourselves. They are no longer men with tendencies seen as shocking today, and we don't wish to think about it. Washington was not considered the best officer in his early military career, and there were many who tried to dismiss him early in the war, but he turned that around to become the military and political leader we needed at the time. Jefferson enslaved people, but he would question the practice over time, just as Franklin and Washington would. Early negotiations with Indigenous people of the country easily transformed into these people being driven out and killed to expand the area for White settlers. And although there were some attempts to peacefully deal with the issue, later administrations moved against them.

The problem in our movies, in how we tell their stories, is that by dismissing elements that upset the balance of the tales we wish to tell, we ignore our own heritage. People are shocked by the evidence of slavery among these men and other issues in which they were involved because we were never taught about them. And our refusal to knuckle down and get involved with our history, both the good and bad, leads us to knee-jerk negative reactions when such evidence is brought to the surface. Suddenly these men become monsters because we hear the words without understanding the history behind it. This can be flipped over, as well: Dickinson in 1776 is given to us as the villain when not only would he fight for the country's independence but he also would free all his slaves in 1777, long before many others from the convention would do so if at all. Yet if we saw the movie and knew nothing more, then that history matters little, and Dickinson remains the smug upstart in the film.

Dickinson wasn't alone in achieving highly progressive things for the times, and the Founding Fathers did what they could with their limited understanding of their issues. Many believed slavery was not good, but

they did not have the tools to conceptualize how the country could eliminate the practice. It would take the Civil War before slavery could be
addressed, and we still deal with the ramifications. Looking back from
250 years in the future, we can be proud of the achievements they aimed
for and fulfilled while still admitting that some of their objectives were
backward, and in good humor, we must realize that 250 years from now,
future generations will think we were just as backward in our own ways.

But movies are made to entertain. The stories we tell of these men
are heroic and epic, and that's the way we want it to be. In one scene of
the 2001 movie *The Patriot*, Heath Ledger's character is a soldier in the
Continental Army lying on the ground with other soldiers. He looks up
to see General Washington go by on his horse. Washington is presented
as if from a painting, with a strong horse under him, his crisp uniform,
and flowing cape, sitting grandly and staring solemnly ahead as he goes
by. In that moment, Ledger's character is looking up at a deity, not a
man. It's how we want to see these early presidents—stainless and all
powerful.

And it's hard to write stories about flawless supermen. Look at the
films discussed here and notice how little suggests that these presidents
on screen are human. Such perfection is hardly the thing to build a story
arc on. Even *Jefferson in Paris*, which tries to bring some humanity to
Jefferson, cannot fully bring Jefferson down to a mere mortal; it would
defeat the aim of the film. So if we cannot have that type of character
development in our movies, then we have other characters near these
men to do it for us. The stories become about John Paul Jones or some
saloon girl or an old friend, with Washington, Jefferson, and others on
the edge of the story, ready to be brought in when needed to push the
story along.

There's the old concept of the MacGuffin in storytelling, usually referred to in Alfred Hitchcock's movies, but the idea had been around for
many years before he began using it. A MacGuffin is an object that has
no other purpose than to be an objective for the characters in the story,
and the plot or resolution is achieved once the MacGuffin is obtained.
When the saloon girl hears about the plot to kill Washington in *Washington at Valley Forge*, for the sake of the story the person she is protecting
could be anyone, but making it Washington gives the story extra weight,
and thus Washington is the MacGuffin. Hannoc of *When the Redskins*

*Rode* spends most of the film fighting the enemy so he can go save Washington in the final scenes. James Madison in *Magnificent Doll* has little to do other than to be the man whom Dolley turns to in order to avoid falling for Aaron Burr. We can't touch the Founding Fathers because they're sacred, as we see in *The Patriot* and *John Paul Jones*, so we make our other characters heroic by pairing them with these holy men, who become little more than objects they must get messages to or save or help in some manner. Hollywood has created presidents in their stories who serve the same purpose as uranium in a wine bottle in *Notorious* (1946) or the blackbird in *The Maltese Falcon* (1941).

It works, but in doing so, we place these men on a seldom-achievable level for those in the real world. We therefore tend to pick individuals as our leaders who we hope will prove themselves to be as infallible as our notions of the Founding Fathers and then criticize them when they can't achieve that purity. The Hollywood gloss on these people whom we know only through their glories prohibits us from allowing our leaders today to be wrong, make mistakes, and then rise and learn from them.

Make no mistake: The MacGuffin presidents who make up our filmic Founding Fathers expand to cover many other presidents in movies, both real and fictional, in the years that follow, and in many cases, those MacGuffin presidents are just as infallible once they are pressed into service in such movies. But Hollywood at times deals with fictional presidents who can make mistakes. They are sometimes secondary to the stories, but other times, they are major players in the movie plots, even more so than the MacGuffin presidents. Most of the time, they are individuals who didn't really want the job in the first place, as explained in the next chapter.

## 2

# THE KIDNAPPING, *THE MAN*, AND THE ACCIDENTAL PRESIDENT

In our system, the vice president is like the queen of England. She can't even get airline tickets without talking to somebody like me.

—*Air Force One* (1997)

In retrospect, Harrison Ford may have been a dubious choice for president. *Air Force One* is an action movie released in 1997 featuring Harrison Ford, at the peak of his action-movie fitness, playing President James Marshall, who helps secure the capture of tyrannical General Radek (Jurgen Prochnow) in a joint American-Russian assault at his stronghold. Given that volatile situation, President Marshall still feels secure in waltzing into Moscow three weeks later with his family in tow to attend a large diplomatic dinner. He then berates others before stating that when Americans see injustice and terrorism now, they will be ruled by the country's moral judgment instead of worrying about what the world thinks. When his security advisor and chief of staff tell him that the sudden policy change may cause issues with the country's allies and Congress, Marshall pushes it off as meaningless because they are doing what is "morally right."

His security detail for the flight back not only contains a mole for a small group of terrorists but also protocol shaky enough that said

**Our action president, James Marshall (Harrison Ford), in *Air Force One* (1997). *Lobby card, author's collection, © 1997 by Beacon Communications Corp.***

terrorists can get onboard and commandeer weapons to hijack Air Force One. Then, after Marshall's staff follow procedures, he can't be responsible enough as the leader of the free world to get into the plane's escape pod and be safely jettisoned, even while several Secret Service members are killed in the process. With shaky diplomatic ground broken that night suggesting "America First" and the president possibly dead or compromised, it is little wonder that his cabinet is ready to invoke the Twenty-Fifth Amendment in order to push the hesitant vice president to begin making presidential decisions.

The Twenty-Fifth Amendment is brought up frequently in the movies ahead, as it deals with how and when the government will respond if the president or vice president is unable to discharge the powers and duties of the office, most commonly due to illness, resignation, or death. It has been invoked a handful of times since being ratified, typically when the president has surgery or medical testing when they must be rendered unconscious for a designated amount of time. The only other times it has been used was during the Nixon and Ford administrations, thanks to Nixon having to replace Vice President Spiro Agnew due to bribes he received while governor of Maryland, then when Nixon resigned, and finally when Gerald Ford (who replaced Nixon as president) selected Nelson Rockefeller as vice president. If the Twenty-Fifth Amendment is used on the grounds that the president cannot fulfill his or her duties, then the president can go to Congress with a rebuttal. Congress will then debate and vote on whether the attempt to replace the president should proceed, as well as if the appointed replacement should take on the role. So while there's a tendency in movies to make dismissing the president sound like a magical "Go Directly to Jail, Do Not Collect $200" card, it's not quite that easy.

Although we hear about the Twenty-Fifth Amendment more often these days when any opponent wants to rattle a saber at a president they don't like, the amendment was not ratified until 1967. Before that, things were a bit more of a mess if a president couldn't fulfill his duties. At the Constitutional Convention of 1787, John Dickinson asked what would constitute the disability of the president for clause 6 of the Constitution, and the response had all the vagueness of a bureaucratic "we'll get back to that." By the time William Henry Harrison died in office in 1841, some in Congress suggested that the clause meant Vice President John Tyler could perform presidential duties only until an election occurred to find a new president, leading Tyler to have the Oath of Office given to himself in order to force senators to abandon the idea of a new election. This helped form the tradition of the vice president automatically becoming the president, end of discussion. It would be another hundred years before rules of succession were even put into place if the president was unable to do their duties with the 1947 Presidential Succession Act: vice president, then speaker of the House, and finally the president pro tempore of the Senate (and not the secretary of state, although then secretary of state Alexander Haig would infamously frame himself as the leader of the country when Ronald Reagan got shot in 1981).

The reason it didn't come up much before the twentieth century was that many people then and still to some extent today see the role of the vice president as window dressing or a person used to garner votes for a presidential nominee who needs to shore up representation for an area of the country (such as commonly perceived when John F. Kennedy picked Texan Lyndon B. Johnson as his vice-presidential nominee).

Sometimes, it was felt that a vice president was not even necessary. James Madison went twice without a vice president for example, and four presidents went through their entire term without one. The concern about having someone ready to be "next in line" changed, however, as death, assassinations, illnesses, and other issues occurred through the years and made the need for such clear directions to put into office someone who was picked not by the public but by the president—and not because they were necessarily the best person to be next in line but because they were best for votes. Thus, if the president died, America was left with a person in charge who got there by chance, an accidental president. And the concept of an accidental president comes up often in films of fictional presidents, especially action presidents, as in *Air Force One*.

*Air Force One* was directed by Wolfgang Peterson, who made other action films that dabbled with political themes, like *In the Line of Fire* (1993), *Outbreak* (1995), and the excellent *Das Boot* series (also starring Jurgen Prochnow). But even at the time of the film's release, it was clear to many that the movie owed a certain debt to the 1988 action film *Die Hard*, directed by John McTiernan and starring Bruce Willis. In that film, as in *Air Force One*, gunmen take over a structure and make demands, with the protagonist secretly moving about the place to take out the bad guys. As a bonus, the wife of the protagonist becomes a hostage, and the hero and villain meet up for an extended time to heatedly snarl at each other before a final showdown. *Die Hard* doesn't have the plot point of a traitor among the good guys, as in *Air Force One*, but that element (along with the bad guys attempting to rescue a general using a plane) can be found in its follow-up, *Die Hard 2* (1990), so *Air Force One* stays within the theme of the earlier series of films at least. *Air Force One* follows most of this with only one major difference: We don't need someone to save the hostages; the president does it himself. There is even quick exposition from his cabinet early in the crisis to establish Marshall's ability for the audience: Marshall is a Medal of Honor recipient, is fluent in Russian, can use a gun, knows how to do hand-to-hand combat, and even (thanks to his helicopter training) can fly Air Force One. (Marshall probably had done so in the past just for kicks, as he easily jumps into the pilot seat.) It's as if the director of Nakatomi Plaza in *Die Hard* had been Bruce Willis's character. He's not just a president;

he's an action president, ready to physically jump in and do what is right to save others, and this concept of an action president returns time and again in the movies to follow.

The action president didn't start with Harrison Ford, however. The public loves a decisive personality in the role as president, and someone who can demonstrate his or her ability through physical actions suggests strength. It's obvious that Washington's success in the Revolutionary War, even if he faltered earlier in his military career, was a major reason he was viewed as the perfect candidate for the presidency. Andrew Jackson was a cantankerous politician known for his mood swings, but he had won the Battle of New Orleans in the War of 1812, which helped get out the votes for him when he ran for office in 1829. Ulysses S. Grant, Teddy Roosevelt, Dwight Eisenhower, and John F. Kennedy all were served well in their political careers by their military record. (Attempts at toughness can also work against such individuals. Michael Dukakis's infamous photo of him riding in a tank helped kill his 1988 campaign for office, while George W. Bush's landing in a jet to give a speech with a "Mission Accomplished" banner behind him in 2003 would be ridiculed for years afterward.)

The movies are no different about showing such physical abilities for the presidents. Many of those featuring presidents typically present them earlier in their careers, during the excitement of war rather than sitting in an office years later making decisions. When Hollywood moved on to fictional presidents, the studios were paying to have an actor play the president, and you can't have him just at a desk. There has to be something for the president to physically do, so it wasn't long before one of the easiest concepts came along, which was the question, What would happen if someone kidnapped the president?

*The President Vanishes* (1934) was released by Paramount Studios and based on a novel by Rex Stout, under the alias "Anonymous," that was published earlier that year. This wasn't a completely unusual tactic in publishing political books at the time. Henry Adams went by the pen name of "Anonymous" for his very popular novel about Washington in 1880 called *Democracy*; a collection of questionable gossip about politicians by Drew Pearson and Robert Allen, *Washington Merry-Go-Round* (1931), would also feature the "Anonymous" byline; and in more recent years, there was the release of *Primary Colors*, featuring a lightly disguised Bill and Hillary Clinton, written by Joe Klein but released as written by "Anonymous." Stout did so with *The President Vanishes* for similar reasons as the others—not because the authors needed to hide their identities but because by making the writer mysterious, the readers presumed the author to be someone high up in the government, dishing out information that couldn't be told otherwise. It was only later, when he found success with his series of mystery novels on Nero Wolfe and Archie Goodwin that Stout would admit he was the author.

*The President Vanishes* was successful enough as a novel that it was picked up by Paramount to be made into a feature. William Wellman, the director of *Wings* (1927), the first movie to receive the Academy Award for Best Picture, was signed as director, and Lynn Starling, Carey Wilson, and Cedric Worth were picked as screenwriters (Ben Hecht and Charles MacArthur also contributed to the script). The film follows closely on the plot of Stout's novel: President Craig Stanley (Arthur Byron, *The Mummy, 20,000 Years in Sing Sing, Gabriel over the White House*) is being pushed by Congress and the press to deploy troops to fight in a war in Europe, which he believes is a mistake for the country. Munition makers and other businessmen representing oil, the banks, and even the press are behind the push, seeing dollar signs. There is also a fascist group known as Grey Shirts, not unlike Hitler's Brownshirts and Mussolini's Blackshirts of the era, inciting riots in the streets against anyone opposing the war efforts. Congress is ready to bypass the president and vote for both war and his impeachment, when it is announced that President Stanley has disappeared. The vote in Congress is delayed, and suspicion surrounds everyone, from the radical leader of the Grey Shirts, Lincoln Lee (a conflicted name pulled from the Civil War of its two opposing leaders and played by Edward Ellis), to a dimwitted delivery boy (a part originally offered to the up-and-coming Broadway star Henry Fonda in August 1934 before being passed on to Andy Devine) who was last to see Stanley. Meanwhile, the businessmen push the vice president to assume the responsibilities of the presidency in the president's absence and declare war.

Eventually, it is revealed that the president had intentionally disappeared, with the help of the delivery boy and special agent Chick Moffat (Paul Kelly), in order to stall Congress on the war vote until cooler heads could prevail. To complete the staged kidnapping of the president, Stanley has Chick tie him up in a building connected to Lincoln Lee and then plans to have the police find him to pin his kidnapping on the Grey Shirts and turn public opinion against them. Unknown to both the president and Chick, Lee discovers the defenseless Stanley first and is about to assassinate him, when Chick arrives and kills Lee, just in the nick of time. With sentiment for war dissipating, the novel and film end with President Stanley emerging and delivering a speech to the public on why going to war would not be in the best interest of the United States.

Walter Wanger was a producer at Paramount known for his zealous dedication to his projects, including *Stagecoach* (1939), *Invasion of the Body Snatchers* (1956), and *Cleopatra* (1963), and infamously remembered for shooting the agent of his wife, actress Joan Bennett, in the groin over a suspected affair. Wanger had previously turned his attention to two other fictional films about Washington before *The President Vanishes*: *Gabriel over the White House* (1933 and discussed in chapter 10) and *Washington Merry-Go-Round* (1932), based on Pearson's and Allen's book. *The President Vanishes* was a natural for Wanger, who was very left leaning and passionate about corruption seeping its way into politics, as seen in Stout's novel, with the businessmen sealing deals to start a war in order to profit from it. With the film dissolve early in the picture from the businessmen to a flock of vultures picking over remains, it is clear where Wanger's allegiance lay.

There are some minor changes from the books to the screen: In the novel, it is assumed that Stanley has only disappeared, while the movie quickly suggests he has been kidnapped. The movie also spends more time setting up his disappearance and the aftermath with the delivery boy and Chick, while consequently, the president's speech after he's found that explains why America should not fight is considerably shorter in the film than in the book (the novel's speech goes on for pages and demonstrates a young writer spinning his wheels). While making the film, Wanger managed to sidestep the Production Code Administration (PCA) in their request that he tone down the dealmakers from being involved in certain industries that could hurt the marketing of the film. He did, however, make a rather minor change to the vice president in the film. In the book, Vice President Robert Molleson (Robert McWade) is an emotional mess who eventually has a breakdown when pushed by the dealmakers to declare himself president and commence with the war.

The PCA did not think depicting the vice president in such a manner would be a good idea, and Wanger changed the character to avoid any hint of a psychological collapse. After filming was completed, he also ran into issues with the Hayes Code, which in 1934 was a self-censoring body for the Hollywood studios to avoid releasing questionable content. The Hayes office delayed giving the film its approval until Wanger toned down some violence in the Grey Shirts scenes.

Although *The President Vanishes* was a successful novel, the movie did not do well at the box office, losing over $100,000 (close to $2 million today) for Paramount, even with an ad campaign that included grand reviews by Cecil B. DeMille, Ernst Lubitsch, Ed Sullivan, and Walter Winchell. Wanger was always proud of the film, however, and boasted for years about the movie being banned from countries like Japan, France, Germany, and Italy due to its political tone. "It was too far ahead of its time," he proudly told the Des Moines Ad Club in 1940. "While Americans may not have appreciated some of our films, our enemies always have." If the film is remembered at all these days, then it is due to a very early role for Rosalind Russell, who appears briefly near the beginning of the film as a lobbyist's wife whose main function is exposition about the dealmaking villains in the movie.

What's interesting in this very early depiction of a fictional president of the country is how in control President Stanley is. Stanley initiates the disappearance with only two other men readily knowing his whereabouts, and he depends on them to help him succeed in a rather outlandish plot to turn public opinion away from going to war. He also intentionally dooms the Grey Shirts by allowing himself to be bound, gagged, and left alone in their stronghold and luckily draws in the death of their leader, Lincoln Lee, to help cement their participation. It's rather a dastardly plot by the president to lie to the public about his disappearance that leads to chaos in the streets and more than one death, but evidently, the ends justify the means in the eyes of President Stanley. Further, he takes the physical risks himself rather than forcing others to do it for him, making him a very early example of the action president, much like President Marshall in *Air Force One* more than sixty years later.

Besides probably the first instance of an action president, *The President Vanishes* also offers up one of the first depictions of what would be common characteristics of the accidental president. As mentioned, the PCA wanted Vice President Molleson to not be depicted as a "drunkard, a weakling," as in the novel, when he has a breakdown because the cabinet refuses to seat him as president (the cabinet decides that clause 6 of the Constitution, detailing succession of the presidency to the vice president, has not been fulfilled because as far as they know, the president is still fit to hold his office, even if he isn't there). Instead, Wanger makes Molleson a vain man who is easily manipulated by the oil man's proclamation that joining the war was the way to show his leadership. If it was not for the sudden reemergence of the president, the country would have gone to war, thanks to the mistaken Molleson.

Molleson's actions are very similar to two television movies featuring a disappearing president, both (oddly enough) with Rip Torn in pivotal roles: *The President's Plane Is Missing* (ABC, 1973) and *Dawn's Early Light* (HBO, 1990). *The President's Plane Is Missing* has Air Force One crashing just as a potential war is flaring up between China and the United States (in fact, the movie was delayed a year in airing on ABC, as Nixon was traveling to China in 1972 to help deescalate tension between the two countries, and the network decided the timing was wrong to show a movie with China as potential bad guys). With the president (Tod Andrews) missing, the vice president (Buddy Ebsen) begins getting conflicting advice on how to handle the Chinese, with the national security advisor (Rip Torn) adamant that the president was planning to go to war. Just as the vice president is about to authorize a preemptive strike against China, the president appears to countermand the orders. It is then revealed that, much like in *The President Vanishes*, his disappearance was deliberate, as he was secretly meeting with the Soviets to forge a treaty of solidarity against China. Thus, without the president once again popping up at the last second, it is possible the accidental president would have made a massive mistake.

Rip Torn returns in *Dawn's Early Light* to once again be a military advisor who attempts to get the country into war, only this time against the Soviets. In this case, the president (Martin Landau) goes missing when Marine One crashes after being hit by blast waves of a bomb. With the president missing and many others in the line of succession killed in various bombings, the secretary of the interior (Darrin McGavin) is the next in line for the presidency. The secretary, convinced by Torn's character that the president would want a bombing of the Soviet Union, nearly succeeds, until the real president, heavily injured and blind, turns up and countermands the order, stopping global destruction.

Making a mistake is a condition of the accidental president in subsequent films as well, such as Vice President Bennett (Glenn Close) in *Air Force One* being pushed to sign a document relieving President Marshall of his duties via the Twenty-Fifth Amendment. Both accidental presidents are hard pressed by others to do things they are initially reluctant to do, only to be saved in the final moments by the return of our strong action president to correct them. (A side note: Bennett was to sign the document in order to nullify the release of the general that Marshall okayed when his family was threatened by the terrorists, but she does not have to do so, as Marshall kills the terrorists and rescinds his order, thus making Bennett's actions in the film little more effective than staring at a phone and trying to keep Dean Stockwell from chewing the scenery.) As such, there is an inclination for the vice president (or subsequent accidental president in some films, as is discussed later) in the movies to be used to visualize our worst fears: an inept leader who is going to send us down the wrong path.

In some cases, such gaffes are fixable and used to educate the person so they will become better presidents in the resolution to the story. For example, *The Day after Tomorrow* (2004), directed by Roland Emmerich (a name that will pop up a few more times in the chapters ahead) deals with a drastic climate change that will cause the northern half of the United States to be subjected to rapid freezing, creating a new ice age. In the movie, our hero, Jack Hall (Dennis Quaid), meets to discuss the crisis with Vice President Raymond Becker (Kenneth Welsh), an obvious Dick Cheney clone in both looks and actions to the George W. Bush–like President Blake (Perry King). Becker ignores the concerns, and soon enough millions are killed, including the oblivious president, who is told of the imminent danger only after it is too late to do anything. Becker, who is now president of a diminished United States (a large portion of the population has fled to Mexico), goes on television, humbled and admitting his grievous mistakes in dismissing the crisis but aiming to prove himself a better president than he was a vice president.

One of the best examples of the accidental president truly comes about by coincidence, which is in the 1972 film *The Man*, directed by

Joseph Sargent (*The Taking of Pelham One Two Three, MacArthur*) and starring James Earl Jones (*Dr. Strangelove, The Great White Hope*) as the country's first Black president. The script, written by Rod Serling (*Twilight Zone, Requiem for a Heavyweight*), was based on a novel by Irving Wallace, a nonfiction writer who had begun producing novels in the late 1950s that were heavy on character exposition to explain plot concepts, along with dashes of sex, coarse language, and violence—like if your history teacher at school suddenly became Sidney Sheldon.

The novel is based on a visit Wallace made to John F. Kennedy's White House in 1963, and his president in the novel, addressed only as T. C., is an idolized leader, much like how Kennedy would be remembered. The book opens with the president and speaker of the House being killed in an accident while in Germany for an important meeting with the Soviets on a pact with Africa. With the vice president having died of a coronary shortly before the trip, the presidency is now in the

*The Man* (1972), starring James Earl Jones as Douglass Dillman, the nation's first Black president, per Irving Wallace's novel from 1964. *Lobby card, author's collection, © 1972 by Paramount Pictures Corp.*

hands of the president pro tempore of the US Senate, Douglass Dilman. It is only as Dilman is given the oath of office at the end of chapter 1 that readers discover Dilman is a Black man.

The novel follows his story as he begins the last year and a half of T. C.'s term, facing a cabinet that sees him strictly as a straw man to help push the agenda established by the deceased president. Dilman also faces public distrust and his own inadequacies on how he became president as well as personal issues with family and friends due to his rise in power. Dilman must further deal with racism from all sides: with Whites who see him as inferior for his skin color and Blacks who assume he is working for "the man." At first, Dilman is satisfied to simply sign off on T. C.'s old projects, but his discovery of a bill to keep him from dismissing members of the cabinet and plans to allow the Soviets to overrun an African country puts him at odds with his staff and in particular the secretary of state, leading to an impeachment trial. Dilman is cleared of the charges, and his gambit against the Soviets in Africa succeeds, but when asked if he will seek another term as president, Dilman declines, deciding to be the man he wants to be instead of hiding his own interests to satisfy politicians in Washington.

The novel was published in 1964, and film rights were quickly picked up by Sammy Davis Jr., with the aim to have Sidney Poitier star as Dilman, and two scripts were written by William Attaway (author of *Blood on the Forge*, 1941, and *Hear America Singing*, 1967). Davis sold the rights to singer Eddie Fisher, who planned to make the film in 1968 with Jim Brown as Dilman and Bud Schulberg (*What Makes Sammy Run?* and *On the Waterfront*) as scriptwriter, but then the production moved to the ABC television network, and what was to be a television movie began filming in 1971. While filming was being completed, *The Candidate*, starring Robert Redford as an idealistic candidate for office who finds his platform and personality compromised in order to win the election, was rushed into production so the movie could be out before the presidential election in 1972. ABC, sensing a chance to piggyback off the interest of *The Candidate*, decided to release *The Man* into theaters the month after Redford's film was released.

As James Earl Jones discusses in his 1999 introduction to a reprint of the novel, everyone who worked on the film was proud of what they had done with a television movie. But a theatrical film would have had many more opportunities to cover adult topics, situations, and language found in the book than could be done on network television in 1972. Certainly, more money would have been spent on the look of the film, if nothing else. Those connected with the movie tried to convince ABC not to release into theaters what was and looked like a television-budgeted, twenty-day-shoot, sanitized version of the novel, but the network didn't listen and pushed ahead with the theatrical release, only to see it flop in theaters for these same reasons. The timing of the film is a shame in a way; if the project had been made in the late 1960s, when the studios were looking to do more challenging material, or on television in the later 1970s, when the "novel for television" miniseries were popular and a more relaxed attitude toward discussing racial issues was prominent, then *The Man* might be better remembered today. As it is, it stands as a curious "what if" of the time but doesn't pay off on its promises.

As expected, many changes were made to the story. For example, subplots dealing with Dilman's daughter passing for White and his son looking to join a radical group whose leader had just killed a racist White judge are dropped; instead, in the film, Dilman has only a militant-leaning daughter who eventually comes around to his way of thinking. Another completely abandoned subplot deals with the widowed Dilman trying to hide his relationship with a light-skinned Black woman because he fears "not being Black enough." An assassination attempt foiled by a racist Secret Service agent is deleted as well as an unnecessary false rape charge against Dilman during the impeachment trial. Dilman working to stop the Soviets from their attack on an African country because they assume Americans will not fight to save the nation for racial reasons is stripped from the film, as well. The biggest variation is that a Black militant group that pressures Dilman to save their leader from execution after killing a judge is changed to a Black American citizen, Robert Wheller (Georg Stanford Brown), who is wanted for extradition because he is suspected of attempting to assassinate a defense minister in South Africa. The story's temperature is cooled by moving politics from the US Deep South to another nation, one that Americans knew of but didn't take enough interest in at the time. After all, the network had to deal with areas of the United States where even the topic of a Black president would be cause for tension with station owners, so lessening the crime and moving it to another part of the world made the country look more progressive than it was. Even the most racist of senators in the novel, Senator Watson, played by Burgess Meredith in the film, is redeemed because he despises the level of bigotry of the South African ambassador who gives him footage of Wheeler shooting the defense minister. Americans may have their differences, but according to ABC, they could never be as bad as "those foreigners over there."

Jones in his introduction says they were missing a chance to confront the issue of Apartheid in South Africa by not having Dilman at least meet with the ambassador, but when he talked to scriptwriter Rod Serling about doing so, Serling's reply was, "No, Jimmy, that would be another story." What he meant by that is there simply was not the time in a ninety-minute television film to get in all the other points possible in such a scenario when the focus of the story had to remain on Dilman and the broader canvas of him fulfilling his role as president. When Dilman turns Wheeler over to the South African government after Wheeler confesses to his crime, Wheeler derides him for not protecting him. Dilman, however, sees Wheeler as a man who is just as wrong as those he was fighting against, and assuming that because of his skin color, Dilman will play favorites with Wheeler is as racist as those in his cabinet who felt he could be confined to doing what the White man wanted.

This last plotline gets us back to the general concept of the accidental president, which ironically, the novel's Dilman does not face because he is proven right in all his actions. The movie's Dilman early on actively tries to take his own route with his new role, even forgoing prepared answers given him by his cabinet for a press conference. Yet because he attempts to follow his heart without much consultation, he at first willingly gives sanctuary to Wheeler, believing Wheeler when he says he did not attempt to assassinate the minister. Dilman even goes public with his defense, and thus when it turns out there is clear evidence Wheeler did commit the crime, Dilman must face up to that mistake in front of the world. He does so and yet refuses to back away from his duties that he may not have wanted but needed to do as president. Unlike his novel counterpart, this accidental president is on his way not only to recover from his mistake but also to be a better president because of it, and when asked if he will run in the upcoming election, he proudly states that he'll seek the nomination. Incidents like this are a common trait for the accidental president in many films: making a mistake that escalates into a crisis, with the president either recovering like Dilman in *The Man* to become a better leader or being driven out like Molleson of *The President Vanishes*.

After *The President Vanishes*, the concept of kidnapping a president went on the backburner for a few years, although it would briefly pop up in *Seven Days in May* (1964). The film, based on a book by Charles W. Bailey and Fletcher Knebel from 1962, features another screenplay from Rod Serling and was directed by John Frankenheimer. *Seven Days in May* deals with the Joint Chiefs of Staff (JCS; the leaders of the Department of Defense) initiating a coup attempt against the unpopular president Jordan Lyman (Fredric March) after he signs a nuclear disarmament treaty with the Soviet Union (presidents looking to agree to peace are usually the trigger for many of the movies here). Colonel "Jiggs" Casey (Kirk Douglas), the JCS's director, stumbles on the JCS chairman, air force general James Mattoon Scott (Burt Lancaster), setting up the coup with the abduction and deposition of the president to occur during a planned military exercise. When associates of Scott are filmed scouting out a means to kidnap him, Lyman is convinced of the coup, but he has little evidence to bring to the public. The rest of the film involves Casey, Lyman, and others working to corner Scott and his associates, including a tense meeting between the president and the general, and the very modern concept of the general planning to use mass media to get the public on his side when the coup begins. Eventually, a signed confession from an admiral (John Houseman) is located, and most of the JCS resign in haste, ending the coup attempt.

The book was released in 1962 and had been picked up by Kirk Douglas's production company, but he at first had trouble finding a studio for the project, as most of the studios were anxious over how Washington would view a movie that put the Pentagon in an unfavorable light. The success of the novel changed their minds as well as news that President Kennedy had enjoyed the novel and felt it was timely. Some have suspected this was due to General Edin Walker's resignation from the JCS in 1961. Walker promoted an anticommunist agenda in the military and suggested that every president since Franklin D. Roosevelt was possibly a communist and weak, which no doubt reminded Kennedy of the general in *Seven Days in May*. Because of this link, the White House

**Fredric March as President Jordan Lyman in *Seven Days in May* (1964). In avoiding a coup and a kidnapping, he becomes an action president in his own way. *Official press still, author's collection, © 1963 by Joel Productions, Inc.***

offered a certain amount of access to the film production, including allowing filming of a sequence showing competing demonstrations outside the White House that end in a riot, although the Pentagon refused to be involved, and John Frankenheimer had to sneak footage of Douglas outside the Pentagon building for the film.

President Lymon is presented as unhealthy, but in his own way, he performs as the action president by willingly confronting Scott face to face and initiating the resignation requests to stop the coup. And for the vice president? In this case, the vice president may be second in line of command but is a fifth wheel in terms of the plot, and for the sake of the novel and film, he is removed to Italy for the duration. A 1994 television remake for HBO entitled *The Enemy Within*, featuring Forest Whitaker as Casey, Jason Robards as the general, and Sam Waterston as the president, creates a more active role for the vice president (played by Dakin Matthews). His function, however, is very similar to the one found for the vice president in *The President Vanishes*, only with the addition of the Twenty-Fifth Amendment, and then the general and the others plan to run the country "behind the throne." Perhaps the vice president was better off overseas like in the earlier version, as this case of an accidental president is more intentional and for all the wrong reasons.

Hollywood's dismissal of the vice president holds true when Burt Lancaster once again tries to kidnap the president in the film *Twilight's Last Gleaming* (1977), and here, the vice president simply isn't needed, as all questions confronting the characters are handled by the president's cabinet. The movie is based on a novel called *Viper Three* by Walter Wager (who also wrote *Telefon*, which was later made into a 1977 film with Charles Bronson, and *58 Minutes*, which was adapted to become *Die Hard 2*). The novel has Lawrence Dell, a former general sent to prison on trumped-up charges who then escapes from death row with five other prisoners. Using Dell's knowledge of a nearby military silo, the prisoners hijack the base with a demand for $5 million, a flight out of the country, and the president as a hostage, or else the nuclear missiles at the silo will be launched.

Lorimar, a studio known for their television programming, bought the rights to the book and asked director Robert Aldrich (*Whatever Happened to Baby Jane?* and *The Dirty Dozen*) to look at it, as actors and other directors passed the project by. Aldrich spotted the issue, as he told *Film Comment* in 1977: "Two guys hijack the President, they hold him up for some money, they get killed and the President gets off free. There was no social impact. The kidnappers had no interesting motivations. The reasons they wanted to get the President weren't even PLO-type reasons. They just wanted the money. That didn't seem to me to make much sense."

With screenwriters Ronald M. Cohen and Edward Huebsch, Aldrich upped the stakes for Dell: $10 million, passage out of the country on Air Force One with the president as a hostage, and for the president to go public with secret documents proving the United States continued fighting in Vietnam even though they knew the war was unwinnable. Charles Durning, who commonly played slightly confused or put-upon secondary characters, is quite good as President David Stevens, a man who looks like he's very close to physically attacking members of his cabinet who freely admit their role in hiding the material and sending Dell to prison on false charges to keep him silent. Sympathetic to Dell's plight, Stevens arrives at the silo with Air Force One, announces he will release the document, and bravely agrees to be a hostage for Dell and the one remaining prisoner still with him. The government has other plans, however, and once outside the silo, snipers take out Dell and his assistant, with the president fatally wounded. As he lies dying, the president asks the secretary of defense (Melvyn Douglas) if he will release the document, only to receive no response from the secretary.

It's a cynical 1970s ending to the film that invokes the spirit of those films of the 1930s, like *The President Vanishes, Washington Merry-Go-Round*, and even *Mr. Smith Goes to Washington*, where we feel powerless against an uncaring government. In 1964, a president could almost single-handedly stop a coup in *Seven Days in May*, but less than fifteen years later, he can't even expose the truth about a topic many already suspected to be true without "accidentally" being killed. Aldrich in his *Film Comment* interview wanted audiences to think most probably it was an accident, but in that age, as is now, we are conditioned to think the worst. The most powerful man in the land was not safe from the government, and if he wasn't, then how can any of us be?

The vice president takes a more active role in the next movie to feature a kidnapping of the president. In fact, it's right there in the title, *The Kidnapping of the President* (1980), which also reinforces the role of the Secret Service agent who some may not see as competent, but who nevertheless saves the president, as seen earlier in *The President Vanishes*. This Canadian production with a predominately Canadian cast and crew stars William Shatner as Secret Service agent Jerry O'Connor, who suspects that a trip to Toronto by President Adam Scott (Hal Holbrook) is likely to end in an attempt on the president's life after the sighting of a presumed-dead terrorist named Roberto Assanti (Miguel Fernandes). The president has other concerns, though, after receiving proof that Vice President Ethan Richards (Van Johnson) was on the take when governor and is still getting payments. The president asks for Richards's resignation before heading off on his Toronto trip. Further complications occur when the head of security for the trip suffers a heart attack on the flight, forcing O'Connor to take over the details, to the chagrin of the CIA director (Gary Reineke), who believes O'Connor is incompetent.

As it turns out, O'Connor is right. Assanti appears in the crowd in Toronto and handcuffs himself to the president, wearing a vest with explosives. Everyone backs off as Assanti guides the president to an armored truck that is set up with sound, heat, and motion detectors rigged to set off explosives if disturbed. Assanti then demands $10 million in diamonds and two planes for himself and his assistant hidden in the crowd, Linda (Cindy Girling).

Robert Trussell of the *Kansas City Star* in 1980 raved about Holbrook's performance "as the no-nonsense common-sense chief executive, [who] looks like better presidential material than any of the current crop of candidates," and it's an accurate description. His Scott wants no negotiations with the terrorists, and even though he is handcuffed inside the truck, he still picks at the walls and floor of the truck by hand to get some idea as to how he may be able to get out (he never sets off the motion detector, but he's not aware of them). He's responsible and ready to do what is needed for the best of the country.

It is at this point in the film that the vice president gets to do a bit more than normal for such films. It's no accident that Richards is being asked to resign over bribery, as Richards is clearly based on former Maryland governor Spiro Agnew, who had to resign in 1973 from the vice presidency due to similar charges. After the president is kidnapped, the audience is given a scene amusingly featured in many such movies where the Cabinet reads the Twenty-Fifth Amendment as if no one has heard of it before or knows what would happen if the president is not around. Richards is unsure of his actions and keeps asking O'Connor by phone what to do, but O'Connor feels reluctant to make decisions for Richards. The cabinet reads a quote from Richards about not nego-tiating with terrorists, as the President himself has made clear, as well. However, the CIA director refuses to follow O'Connor's lead, and a timer in the truck is activated that will cause it to explode in three hours, pretty much taking the matter out of Richards's hands. A last-ditch effort by O'Connor to turn Linda against Assanti works too well, with Linda killing the terrorist, which forces O'Connor to take drastic measures to secure the president in the time remaining before the truck explodes. The plan works, and after being saved, Scott calls Richards to commend his dedication during the crisis and to forget about the resignation.

The movie has a television-film quality to it that many movies from the late 1970s and 1980s suffered from. (If Shatner did not on occasion drop an F-word here and there, it would be easy to wonder where the commercial breaks would be.) Still, as mentioned earlier, the actors do fine work, and there are some solid moments of tension, such as an early stop to fix up the armored truck leading to a shoot-out at a gas station and a later moment with O'Connor trying to stop a fanatic from crossing a melting ice rink and reaching the truck before a sniper can take the person out. The movie also sets up many of the principles of later films of this sort:

1. The president is aware of approaching danger but is assured things aren't that bad. (The CIA director tells the president to ignore O'Connor.)
2. Things really are that bad, and he is soon in danger. (See the title of the movie.)
3. Nevertheless, the president is resourceful and does what he can to stop the terrorists. (Scott picks his way through the truck while waiting, and he instructs the cabinet not to pay the ransom.)
4. There is a third party who will try to throw all plans into chaos. (The CIA director arrests Linda, which triggers the timer to be started on the explosives.)
5. An officer/lone-wolf cop/ex-CIA agent/fallen Secret Service agent who is not trusted by those in power but who has special knowl-

edge that makes him or her indispensable is the only one who can save the president and is trusted by him or her. (The CIA director does not trust O'Connor, but the president does.)

6. The president faces a final danger before the resolution. (The cheap edit done to make it momentarily appear as if the truck has blown up with the president still inside.)

This formula is played out through many movies to come, especially in cable and streaming-channel movies and direct-to-video films that seemed to grow in number after the release of *Air Force One*. Here's a sampling:

- *Executive Target* (1997), with Michael Madsen out to save Roy Scheider as the president
- *The Peacekeeper* (1997), with Dolph Lundgren out to save Roy Scheider as a different president
- *Strategic Command* (1997), with Michael Dudikoff out to save the vice president
- *Loyal Opposition: Terror in the White House* (1998), with Joan Van Ark as the vice president out to save Lloyd Bochner as the president
- *First Daughter* (1999), with Mariel Hemingway out to save Gregory Harrison as the president
- *Agent of Death* (2000), with Eric Roberts out to save John Beck as the president
- *Chain of Command* (2000), with Patrick Muldoon out to save Roy Scheider as a completely new, absolutely different president
- *First Target* (2000), with Daryl Hannah playing Mariel Hemingway's character out to save Gregory Harrison again
- *First Shot* (2002), with Mariel Hemingway back to save Gregory Harrison one final time
- *Air Force Two* (2006, also known as *In Her Line of Fire*), with Mariel Hemingway not playing that Secret Service agent but a different one—swear to God—who is out to save David Keith as the vice president

- *Airline Disaster* (2010), with Scott Valentine as the brother of the president, played by Meredith Baxter, and who (here's the twist) must save himself
- 3 *Musketeers* (2011), with three Secret Service agents out to save Andy Clemence as the president
- *America Has Fallen* (2016, also known as *Rising Fear*), with Tom Getty out to save Chuck Getty as the president

Of course, tweaks to that format are bound to occur, and a movie released in 1981 gave us a more futuristic look at such a concept with John Carpenter's *Escape from New York*. Most elements of the "kidnapped president" film are here, with Snake Plissken (Kurt Russell) established as a decorated hero of the government who had turned against them for vague reasons. He is given a chance for a pardon, however, when Air Force One is taken over by terrorists (obviously not the last time that's going to happen in a movie) and President John Harker (Donald Pleasence) uses an escape pod to abandon the plane, only to land in Manhattan. The problem is that Manhattan, in the future year of 1997, is now a maximum-security prison with the most ruthless criminals inside, and when security arrives to extract the president from the pod, they find that he is missing and being held for ransom by the Duke (Isaac Hayes). The Duke, also known as "A-Number One," plans to use Harker as a means for a mass escape from the prison, but he's going to take his time torturing the president first. The offer is made to Plissken to enter Manhattan to rescue the president and a cassette tape in his briefcase with information about nuclear fusion that he plans to produce at a peace summit in twenty-two hours. With explosives placed in his body that will detonate in twenty-two hours if he is not back with Harker and the tape, Plissken has a better incentive to complete the mission.

Plissken tracks down the whimpering President Harker and, with friends sacrificing themselves in the process, helps him escape. At the wall of the prison, where guards have set up a pulley system to draw them up and over, Plissken sends the president first. Soon after, when he is halfway up the wall, Plissken's ascent is stopped by the president in order to draw out the Duke, who has followed them, into the open so the president can gleefully execute him with a gun. After finally making his way over the wall and having the explosives in his body deactivated,

**The conniving President Harker (Donald Pleasence) from *Escape from New York* (1981) is about to be sent out via escape pod from Air Force One. Official press still, author's collection, © 1981 by Avco Embassy Pictures Corp.**

Plissken discovers that Harker has little concern for the people who died trying to rescue him. Seeing the president's disregard, Plissken walks away a free man while destroying the tape that the president planned to use in the summit.

Typically, if there's a negative political figure in one of these movies, it's the vice president or some type of military leader but not the president himself. *Escape from New York* is a rarity in showing us a negative image of a president. Harker is narcissistic in the final moments of the film and somewhat sadistic with his willingness to strand Plissken in order to draw out the Duke, taunting him as he riddles him with bullets. Harker also is hardly the action president we're used to seeing in these films. He acts presidential only when he is secure in the knowledge that no harm can come to him. Once security is gone, he's a coward; once the tape is gone, his control over the peace conference vanishes, and he has nothing to say. It isn't a presidential image, that's for sure, although considering the abuse he's just been through, one could almost excuse him for wanting to personally deal with A-Number-One. (Interestingly, Carpenter in his commentary for the movie on video mentions that Donald Pleasence, as a pilot during World War II, had been captured and used some of that emotional baggage in his reactions as the president in the film.)

Harker can be given somewhat of a pass for his actions after being tortured by the Duke and perhaps even be excused for having more pressing concerns about saving a peace conference for the country after his ordeal than worrying about those who died. At least he isn't the insane commander in chief who would appear in the sequel film by John Carpenter featuring Snake Plissken, *Escape from LA* (1996). That film, written by Kurt Russell and John Carpenter, is set in 2013 and has Plissken being sent to a new prison, which is on an island that used to be Los Angeles and is now cut off from the rest of the state of California after a massive earthquake. Times have changed, with the prison set up to contain anyone who does not fit the new morality of the nation forced upon it by the president (Cliff Robertson, who played John F. Kennedy in *PT 109*). Made president for life in 2000 after predicting the earthquake that cut off Los Angeles, the president pushes hard-core conservative values by outlawing smoking, alcohol, red meat, profanity, sex outside of marriage, and any deviation from strict Christian values. Men, women, and children convicted of crimes against the state are given the opportunity to either be electrocuted or deported to the LA prison for life.

The president's daughter, Utopia, is brainwashed by a terrorist named Cuervo Jones to steal a remote-control device for the Sword of Damocles satellite, which can destroy all electronics in a designated area, from a city block to the entire world, with just the touch of a button. Utopia launches the escape pod from Air Force Three (evidently in the future, the president's kid gets her own plane designation) with herself and the remote inside so that she will land inside the LA prison where Jones is located, leaving a message that the country needs to revolt against her father. The president had plans to use the device to stop an invasion by several other countries already in progress. Now, however, Jones plans to use the device to help knock out American military forces and allow the advancing enemy forces to take over the United States in the next ten hours.

The president, a sadistic religious fanatic gloating about how superior he is to those around him, has no concern for his daughter, whom he sees as a traitor to him and America, and tells Plissken to kill her if found. All he wants is the remote control back. Plissken manages to complete the mission and bring back Utopia, only for the president to immediately send her to be executed for her crimes against him. He then goes on international television to bellow that he will use the satellites as a "final solution" unless forces are withdrawn immediately. The remote given to him by Plissken turns out to be a fake, however, and the president demands Plissken be executed live on television for the betrayal. When the president tells him that it is "us or them," it solidifies Plissken's view that a world without people like the president holding that kind of power may be for the best, and he activates the device to destroy all electronics in the world so no one can have that kind of power.

*Escape from LA* was not a success at the time, although some fans of the original liked it even with the repetitive setups and weak CGI effects. A kidnapping occurs, albeit the victim is the president's daughter, and once again we have an ex-serviceman save the day to help fulfill the common grounds of such films. One could even say we have an action president. Even the president here, who is never named, is drawn from our worst nightmares of leaders, obviously born out of fears of the growing religious Right movement from the 1980s and 1990s, just as Harker seems drawn from the early days of the Reagan era, where appearing to act tough was just as important as actually being tough. The president of *Escape from LA* thinks he has God on his side and no doubt has his public believing that his proclamations will turn the tide against those who are ruining the country from within and who need to be locked away and forgotten. And even though some question the president's desire to publicly execute Plissken on television, the president knows that he can get away with it because his public will believe he is doing what is right. After all that, Plissken's actions may be severe, but it is the only thing to give the world time to come to their senses as this deranged president vanishes, at least from all electronic devices for the time being.

One of the few other negative portrayals of a president involving a kidnapping outside of Carpenter is in David Mamet's 2004 film *Spartan*, starring Val Kilmer as a former soldier searching for the president's daughter, who has been kidnapped and forced into an international sex ring (no, really). In that movie, information suggests the president allowed his daughter to be kidnapped to cover up his extramarital affairs related to the sex ring, only for him to be able to use the soldier's saving of his daughter as a positive political spin on a possible scandal. Yet in the case of *Spartan*, we are never even shown the president and must go by what other characters say of his involvement, so it doesn't quite fit this category here, even with a kidnapped president's daughter. As for Snake Plissken, the lack of success of the second movie meant no more Plissken confrontations with the president, negative, kidnapped, or otherwise.

At least not by Carpenter himself. In 2012, a science fiction action movie called *Lockout* was released, with Guy Pearce as Snow, a man in 2079 convicted for a crime he didn't commit and given a chance to save the kidnapped daughter of the president. The problem is that the daughter, Emilie (Maggie Grace) is in MS One, a penitentiary out in space, investigating rumors of prisoners being experimented on. Alex, one of the prisoners on the station, then kidnaps the president's daughter during a riot at the station and demands the release of the prisoners. Snow at first refuses to go until he is told that one of the prisoners can prove his innocence, giving us the usual Plissken incentive to agree to a mission. The resemblance to Carpenter's Snake Plissken and the two *Escape From* movies is so close that it led to a plagiarism suit in France by Carpenter, which he won. At least in the case of *Lockout*, the president (played by Peter Duson) is trying to do the right thing and wants his daughter safely back, unlike the previous two films with kidnapped president's daughters here. He refuses an attack on the station, fearing that his daughter may be killed and hopes Snow can do the job instead. This leads to the rather ludicrous plot twist of the Secret Service director producing a Twenty-Fifth Amendment paper from seemingly nowhere to relieve the president of his duties so the Secret Service director can bomb the station and kill everyone there. At least earlier movies tried to present a cabinet working through the idea of using the amendment. Here, it is evidently an easy online legal print-off you can get with no delay. That's the convenience of 2079 for you.

Snow does save the president's daughter; the prisoners all get blown up; the president gets reinstated; Snow gets proof of his innocence; and in a final moment resembling Plissken, Snow walks away from the event with the secret information on him that the government had been look-ing for all along. While we don't get the action president, we do get the Twenty-Fifth Amendment in fast-food form, and the daughter of the president dodges an escape pod like Marshall in *Air Force One* in order to go back in the station and help save Snow, our ex-agent in peril. In this case, however, the president himself doesn't have much to do but sit in a room and listen in on events happening around him.

Escape pods crop up a few times in these movies, including three times from Air Force One and once from Air Force Three in the case of *Escape from LA*. (There's also an escape pod used by the president, played by John Savage, in the straight-to-video monster movie *Bermuda Tentacles* from 2014, but the greatest horror is that a great actor like John Savage is performing in a straight-to-video monster movie.) When asked, the White House is clear that an escape pod is a work of fiction, and there is no such device on Air Force One. Of course, maybe that's just what they want us to believe. If so, that hasn't stopped their use in the movies, and there is one more example of it being used by the president to avoid terrorists kidnapping him: the 2014 Finnish film *Big Game*, starring Samuel L. Jackson as President Alan Moore and written and directed by Jalmari Helander, who had previously done the endear-ingly strange Santa Claus movie *Rare Exports: A Christmas Tale* (2010).

The movie has Ray Stevenson (*Punisher: War Zone, Thor*) as Morris, a Secret Service agent who gets the lame-duck president to the escape pod when Air Force One is attacked by terrorists. Yet Morris is not our ne'er-do-well agent who will prove himself by saving the president. Instead, he's the mole who is helping the bad guys, like in *Air Force One*. The cast-out hero instead is Oskari Kontio (Onni Tommila, the star of *Rare Exports*), a thirteen-year-old boy from a Finnish village who doesn't appear to have the famous hunting skills of his father. Sent out to collect a deer as part of a village initiation into adulthood, he avoids the crashing Air Force One in the forest, chances upon the escape pod, and releases the president from inside. The pair take off on the run through the woods and mountain terrain, with Morris and the bad guys in pursuit. Back in Washington, the vice president (Victor Garber), ter-rorism expert Fred Herbert (Jim Broadbent), and others try to track down the president and the terrorists. The rest of the film is a cat-and-mouse game as Oskari helps the president repeatedly avoid capture.

Although a foreign film using the concept of the American president, the position is never made fun of as one would expect another country would attempt to do. Jackson as President Moore does get the brush-off from Oskari early in their adventures, when Moore attempts to use his clout to commandeer the boy's ATV, but is paternal to Oskari when the boy discovers that the map his father gave him as a guide to finding the best hunting place takes him to a prepared deer head. Thus instead of the agent no one trusts, we have the boy hunter that no one in his village, including his father, thinks is a hunter. Moore is also out of shape, not good in a fight, doesn't know how to use a gun, and thus lacks elements of the action president, but he is still a nice switch-up to the more physical characters Jackson commonly plays. He is protective of Oskari, however, and tries his best to hold off Moore to give the boy a chance to safely get away. He later makes a point to Oskari's father as to how good of a hunter his boy is.

The attack is finally disclosed as being the work of the vice president and the terrorist expert Herbert, who had planned for the death of the president to propel the vice president into the Oval Office and incite the public to pour more money into fighting terrorism. Once again, we have a vice president who is easily swung over to the wrong side, which seems to be a rather preoccupied position for vice presidents in many of these movies. Surprisingly, the film allows the main hidden villain, Herbert, to duck out of any repercussions by killing the vice president in a staged accident in order to avoid him telling anyone of their actions.

An additional example of a vice president looking out for himself in hopes of taking over as president is in *Iron Man 3* (2013), which has Vice President Rodriguez (Miguel Ferrer) secretly working with the supervillain Aldrich Killian (Guy Pearce from *Lockout*) to have President Ellis (William Sadler) eliminated so that Rodriguez can take over. That movie also gives us a chance to briefly see Ellis in action-president mode. He initiates contact with the Mandarin (Ben Kingsley), a front for Killian, to try to stop an execution, even though others advise him not to do so. He also attempts to use a gun to protect himself when Killian initiates his kidnapping on Air Force One midway through the movie. Finally, near the end of the movie, while trapped inside the War Machine/Iron Patriot suit normally worn by Stark's associate James Rhodes, Ellis momentarily helps fight Killian with Stark and the others.

It's a rare appearance of a president in more than two dozen movies made based on the Marvel Comics superhero staple that began with *Iron Man* in 2008, which is surprising, considering how often the actions of the heroes involve international and other-worldly events. Ellis is briefly alluded to in *Captain America: The Winter Soldier* (2014), pops up momentarily in a deleted scene from *Ant-Man* (2015), and appears a handful of times in the Marvel television series *Agents of S.H.I.E.L.D.*, but some question if that series is canonic to the storylines featured in the theatrical movies. Instead, most political events seen in the Marvel films are handled by members of the military, while other common political figures turn out to be hiding ulterior motives, such as Alexander Pierce (Robert Redford), the secretary for the World Security Council, and Senator Stern (Garry Shandling) in *Captain America: The Winter Soldier*, who both turn out to be working for the evil organization H.Y.D.R.A. (To go back further, one could count the mutant-hating Senator Robert Kelly, played by Bruce Davison, in *X-Men* from 2000.) There is one major exception to this for Marvel (beyond *X-Men: Days of Future Past*, covered in more detail in chapter 9) and it involves another kidnapping of the president. It just happens to be a movie not considered part of the Marvel Cinematic Universe.

*Captain America* from 1990 was supposed to be a fresh attempt to develop the Marvel superhero character after two television attempts in 1979 failed. The movie tries to stick somewhat with the origin given to the character in the comic: a soldier (Matt Salinger) who is sickly gains superstrength via a special serum to become Captain America. In fighting the Red Skull (Scott Paulin), Captain America saves Washington, DC, in 1943 but ends up frozen in ice until 1993, when he is revived to continue his battle against crime.

As it turns out, the president, Tom Kimball (Ronny Cox), was once a boy who idolized Captain America and photographed him in 1943. Kimball falls into the line that we see of President Marshall in *Air Force One*, as he is a Vietnam War hero who takes aggressive action against the status quo in Washington and turns others against him as president. In his case, Kimball is an environmental president seeking to pass legislation that goes against military buildup supported by an American general (Darren McGavin) and Captain America's old nemesis, the Red Skull. The Red Skull has the president kidnapped in order to brainwash him to do his bidding, but Captain America is on the case and eventually tracks the Red Skull to his lair, where the president is busy trying to break himself out. The president and Captain America then work together to fight the Red Skull's henchmen and stop the Red Skull from setting off a nuclear bomb.

The movie was written by Stephen Tolkin and directed by Albert Pyun and looks very cheap (as many have noted, Captain America in costume has plastic ears where the actor's real ears should appear). Originally to be released to theaters in April 1990, it got pushed back to August of that year and then quietly released overseas in 1991 before eventually turning up on video in 1992. It does give us a president working to get out of his cell at the Red Skull's hideout and who is handy with various weapons when given a chance late in the movie. He gets a thumb's up from Captain America, his boyhood hero, before the movie is over, and affirms our continued hope that a president would prove to be the leader we would want.

The vice president in *Sudden Death* (1995), starring Jean-Claude Van Damme, isn't out to get anyone for once, although he and several others do get kidnapped during the Stanley Cup Final by a group of terrorists. Van Damme (whose main stunt in the film is being worked into the plot as a French Canadian fire marshal in Pittsburgh) works through a *Die Hard*–type scenario, only with a crowded arena full of people watching the game in addition to hostages to save. Van Damme saves everyone and even gets to play in the hockey game at one point, showing how amazing he is (or how somewhat silly the whole enterprise is). Power Boothe plays the obvious Secret Service mole working with the terrorists, a character we've seen before and will see again in the following movies.

Two films showing the White House being taken over by terrorists and the president being kidnapped came out in 2013: *White House Down* and *Olympus Has Fallen*. Both feature a mole in the White House's security who helps terrorists infiltrate the area, kill the vice president (to prove how dastardly the villains are), and destroy the premises. There is a lone officer who is the president's only hope, a child in danger who sees the officer as a father figure, and a president willing to jump in and take physical action when given a chance. Once it was realized that both films were plotting similar courses, they were in competition to see which could get released first, with *Olympus Has*

*Fallen* getting to theaters in the spring of 2013 and *White House Down* following that summer.

*Olympus Has Fallen* is the more sophisticated in plot of the two, although *White House Down* is more fun to watch. *Olympus Has Fallen* stars Gerard Butler as Mike Banning, a Secret Service agent who was pushed down in rank when he failed to save the First Lady during an automobile accident. A visiting South Korean congregation turns out to be a front for a terrorist infiltration of the White House, and they kidnap President Benjamin Asher (Aaron Eckhart), the vice president, the secretary of defense, and the chairman of the Joint Chiefs of Staff and hold them in the Presidential Emergency Operations Center (PEOC), which is a reinforced bunker deep under the White House used for emergencies. Speaker of the House Allan Trumbull (Morgan Freeman), working as the leader of the country with the president and vice president under duress, initiates an assault on the White House to stop the terrorists. Meanwhile, Banning manages to slip inside the White House and begins to *Die Hard* his way through the place to save, first, the president's son and, then, the president, before deactivating the missiles at the last second.

The film is pretty cookie-cutter for an action movie—it even features the destruction of a helicopter that supposedly has the lead terrorist on it so he can sneak away with everyone thinking him dead, much like in *Die Hard*. Trumbull, as the accidental president, has his burden of mistakes when he is first talked into a siege on the White House that not only wipes out the soldiers but also leads to the vice president being killed in retaliation, while a pull-back of US troops in Korea only leads to the terrorists activating the United States' nuclear arsenal in order to kill everyone. There are moments of the action president, as well, which are introduced in the beginning of the film, when the president is shown working out with Banning, and eventually fighting the terrorists near the end to allow some payback for the abuse he received from the head terrorist.

*Olympus Has Fallen* was a big enough success to lead to two sequels, *London Has Fallen* (2016) and *Angel Has Fallen* (2019). *London Has Fallen* has Aaron Eckhart again as President Asher and Gerard Butler as Mike Banning, only this time he's leading security for the president on a visit to London to attend the funeral of the British prime minister. The funeral turns out to be a set-up: The Prime Minister was poisoned

Gerard Butler plays a bodyguard for the kidnapped President Asher (Aaron Eckhart), while Allan Trumbull (Morgan Freeman) takes on the role of accidental president in *Olympus Has Fallen* (2013). *Official movie poster, author's collection.*

to bring world leaders to London to be executed around the city by an international arms trafficker, Aamir Barkawi (Alon Monni Aboutboul), who was thought to have been killed in an attack two years prior that took out most of his family. With Barkawi's cabal having infiltrated the police and the government telling everyone to stay inside, Banning and Asher are on their own in a deserted London, with only the bad guys out on the streets looking for them. Back in Washington, Trumbull is now the vice president (after the death of the vice president in the previous film) and works to locate Barkawi's people in the city. Once again, a mole, in this case the chief of counterintelligence for MI5, puts much in motion for the villain, but at least this time, it's not an inside job from the good ol' USA. Asher, perfecting his inner action president, helps Banning to take out the cabal in London, while Trumbull learns from earlier mistakes he made in *Olympus Has Fallen*; locates Barkawi's hideout; and destroys it, killing Barkawi and his followers.

The final movie in the series, at least so far (there are still rumors of at least three more movies to be made, with the next being *Night Has Fallen*) is the 2019 film *Angel Has Fallen*. In this one, Asher is no longer president, and Trumbull has been elected. Trumbull plans to have Banning made the head of the Secret Service, when the pair are attacked on a fishing trip that leaves the president in a coma, and evidence is falsified to make it look as if Banning attempted to kill the president on the directive of the Russian government. Banning goes on the run to prove his innocence, meeting up with his father, played by Nick Nolte (Thomas Jefferson in *Jefferson in Paris*). It turns out that an old trainer for Banning put together a deal with the vice president (Tim Blake Nelson), who once again is found to have gone rogue. His plan was to have the Russians blamed for Trumbull's death in order to kick off another cold war, profit in arms sales, and no doubt win at a game of Presidential Kidnapping Bingo.

Being in a coma for most of the movie, the president doesn't get much of a chance to have any action beyond being moved out of a hospital rigged to blow up. The film is more about Banning, with the president given little to do, and considering how famous Banning must be for already having saved the president twice by that point, it is curious anyone would suddenly suspect him of attempting to assassinate one, but when you're on your third film, you do what you can to keep things rolling.

*White House Down*, directed by Roland Emmerich of *The Day after Tomorrow*, is the other "president kidnapped in the White House" film from 2013. It deals with President James Sawyer (Jamie Foxx) working to have US troops pulled from the Middle East (another peace attempt leading to an assault on the presidency). An attack on the Capitol building leads to President Sawyer being moved to the PEOC by Secret Service head Martin Walker (James Woods), while Vice President Alvin Hammond (Michael Murphy) is transported to Air Force One, and Speaker of the House Eli Raphelson (Richard Jenkins) is moved to a secure location at the Pentagon. It turns out, as always, that there is a mole who is helping the attackers, and it is Walker, who is looking for retribution after his son was killed while serving in the Middle East in a war that now has been made redundant by the president. Sawyer finds out that Walker, who is dying of cancer (very much like Moore in *Big Game*, who needs pills to stay alive and wants to take down a president he sees as weak before he dies), wants him to use the nuclear football (a device commonly seen in a briefcase handcuffed to a member of the president's party that allows the president to activate a nuclear strike if needed while away from the White House) in order to bomb targets in the Middle East.

As a group of mercenaries take over the White House with Walker's help, a group of tourists are made hostages. The hostages include the daughter of a police officer, John Cale (Channing Tatum), but Cale manages to slip away momentarily right before the hostages are taken, allowing him to *Die Hard* his way around the White House, much like Banning does in the other film. Distracting Walker long enough, Cale and the action president Sawyer attempt to escape, only to appear to have been killed in a limo explosion.

When this occurs, the Twenty-Fifth Amendment is once again brought up, and Vice President Hammond is made president only moments before a hacked missile is sent into Air Force One, killing him and thus making Speaker of the House Raphelson the new president. As it turns out, this was always part of the plan, with Raphelson sending Walker the codes for the nuclear football in order to set off the missiles. Walker manages to get Sawyer's thumbprint to activate the nuclear football and is about to press the button when Cale arrives and kills Walker. President Sawyer is saved, and the accidental president Raphelson is found to have started the whole scheme in order to become president so he could stop a peace treaty.

*White House Down* takes us to the edge of disaster with the wrong person having control of the nation, only for salvation to come in the form of a president we know will set things right. The common feature of all these movies is that our superhero, the action president or someone working for the president, jumps in and fixes the nation and the world for us, and even the accidental presidents learn and are reborn as action presidents in their own right. It's the comic book ending we need. Hollywood tends to avoid negative portrayals of presidents because our own historical values have presented us with presidents who were not good for the nation but who were in due course defeated and replaced with someone who rectifies those problems. And if we can't have that in reality, then at least let us have it in our fantasies.

But the real world is calling. We left the presidents in chapter 1 only a few years into the nation's birth and with many adjustments to prove itself a strong nation. We return to 1825, when America is about to go through some of its deepest growing pains over the next forty years.

**3**

# ADAMS THROUGH PIERCE

The Messenger and the Downgrading of the President

We've come to understand that who we are is who we were.

—John Quincy Adams in *Amistad* (1997)

In 1825, the Founding Fathers had moved on, and the next generation was taking on the roles of the government, with the election of John Quincy Adams in 1825. Adams, the son of John Adams, was born on July 11, 1767, and witnessed much of his father's diplomatic history by traveling with him. That experience, along with his education as a lawyer after graduating from Harvard, led him to an appointment by Washington to be an ambassador to the Netherlands in 1795 and then to Prussia, before returning in 1801 and becoming a senator for Massachusetts in 1803. Although voted in as the Federalist Party's candidate, Adams became known for defying his own party when voting in the Senate, which led to the party picking a replacement six months before his term was over and his resignation from office. Adams was offered an appointment to the Supreme Court in 1811 and refused, deciding to continue his work as an ambassador overseas and leading to his large contribution in negotiating the end of the War of 1812. He finally agreed to return to the United States to become secretary of state for James Monroe, where he helped create the Monroe Doctrine (discussed in chapter 1) and worked on sealing the deal with Spain for Florida in 1819's Adams-Onis Treaty, which Adams considered one of the most important events in his life.

Adams would run for the presidency in 1824 against Henry Clay, W. H. Crawford, John Calhoun, and Andrew Jackson, with Jackson winning the most electoral votes and popular votes but not enough to claim a majority of the 261 electoral votes. Henry Clay, not liking Jackson, threw his votes to Adams, securing the votes needed to win the House vote that followed when the electoral vote did not conclude a winner.

Such a decision like Henry Clay's to swing his votes to another candidate is much more common today in the party nomination process, with candidates who know they will lose releasing the delegates dedicated to voting for them and suggesting they vote for another candidate instead. *The Best Man* (1964), written by Gore Vidal and directed by Franklin Schaffner (*Patton, Nicholas and Alexandra*) deals specifically with this concept. The film has multiple candidates running for the Democratic Party presidential nomination, including William Russell (Henry Fonda), Joe Cantwell (Cliff Robertson), and John Merwin (William Ebersol). Cantwell is a hustler, willing to do anything to get what he wants, Russell is a more sedate and serious candidate, and Merwin is seen as a good man but without the personality of the other two. A former president who is near death, Art Hockstader (Lee Tracy, who won an Academy Award as Best Supporting Actor here), refuses to help swing votes, with Russell and Cantwell in a virtual tie. He sees Cantwell as determined but too volatile, while Russell is too reliant on principles and not willing to play dirty as Hockstader feels all politicians should. Both major candidates have skeletons in their closet that can damage their careers, as well. Russell suffered an emotional collapse a few years prior, while Cantwell participated in a same-sex affair during World War II. When Russell refuses to use Cantwell's scandal to turn votes against him, Cantwell think he has the nomination in the bag, little realizing that Russell will instead endorse his delegates to the third candidate, thus giving John Mervin enough votes to win the nomination.

In the case of *The Best Man*, such a decision unifies the party. The similar decision by Clay for Adams may have allowed Adams to take office but would split the Democratic-Republican Party over what some saw as Adams making an under-the-table deal with Clay to get his votes.

**Henry Fonda and Cliff Robertson, presidents in a number of other films, fight for the nomination in the 1964 movie *The Best Man*. Original movie poster, © 1964 by Millar/Turman Production, Inc.**

With Clay announced as secretary of state under Adams, it was not easy to dismiss that notion. The issue would directly lead to the Democratic-Republican Party splitting into two, with Republicans following Adams and Jackson obtaining interest from the Democrats. Adams would also find it difficult to get Congress to move on any of his objectives during his term, with many of his requests to advance education, a national bankruptcy law, infrastructure, and diplomacy with Mexico and South America ignored. In the next election, he lost to Andrew Jackson and initially planned to retire from politics, when he was elected to the House of Representatives for Massachusetts, where he would spend the rest of his career, until his death in 1848.

Although people tend to remember John Quincy Adams as a president, it is namely due to his namesake more than the actions he took in office. That is not to say that the things he did are entirely dismissed, as he certainly did strive to advance the nation, including working to reduce the country gaining more slave states and helping to promote discussion of the issue (e.g., due to his influence, a gag rule that kept members of the House from even discussing slavery was removed in 1845). What is at issue, as is increasingly common to see, is that he did his best work behind the desk and not in a pursuit that drew attention to him. Because of this, the best representation of John Quincy Adams is really in the 1976 PBS television miniseries *The Adams Chronicles*, which devotes four episodes to him. Theatrical pickings are slim, however, with a quick shot of Grant Mitchell as Adams in *The Monroe Doctrine* (1939), discussed in chapter 1, and then a large secondary role for Adams in the 1997 Steven Spielberg movie *Amistad*.

*Amistad* is based on a real-life incident where a group of enslaved Africans took over a ship called *La Amistad* in 1839. The ship was captured by the American Navy, and a court battle commenced, with many parties claiming those enslaved as cargo they owned, including Secretary of State John Forsyth (David Paymer), who represents Spain's claim, per the request of President Martin Van Buren (Nigel Hawthorne). Abolitionists Lewis Tappan (Stellan Skarsgård) and Theodore Joadson (Morgan Freeman) hire Roger Sherman Baldwin (Matthew McConaughey) to defend those enslaved and earn their freedom. Baldwin finds evidence that the people were kidnapped to be illegally sold in America and should be freed, only for the US government to replace the judge and attempt a different tack to win the case for Spain. With help from an interpreter, Sengbe Pieh (Djimon Hounsou), who can speak to the leader of those enslaved, the case expands to deal with a slave fortress in Sierra Leone and stories of torture and cover-ups. Even with the new judge, the verdict is to set the Africans free, which leads to the United States pushing the case to the Supreme Court in 1841.

Prior to this point, the film periodically checks in with John Quincy Adams (Anthony Hopkins), introduced as dozing in the House although very much aware of the discussion occurring around him. Joadson and Baldwin routinely visit Adams for advice on the case, and although Adams sympathizes, he shows little interest in getting involved until asked to help when it reaches the Supreme Court. Adams, a known abolitionist, then rallies for nine hours while presenting to the Supreme Court why the Africans should be free and helps win the case. Hopkins plays Adams similarly as a handful of other characters he has done before and after, as a man with an air of indifference that hides a man lost in thought who has much to say when motivated to do so. This is clearly the thrust of the Supreme Court case seen in the movie, as well; while not seen, in reality, Baldwin presented the case to the justices, with Adams on the sidelines until concluding arguments. Because of this omission, however, it makes it appear that Adams swooped in and won the case, making his role a touch more important than it may have been.

The film's depiction of the trial also makes it appear that the Africans were then immediately returned by the US government to Africa, which was not the case, nor was this a fatal blow to slavery in the United States. An enslaved individual who was seen as the property of the captain of the ship was ruled to remain enslaved and returned to Cuba (records suggest that abolitionists helped him escape to Canada before he could be sent back), while the remaining Africans, of which there were fewer than forty, were returned to Africa only when members of the public, not the government, made a collection. Although the case touched on slavery on a national stage, it did more to show the complexity and instability of slavery in an international market when more and more countries were turning away from the practice than any public reconsideration of slavery as suggested by the movie.

The film also maligns the image of President Martin Van Buren, born in 1782 and rapidly moving through the ranks of senator from New York, secretary of state, vice president to Andrew Jackson, and finally the eighth president of the United States in 1837. *Amistad* portrays Van Buren as being dictated to by the eleven-year-old Queen of Spain (Anna Paquin) and former vice president John Calhoun (Arliss Howard), who had the ear of the Southern states as a senator for South Carolina. Reality shows that Van Buren merely wanted to keep Spain happy by at least fighting the case for the queen, no matter the results. As for Calhoun, while he did represent the South, he had such a long, turbulent history with Van Buren that the president would have happily ignored his advice.

It is also insinuated in the movie that Van Buren lost his reelection because of the *Amistad* case, when it was more due to the Panic of 1837, which was the first major financial depression to hit the country. (His opponent in the 1840 election, William Henry Harrison, successfully portrayed Van Buren as a rich aristocrat ignorant of the common man based on the depression.) His refusal to annex Texas for fear of making it a slave state and giving Southern states even more leverage in Congress caused Andrew Jackson to pull support for him in the election, as well, which was a death knell to a second term. It is true that Van Buren is not remembered as an excellent leader; his dedication to continuing the policies of Andrew Jackson that deepened the depression, relocating the Cherokees, and continuing a war with the Seminole Indians in Florida that ended badly and helped steer Florida toward becoming a slave state in 1845 are all detrimental to Van Buren's legacy. However, after leaving office and breaking away from the Jackson agenda, it was also clear that he was an abolitionist who would leave the Democratic Party, running as a presidential candidate in 1848 for an antislavery party named the Free Soil. Once the Civil War started, Van Buren threw his support to Lincoln, the Republicans, and the Union, before dying in 1862. There is much more to the man than is seen in the movie, but as with John Dickinson in 1776, every film needs a villain, and Van Buren was an obvious choice for *Amistad*.

Beyond *Amistad*, Van Buren's appearances in movies were nearly as brief as that of John Quincy Adams. He appears in the 1936 Joan Crawford movie *The Gorgeous Hussy*, with Charles Trowbridge in the role, and a blink-and-miss-it bit in the 1939 picture *Man of Conquest*, but both concentrate more on Andrew Jackson anyway. Perhaps it's not surprising that a man who chose to live in the shadow of Jackson would be remembered in much the same manner. Then again, it is hard for most people to not live in the shadow of Andrew Jackson because whether people believe him to be one of the best or worst presidents of the country, he certainly stood out, and his flamboyant style and actions made him a natural for the silver screen.

For many years, Jackson would be seen by the public as the second coming of George Washington: a man who won against the British in the War of 1812 (even though the war was officially over by the time Jackson beat the British at the Battle of New Orleans); fought for the common man by being dismissive of long-time, money-hungry politicians; paid off the nation's debt (the only president to do so); worked to keep the union together when South Carolina looked to secede in the early 1830s; helped set up the annexing of Texas; and was the first president to face an assassination attempt (on January 30, 1835, Richard Lawrence fired two pistols at Jackson, with both misfiring; Jackson responded by nearly killing the man with his cane before Davy Crockett and others could split them apart).

There was a darker side to Andrew Jackson, as well, that tarnished his reputation even while alive. Jackson took part in the Creek War (1813–1814), a series of battles by the US government and several tribes (including the Creek) against a Creek tribe known as the Red Sticks, who were getting assistance from the British and Spanish to hold onto land in the southeastern part of the country. The victory against the Red Sticks would help elevate Jackson's career, but the peace treaty, the Treaty of Fort Jackson, forced many Creek tribes who fought alongside the US troops, as well as the Red Sticks, to give up their land, allowing White settlers on to their land in what would become known as Georgia and Alabama. Jackson would go further in his eradication of Native Americans in the area with the Indian Removal Act of 1830. The act gave the president unusual powers and money to move—sometimes by force—Native American tribes from their homelands to areas west of the Mississippi River. The relocation, which many protested, would last into Martin Van Buren's administration and see the death of tens of thousands, namely Cherokees, forced on the Trail of Tears (the route taking them out West) during harsh weather with few supplies and little assistance.

As someone known to have those enslaved by him beaten and who once ran an advertisement in 1804 offering "$10 for every 100 lashes doled out" to a person who escaped his planation, Jackson shied away from dealing with slavery expanding to the west. While some in Congress squirmed over annexing Texas due to Southern influence, Jackson had no qualms about Texas being a slave state. The issue was that he didn't want to deal with the uproar that would come with it and thus allowed the option to sit for years, frustrating people like Sam Houston, who had to deal with determining if Texas should become an independent country or even join up with Mexico. Elsewhere, Jackson would ignore attempts to prevent slavery in the western territories and saw abolitionists as "monsters" who were only trying to stir up trouble. In balance, Jackson was not that much different from other presidents before and after him, who believed any resistance to slavery in new states would bring about civil war and talk of secession from the South, but Jackson's outspoken public stance on the issue did not age well.

On a more personal note, while Jackson could be kindly and thoughtful, he was seen by many as narcissistic, judgmental, and quick to anger, bestowing favors on his friends but instantly turning against anyone he felt was mistreating his friendship. He was known for demanding duels (some estimates are of a hundred or more) for any number of reasons, most notably when gossip was made about his wife. Many were resolved before any shooting started, or shots were fired into the air to put an end to the discussion, but he did kill one man in such a duel. Jackson was also famous for perpetuating the "spoils system" after being elected, with him giving federal positions (made vacant when experienced individuals were fired) to friends and supporters, many of whom were perhaps not beneficial to the country. Jackson vetoed the renewal charter for the Second National Bank in 1833, as he felt it was tyrannical and favored the rich over the common man. The brinkmanship that followed between Jackson and those in favor of the bank, along with attempts to maneuver money around in state banking, led to the four-year-long Panic of 1837 that Van Buren had to endure as Jackson's replacement.

Yet in 1828, when Jackson was running for president for a second time after first losing to John Quincy Adams in what some saw as a rigged election in 1824, many voters saw only the pride of the War of 1812, the victor of the Battle of New Orleans and the Creek War, and a man who seemed not of some higher aristocratic nature like those before him but one of us. It is that legacy that we came to see in the movies about him, as well. Perhaps not surprisingly, as national interests during the civil rights era in the 1960s turned against some of Jackson's biggest achievements, the interest in portraying him in films dramatically diminished as well, with the last theatrical film featuring Jackson being in the late 1950s.

Born in 1767 in Waxhaw, South Carolina, Andrew Jackson joined a militia at the age of thirteen so he could fight in the Revolutionary War. He became a prisoner of war along with his brother and was once struck down by an officer with a saber for refusing to clean the man's boots, leaving scars on his left arm and his head and changing his attitude toward the British that remained for the rest of his life. By the age of twenty-one, Jackson was an attorney in what would become Tennessee, where he accepted land in exchange for fees for his services, making him a large landowner at an early age. In Nashville, Jackson met Rachel Donelson Robards, a woman who was entangled in an abusive marriage with a man named Lewis Robards. A relationship blossomed between Andrew and Rachel, and in 1790, Jackson spirited Rachel away from her husband. When word reached them that her husband had petitioned for divorce, the pair married in 1791 (although there is some evidence to suggest that they lived together before the petition of divorce became known). It was not until 1793 that they became aware that Lewis had purposefully delayed the divorce in order to damage their reputation. With the divorce finalized, the pair married again in January 1794, but it remained a constant source of ridicule to the Jacksons that some have suggested led to health issues for Rachel and certainly episodes of anger from Andrew. Rachel died six weeks after Jackson was elected to the presidency and was buried in the dress she planned to wear at the inauguration.

Their relationship is the basis of the only movie dealing solely with Jackson, albeit it ends just as he becomes president. *The President's Lady*, based on a 1951 novel by Irving Stone (*Lust for Life*, *The Agony and the Ecstasy*), was picked up by Twentieth Century-Fox to be directed by Henry Levin and written by John Patrick. Charlton Heston, freshly minted as a lead in movies thanks to *Dark City* (1950) and *The Greatest Show on Earth* (1952), was starring in a slew of films placing him in the Old West or as a frontiersman, and *The President's Lady* fit perfectly into that cycle of movies. Susan Hayward (*I'll Cry Tomorrow*, *I Want to Live!*) played Rachel.

The film has an interesting voice-over narrative, as it begins with Rachel introducing the audience to Andrew and periodically filling in details of their history, but the ending voice-over is by Andrew at his inauguration as president, remembering her after her death. While based on a novel, the film sticks close to the historical records of their relationship, their marriage, and Jackson's pursuit of his career that left Rachel on her own for long periods of time, although the order of events are shuffled a bit. The movie plays up a clichéd meet-cute for the pair and is refreshingly open about the idea that the two were unknowing bigamists in a period when such ideas were normally not touched on in Hollywood due to censorship. The movie misrepresents information

about their three adopted children, with the emphasis on their second
son, Lincoya Jackson, a wounded orphan Native American child given
to Andrew Jackson during the Creek War. Lincoya in the film dies suddenly as a child but actually lived to be seventeen years old and died
from long-term tuberculosis in 1828. A duel with Charles Dickinson is
depicted after Lincoya's death, when the duel actually occurred twenty-
two years before that in 1806, and although the duel appears to be about
Rachel, historically the duel came out of the horse race depicted in the
film (there's also no mention that many people thought Jackson cheated
Dickinson in the duel by recocking his gun when it misfired the first
time). Jackson then joins to fight in the War of 1812 and soon after asks
to run for president, although his campaign began thirteen years later in
1825 for the election in 1828. The movie ends with Rachel overhearing
people in a crowd accuse her of being a prostitute and Andrew a murderer. Andrew is physically held back from attacking the accuser, while
Rachel becomes sick and bedridden from the stress, eventually dying
just as Andrew tells her he has won the election. Jackson then reflects on
their life together as he gets ready for his inauguration in the final scene.

Heston is as Heston does. That's not a slight because Heston typically was excellent, even if he tended to stick with one personality in
every movie: a rough but fair man who is good-natured to those who are
decent at heart and dismissive of those who treat others unfairly. Such
a persona worked perfectly for such a role as Andrew Jackson, who appeared to many as a friend of the working class who may have bouts of
anger but fair reasons for that anger. Tall, regal, and athletic, Heston
looked every bit what people wanted Jackson to look like, who in real
life was dour and hawklike. Naturally, the film plays to Jackson as the
hero, even if there are hints of his tendency to quickly boil over in anger.
The film shortchanged Susan Hayworth in the role of Rachel, with more
than one critic pointing out that she spends most of her scenes collaps-
ing in either exhaustion or tears. Nevertheless, the script attempts to
portray Rachel as trying to keep their home and family together while
Andrew is off fighting skirmishes in war or politics.

Andrew Jackson dealing with rumors about his wife plays into another
controversy in his career, the Petticoat Affair (1829–1831), which forms
the basis of a Joan Crawford movie from 1936, *The Gorgeous Hussy*. In
the movie, Crawford plays Peggy O'Neal, the daughter of a tavern and

boardinghouse owner well known to politicians in the Washington, DC, area. Peggy was popular as a hostess of the tavern, with a flirtatious style that rankled outsiders. She married John Timberlake (Robert Taylor), an older man who was heavily in debt, and the couple became friends with John Eaton (Franchot Tone), the senator from Tennessee who was also friends of Andrew Jackson (Lionel Barrymore). Eaton tried to help the Timberlakes with their debt, eventually getting John a position in the US Navy as part of their Mediterranean Squadron, where John later died of pneumonia. After this, John Eaton romanced and eventually married Peggy, which led to the worst kind of rumormongering, suggesting that Eaton sent Timberlake off so he could have an affair with Peggy and that Timberlake committed suicide over his heartbreak when he found out about the two.

When Jackson became president, he suggested the two get married to avoid any innuendo about them together, which did little to calm gossip. Educated but outspoken, Peggy rubbed the elite in Washington the wrong way, and when Eaton became secretary of war, the wives of the members of Jackson's cabinet gave Peggy the cold shoulder, so Eaton was on the outs with the men of the cabinet, as well. Martin Van Buren (Charles Trowbridge), who was then secretary of state, and John Calhoun (Frank Conroy), who was vice president but had designs for the presidency himself, pitted themselves on both sides of what became known as the Petticoat Affair (because it was all to do with the wives rather than the men), with the widower Van Buren siding with Jackson and the Eatons. The situation heated to the point where Jackson dismissed all but the postmaster general of his cabinet, and for this affair and other deeds that Jackson rightly saw as trying to undermine his authority as president, Jackson replaced Calhoun with Van Buren in his second term of office.

Just as *Magnificent Doll* invents romance for Dolley Madison, *The Gorgeous Hussy* takes Peggy's story and creates events to make the situation more adventurous. Although Jackson knew of Peggy from the tavern, they were not particularly close, and he certainly was not the playful "Uncle Andy" seen in the film. The movie has Lionel Barrymore's Jackson doting on Peggy every scene they are in together and eventually making Peggy a close confidant and hostess in Washington, which was simply not the case. A large subplot is made of Peggy's turbulent affair with John Randolph (Melvyn Douglas), a real-life senator from Virginia, which ends with his death at the hands of a man planning a rebellion against the federal government, which he informs Peggy about to pass on to Jackson. This is complete fiction. John Randolph was known for having no interest in women, let alone having even spent time with Peggy, and he would die of natural causes soon after returning from Russia as an ambassador in 1833, four years after Eaton married Peggy. Yet the filmmakers here obviously felt they had to give Peggy something monumental to do, worthy of Jackson demolishing his entire cabinet, so saving the nation, thanks to her love for Randolph, fit the bill. The movie implies that others saw a childhood friend of Peggy's with her as she rushed to be at Randolph's side and insinuates that she was with other men, furthering the gossip and directly leading to Jackson dismissing his cabinet, yet Jackson fired his cabinet in 1831, two years before Randolph's death. The Eatons also did not go directly to Spain, as shown in the film, but rather back to Tennessee and then to Florida, where Eaton served as governor, before finally heading to Spain in 1836 as an ambassador. The couple was together until his death in 1856. Peggy remarried in 1859 to a man who later took off to Europe with most of her money and her granddaughter, leaving Peggy to die in poverty, but that's not the Hollywood ending we all want, especially in 1936, so we'll leave the Eatons happily on their way to Spain as the movie ends.

Just as with John Randolph (who was boyish, with a falsetto voice and nothing like Melvyn Douglas, who plays him), the film has several characters who do not represent their real-life counterparts or are imaginary, such as Peggy's friend "Rowdy" Dow, played by Jimmy Stewart, and the villain Sunderland (Louis Calhern), who in this fictional world kills Randolph. Barrymore is still somewhat slim and fit at this point, walking (the two accidents that put him in a wheelchair were still to come at this point) and rightly cantankerous as President Andrew Jackson, who is given enough material in the movie to make him a good secondary character to the action. It's a role he returned to briefly thirteen years later in *Lone Star* (1952), which paradoxically leads us back to the past.

While one can understand the need in *The Gorgeous Hussy* to stick with Jackson's years as president, the more biographical *The President's Lady* spends little time discussing the War of 1812, where Jackson was pushed into the mainstream of public knowledge, thanks to what was seen then as heroic actions against the Creek Indians and later the Battle of New Orleans in 1813. It was during this time that Jackson met up with individuals who spawned movies of their exploits featuring Jackson in minor roles: Sam Houston (1793–1863), Davy Crockett (1786–1836), and Jean Lafitte (1780–1823).

Sam Houston fought alongside Jackson in the Creek War in the battle that ended the war, the Battle of Horseshoe Bend, where Houston was severely wounded. Houston at one time represented Tennessee in the House of Representatives and as governor, before eventually moving on to the territory that became the state of Texas. As mentioned, Texas was a hot potato in Washington, with issues with Mexico, Native Americans, and—most pointedly—the question of annexation. Houston, as president of Texas, juggled many of these balls while trying to keep the area from seceding from the Union and finally saw the annexation of Texas in 1845. He became the first senator for the state in 1846, but his defiance in supporting Native American rights and his attempt to keep Texas out of the Confederacy saw the end of his political career, and he passed away in 1863.

With such a remarkable career, it is understandable that Houston is the topic of several movies, with Andrew Jackson popping up to give added flavor to the proceedings, such as *Lone Star*, featuring a cameo from Lionel Barrymore as an older Andrew Jackson (it was his next-to-last film appearance before his death in 1954). Receiving information that suggests Houston is looking for Texas to secede when the US government shows little interest in annexing the area, Jackson calls on Devereaux Burke (Clark Gable) to locate Houston and convince him to "get Texas into the Union." The rest of the film is a standard western, with Gable looking for Houston and Broderick Crawford trying to stop the annexation plans once Houston agrees to them. Barrymore is obviously older, but then again, so was Jackson at this point (only a year or so away from his final exit, as well), so it works here. What the film represents in presidential movies is one of the fundamental roles for propping up real presidents as minor characters: the messenger. Here, as is often the case, Jackson is of no further use in the story beyond setting up the importance of Dev's journey and the mission (or a MacGuffin, in the case of this film) handing off the letter for Dev to deliver to Sam Houston. Once that scene is over (and it is the first scene in the movie), there's no further need for Andrew Jackson, and Lionel Barrymore can take off the wig and head home from the studio.

Jackson gets a bit more to do in the 1939 Republic Pictures film *Man of Conquest*, which has Richard Dix (best remembered for his westerns) as Sam Houston and Edward Ellis (who plays the villain Lincoln Lee in *The President Vanishes*) as Jackson. It is 1814, as Houston tries to rally men to help fight alongside Jackson in the war, with Jackson coming out of the crowd to follow Houston's lead and plead for help. It's a scene that doesn't play much off history, except in the respect that Jackson really was desperately in need of men to fight in the war. The overly dramatic film then jumps to 1829, with Jackson appearing at a rally to help Houston be reelected as governor. Jackson pops up again when Houston comes to Washington in full Native American dress to plead for the safety of the Comanches and then later when Jackson seeks out Houston to get Texas to join the Union. While the Washington visit has some basis in fact, there's not much evidence of Jackson traveling to see Houston about Texas nor a conversation where he tells Houston that he sees him as his adopted son. Even with that big of a dramatic license, the film plays fair in highlighting Houston's first marriage ending in divorce and his subsequent descent into heavy drinking as well as his dedication to the Native Americans and skepticism about Washington. The movie ends on Jackson's deathbed, with the former president being told Texas would become a state, which isn't quite right in timing, as the resolution occurred on March 1, 1845 (Jackson died three months later). Houston arriving moments after Jackson died appears to be true, however, although stories then had him falling to his knees and weeping at Jackson's deathbed, unlike in the film, where he bravely looks upon him before leaving with his wife and son.

Dix looks too old for the twenty-year-old Houston of the Creek War, and his hairpiece is distracting in some parts of the film, but it is obvious he enjoyed sinking his teeth into the part where Houston pleads his case for the Cherokees. Oddly enough, for a movie that is about Houston, the ending is all about Jackson, with him dying after hearing the news about Texas and Houston praising him to his wife and son. Ellis has a slight slur in his speaking voice but comes closest of these early performers in looking and acting the role instead of being an extension of Barrymore or Heston in their typical personas.

As Jackson met Houston during the Creek War, so, too, was Davy Crockett connected with Jackson in the same period, even though they did not meet at that time. Crockett grew up in Tennessee. In 1813, he joined a militia to help in the Creek War in Alabama and then rejoined in the last few months of 1814, doing not much while many had moved on to what became the Battle of New Orleans. In both periods, per Michael Wallis's book *David Crockett: The Lion of the West* (2011), Crockett spent most of this time hunting for food for the soldiers and did little actual fighting. He also never met with Jackson during the war. In 1817, he began his political career as a commissioner in Lawrence County, Tennessee, and moved up to the House of Representatives in 1827. He remained there until 1831, when his stance as an outspoken opponent to the 1830 Indian Removal Act led to his defeat in the following election. The workings of Jackson and Van Buren with the act and other actions so perturbed Crockett that he swore he would leave the country if Van Buren was elected. After losing reelection he declared, as mentioned in his autobiography, "I concluded my speech by telling them that I was done with politics for the present, and that they might all go to hell and I would go to Texas." In November 1835, he would do just that, moving to Texas, which was still not part of the United States at the time. Looking to gain land, Crockett agreed to help defend the Alamo in a multiday battle against Mexican troops, where he died on March 6, 1836.

*Davy Crockett, King of the Wild Frontier* was a reedited version of three monthly episodes of *Disneyland* (the first version of what is commonly remembered as *The Wonderful World of Disney*) that ran between December 1954 and February 1955. *Disneyland* was originally set up as an hour's worth of programming that followed different themes based on the amusement park of the same name, hence the Davy Crockett episodes represent Frontierland. The episodes are "Davy Crockett, Indian Fighter"; "Davy Crockett Goes to Congress"; and "Davy Crockett at the Alamo." The episodes were so popular that the Disney Studio edited them together to release as a theatrical feature in 1955, featuring Andrew Jackson in the first two-thirds of the film (as he is in the first two episodes of the series). The movie takes a few liberties, with Crockett (Fess Parker) working as a scout during the Creek War and having several face-to-face discussions with Andrew Jackson as he proves to be a better fighter than Jackson's men, to the amusement of Jackson. The film has him also fighting Red Stick, a chief of the Red Sticks tribe, which ends with the chief signing the peace treaty; such a treaty occurred a month before Crockett returned to active duty in September, and Crockett never fought a chief named Red Stick. Nor did Crockett ever have a chance to chat with Jackson (Basil Ruysdael), as they were miles apart during the war. About midway through the movie, Crockett meets up with Jackson again, who says he plans to run for president and wants Crockett to run for Congress so he can have "men I know are with me." Crockett replies that he would do what those who elect him want him to do and not take orders from Jackson. This much is true—namely because Crockett didn't much care for Jackson and backed his opponent to the Senate in 1823, having little patience for Jackson's brand of politics. Crockett had already run once for representative and lost before finally winning in 1827, a year before Jackson won the presidency, thus needing no encouragement from Jackson to enter the campaign. He certainly didn't spend time sitting around the White House with Jackson as seen in the film. A comment from Crockett about Jackson having a stable at the White House for his racehorses may not have been an actual quote from Crockett, but Jackson had such a stable at the White House, so that much was true. Further, Jackson responded to Crockett's dismissal of the bill by supporting his opponent in the next election, showing that there was never any love to lose between the pair.

Ruysdael doesn't get much time as Jackson to make an impression, but there's no need for him to be much more than a messenger to show how important Crockett was by having Jackson interact with him more than what really occurred. The film gives Crockett a moment in his ending speech to Congress that suggests Jackson was behind the Act so that White men could profit, but he takes it back. Understandable, really, as many Americans at the time saw Andrew Jackson as one of the greatest presidents, and to show him in any lesser light would have not worked for a kids' show, yet it is still admirable for Disney in even going that far in suggesting manipulations behind the scenes.

Finally, there is Jean Lafitte, a famous pirate and privateer of the nineteenth century who established a base for his ships out of Barataria Bay in the Gulf of Mexico, just off Louisiana. The Embargo Act of 1807 created a gold mine for Lafitte's outfit, smuggling forbidden foreign goods to eager clients in New Orleans. Lafitte also obtained a reputation (whether true or not) for hijacking primarily foreign vessels while also returning ships and crew unharmed after looting them, which made some US officials willing to turn their heads while Lafitte and his crew did their business. In the early days of the War of 1812, an offer of British citizenship and land came to Lafitte and his men if they helped the British fight the Americans. Lafitte, however, not only thought the Americans would win the war, but he also believed he would have a much easier time dealing with the Americans than the British in his line of work. Stating he needed time to think the offer over, Lafitte went to the US government and offered his and his men's services to fight the British. Soon after, however, US forces captured most of Lafitte's men and their ships.

The governor of Louisiana, William Claiborne, had no love for Lafitte but increasingly agreed with others that losing Lafitte and his men as a battle force, with the British on their way to the mouth of the Mississippi near New Orleans, was a mistake. Jackson, upon hearing Claiborne's advice, dismissed Lafitte and his men as "hellish Banditti," but his friend Edward Livingston convinced Jackson that having Lafitte on his side would help swing apathetic public opinion in the area toward him. Further, knowing he had only one thousand barely trained men under his command and little in the way of ships and provisions, Jackson agreed to meet with Lafitte, and they negotiated a deal where Lafitte would use his men, weapons, and ships to fight alongside US forces against the British in exchange for pardons for Lafitte's men, which was sent to President Madison. The repulse of the British in late December, thanks in some part to Lafitte, gained Jackson a much-needed victory, and Jackson personally thanked Lafitte for his assistance. As it stood, the war had already been officially over for days by the time of the battle, but with no knowledge on either side of this, the victory gave the appearance of Jackson's battle being decisive in the Americans winning the war—a factor that helped Jackson's political career. As for Lafitte, he went back to his old ways soon enough and was rumored to have died in 1823 when attacking Spanish ships that were heavily armed.

It's a fascinating story, full of pirates, intrigue, and battles, with a big, splashy ending that gave America a glorious victory. Thus, it was a natural for the silver screen. There are some earlier silent versions of the story of Lafitte, with fleeting usage of Jackson in them (if at all), such as *The Buccaneers* (1913, Universal Pictures), and *Millionaire Pirate* (1919, Bluebird Photoplays). *Eagle of the Sea* (1926, Paramount Studios) features George Irving (Thomas Jefferson in the 1936 film *Hearts Divided*) as Andrew Jackson in a party scene where Captain Sazarac, alias Jean Lafitte, is exposed and given until daylight to leave the city. That party scene, where Lafitte woos a young socialite whom he must leave behind due to his past, no doubt remained with Cecil B. DeMille when he made the first of two films about Jean Lafitte, *The Buccaneer*, in 1938 for Paramount Pictures.

*The Buccaneer* stars Fredric March (*Seven Days in May*) as the slim, devilish, tight-pants Jean Lafitte, with Hugh Sothern as Andrew Jackson. Chapter 1 briefly mentions this movie due to the opening scene with Dolley Madison evacuating the White House as the British arrive to attempt to burn it to the ground. That scene also introduces the audience to the true villain of the film, Senator Crawford (Ian Keith), who is working for the British. The film shows Lafitte becoming aware too late that one of the captains under him, Captain Brown (Robert Barrat), kills all but one person aboard an American ship called the *Corinthian*. Lafitte saves the sole survivor, Gretchen (Franciska Gaal) and has Brown hanged but allows Gramby (Fred Kohler), his second, to live. The British arrive to make their offer to Lafitte, only for Lafitte to go to Governor Claiborne (Douglass Dumbrille) with the papers and offer the services of his men for pardons, which Clairborne is ready to agree to until Crawford convinces him that the papers are forgeries. Military forces capture Lafitte's fleet, but Lafitte escapes. Knowing someone is working against him, Lafitte sneaks in through a window at the mansion Jackson occupies and demands the release of his men or Lafitte will shoot him. The two are at a stand-off, but after receiving news that the British are on their way, thanks to Lafitte being able to communicate with the French-speaking son of a landowner, Jackson is willing to make a deal with Lafitte: pardons for Lafitte's men and a one-hour head start for Lafitte to get out of the area, if Lafitte can get the men to join the fight and Lafitte provides badly needed flints and powder for the upcoming battle. Lafitte agrees and, while later personally setting free the men, kills Senator Crawford.

At a victory ball after the battle, Gretchen arrives unknowingly wearing a dress from the *Corinthian* that belonged to the sister of Lafitte's

The star may be Yul Brynner as pirate Jean Lafitte, but Charlton Heston as Andrew Jackson gets the limelight in *The Buccaneer* (1958). *Original movie poster,* © *1958 by Paramount Pictures Corp.*

love interest, Annette de Remy (Margot Grahame). People recognize
Gretchen as being on the ship, which is known to have disappeared
with the sister and others onboard. Lafitte takes responsibility for the
destruction of the ship and death of its crew and passengers, even
though he was not at fault for Captain Brown's actions. While those at
the party wish to hang Lafitte on the spot, Jackson holds them back and
give Lafitte the promised one-hour head start. We last see Lafitte on
his ship sailing away with a handful of his men and Gretchen at his side.

The basic premise of the film ties in with the facts, but several elements are made up. There was no Senator Crawford, Annette de Remy,
Gretchen, or a ship called the *Corinthian*. While there is legend of such,
there are no records of Lafitte climbing through a window to confront
Jackson about pardoning his men, nor was Lafitte on the run at the
time the two met. Instead, Jackson sent communications to Lafitte, and
the pair met at some point to hash out their positions. Questions over
Lafitte supplying flints and other items have also come up over time.
Lafitte's one-hour lead out of the city afterward is definitely fiction, but
it allows for Lafitte to leave the story as he came in, a man of the sea who
answers to no one, only now with Gretchen at his side.

Fredric March is at his swashbuckling best as Lafitte, dominating
the film. Although a thirty-nine-year-old Randolph Scott, just emerging
from making a number of westerns, tested for and was announced as
playing the role, Hugh Sothern ended up playing Andrew Jackson as
president but a tad too old for the forty-seven-year-old at the time of
the battle. Not that it stops the ladies at a welcoming ball from swooning
over him and asking about why he has the nickname of "Old Hickory"
while glancing below his waist. Jackson's men appear as clichéd fron-
tiersmen, with Walter Brennan as Jackson's assistant and Gabby Hayes
as a substitute who watches after Jackson's health and sneaks up on
Lafitte when the pirate tries to hold a gun to Jackson. Jackson appears
as slightly moody at best and physically ill but always in control, even
at gunpoint, and easily sees through Crawford as a bad guy soon after
meeting him.

Hugh Sothern must have made an impression in the role, for Warner
Brothers soon had him play Jackson again in a short film called *Old
Hickory* in 1939. The short has Sothern as Jackson in four key moments
in his life, including his meeting with Lafitte (George Renavent). There

is no battle footage to go with that, however, just their discussion leading up to Lafitte helping, which may be a disappointment for viewers. Also featured is Jackson talking with Rachel (Nana Bryant) before a duel over insults made about her, his inauguration in 1829, and finally his battle with John Calhoun over South Carolina looking to secede to avoid federal tariffs within the state and his attempt to solidify the union of the United States. Sothern gets some lines, but as was the custom with such historical shorts by Warner, most of the talking is through narration of the action.

*The Buccaneer* was a success for DeMille, and he revisited it in 1958 with Yul Brynner as Jean Lafitte and the return of Charlton Heston as Andrew Jackson, five years after playing him in *The President's Lady*. The new film, also called *The Buccaneer*, was at first reported to have Cecil B. DeMille directing, as well, but his health prevented him from doing so, and he assigned his then son-in-law (and supporting actor in the 1938 version) Anthony Quinn to direct in his place.

It is a rematch for Brynner and Heston, who star together in DeMille's *The Ten Commandments* (1956), which became a big success that solidified the image many have of DeMille's work: melodrama on large, colorful canvases. Brynner had found fame already on Broadway and in the movies with his role in *The King and I* (1956) and continued to have success in movies until his death in 1985, although usually in roles placing him in exotic locations and time periods other than the present. Heston may be last in the starring credits, but his face is on the movie posters, and the man who played Moses just two years before is given plenty of screen time, including the opening scene in the film. There, Jackson good-humoredly lectures a young sentry about his duties before heading back to camp, as he questions their abilities to win considering the few supplies and men available. The following scene then commences where the 1938 version begins, with Yul Brynner in a hairpiece as Lafitte and showing off wares to people for sale. There are some changes in the remake: The last survivor of the ship is no longer the grown woman Gretchen but instead a young cabin boy who becomes a mate on Lafitte's ship. With Gretchen out of the picture, the secondary love interest becomes Bonnie (Claire Bloom), the firebrand daughter of Captain Brown who resents Lafitte killing her father for destroying the *Corinthian*. Lafitte is smitten not by Annette de Remy but by Annette Claiborne (Inger Stevens), scripted as the daughter of Governor William Claiborne (E. G. Marshall). Historically, Claiborne's real daughter would have been two at the time of the Battle of New Orleans, but that didn't stop Jesse Jasky Jr. and Bernice Mosk, the scriptwriters, from making her an adult love interest in the film.

The villain Crawford becomes the less-sinister Mercier (Lorne Greene), who is not in league with the British, as Crawford is in the earlier film, but he does wish for Jackson to surrender to them to save the city. The meeting between Jackson and Lafitte is as in the earlier film, right down to Jackson's frontiersman assistant Peavey (Henry Hull) threatening to shoot Lafitte in the back and the Frenchman arriving, which sets up Jackson agreeing to Lafitte's offer. The battle is won, and the victory ball happens, only this time with the cabin boy being questioned by the attendees and Lafitte admitting his responsibility as the leader of his men in the destruction of the *Corinthian*. Mercier and others are about to string up Lafitte, when Jackson comes in, guns ready, and gives Lafitte his head start. The movie ends with Lafitte and the now-reformed Bonnie heading off to parts unknown.

Brynner is good in the lead, but in many ways the film is a joint venture with Heston, as Jackson has a good amount of time onscreen, considering it's supposed to be Lafitte's story. Heston easily slips back into the role from five years before and looks closer to the age and temperament of Jackson than Sothern before him. As with the earlier film, Jackson is seen as the voice of reason in all the chaos around him, from trying to win a battle that will end the war to stopping the patrons at the victory ball from lynching Lafitte. He shows off a sense of humor in the face of danger, such as when a businessman tells him that the soldiers were using his cotton, he hands the man a musket and tells him, "It's your cotton? Then you'll be ready to fight for it." He's a man of honor, as well, allowing Lafitte to leave, even though it may have repercussions for him with those at the party. We see a bit of Jackson's cantankerous nature as exhibited in history, but it's all for the greater good and in connection with his wisdom, as we would expect with Heston as Jackson. The film, while reminding people of the Battle of New Orleans (some have suggested that the movie helped push Johnny Horton's popular number 1 song "The Battle of New Orleans" in 1959), the film was a critical and commercial flop, making back only half its production value.

Before the 1958 *The Buccaneer*, however, Jackson returned with Lafitte in *Last of the Buccaneers* (1950), released through Columbia Pictures and starring Paul Henreid (*Casablanca*; *Now, Voyager*) as a rather doughy Lafitte. In this case, though, Lafitte's efforts in the Battle of New Orleans are so fleeting at the beginning of the film that we only quickly see Andrew Jackson (played by an uncredited Steve Darrell, who isn't a bad choice for the role, although he's usually remembered as playing bad guys in westerns and crime shows), before the film moves on to a fresh plot that has nothing to do with Jackson and everything to do with pirates and a forbidden love.

Jackson also has a brief "messenger" role in a short from Warner Brothers based on Edward Everett Hale's short story *The Man without a Country* (1937), which was filmed as a full-length film in 1925 as *As No Man Has Loved* from Fox, with Al Hart as Jackson and George Billings as Abraham Lincoln. The 1937 film, based on a piece of fiction, stars John Litel as Philip Nolan, a man tried for treason thanks to his association with Aaron Burr. Defiantly stating on trial that he wishes to never see or hear about the United States again, the judges grant his wish, and he is exiled to sea. During his imprisonment, the woman he loves (Gloria Holden) makes pleas with various presidents to release him, including once with President Jackson, played by Erville Alderson, who does little more than shake his head and passes on any changes to Nolan's sentence. Unlike the story, the short (as in the 1925 version) ends with Abraham Lincoln (played for a third time by Charles Middleton) granting Nolan a pardon, only for Nolan to die at sea before he can return to the country.

Beyond the Lafitte films and *The President's Lady*, there is only one other movie that has Andrew Jackson as a key role: a fantasy film from 1942, *The Remarkable Andrew*. Directed by Stuart Heisler and written by Dalton Trumbo, the movie deals with Andrew Long (William Holden), a mild-mannered bookkeeper for the city council of a small town. Long idolizes Andrew Jackson, whom his great-great-grandfather saved during the Battle of New Orleans. Realizing that $1,240 is missing from the city's budget, Long attempts to bring it to the council's and the mayor's attention, but they want him to just forget about it. Long, however, feels guilty about not resolving the issue, and soon after, the ghost of Andrew Jackson (Brian Donlevy) appears to him. Jackson wants to repay his debt to Long's ancestor by helping the young Andrew with his dilemma and to indulge in the liquor that Long can provide him while they hash out ideas.

Long's girlfriend (Ellen Drew) worries about Long and tries to prove that Jackson is not there, while Jackson's ideas and interruptions lead to people seeing Long as a crank. When the council frames Long with embezzlement to shut him up, Jackson calls in General Washington (Montagu Love), Thomas Jefferson (Gilbert Emery), Benjamin Franklin (George Watts), John Marshall (Brandon Hurst), and Jesse James (Rod Cameron) to help with Long's case. The ghosts manage to find recorded evidence proving the council, district attorney, and even the judge in his trial set Long up, but Jackson accidentally destroys it in his excitement. Fortunately, the ghosts arrive to give Long a detailed transcript from the meeting, leading to the case being dismissed and the resignation of the members of the local government involved with the cover-up.

Brian Donlevy, known for serious roles, obviously relished the chance to play for comedy as the ghostly General Jackson, who creates chaos in Long's life while trying to be of help. Many jokes are either of the "invisible friend others can't see" variety or deal with Jackson learning of modern devices and habits (including the love of household slippers over his military boots). Interestingly, both he and Washington are presented as ghosts from when they were generals and not from when they were presidents, who would seem to be of more benefit in the trial finale. Yet once again, it is the image of the stronger victors of military campaigns that is more visually striking in a movie than the old versions of these men (although Love as Washington looks noticeably older than Washington would have been as a general). *The Remarkable Andrew*, while not a classic comedy, is amusing, and the trial scene readily shows Jackson as a man who fought against the corrupt political structure in Washington. Also, Long details, through quotes from the ghosts, how people need to be able to stand up and question the government when something is found to be wrong, even when those in authority would try to dismiss such charges against them. Although we tend to view Jackson in negative terms much more these days, to moviegoers of the 1940s and 1950s, he represented the fulfillment of an age-old American dream: that a man not born in a powerful family or with influence can someday rise to the level of the presidency and make changes perceived as for the greater good. It's what drives our acceptance of the Hollywood version of Andrew Jackson that resonated with audiences at the time, and only once we get past the 1950s and into the more race-conscious era of the 1960s and onward, our image of Jackson was brought back down to earth, and we are reminded of the many damaging things he did while in office.

Nearly eighty years after *The Remarkable Andrew* came another movie featuring a modern person dealing with the ghost of a president, *Raising Buchanan* (2020). This comedy takes a different tack for the president involved, for James Buchanan commonly ranks near the bottom of the presidents of the country.

James Buchanan, born in 1791 in Pennsylvania, began flirting with state politics after serving in the War of 1812 and beginning a career as a lawyer. He was a representative in Congress for ten years and then was an ambassador to Russia for a year, before returning to spend the next ten years as a senator for Pennsylvania and the following four as secretary of state to President Polk (many agree that Polk's expansion in the territories were due to Buchanan's work). Two and half more years followed as an ambassador to the United Kingdom before his presidency in 1856, all while foregoing a chance to become a Supreme Court justice.

But Buchanan's victory in the election came out of bickering within and between parties, allowing him to win in a split field. His announcement at his inauguration that he would serve only one term instantly made him a lame duck with little to no power to sway Congress. As the issue of slavery was reaching a fevered pitch, Buchanan tried to placate all by calling it a "great moral evil" while also stating that enslaved Black people were better off than "any other portion of the African race." He saw abolitionists as radicals who were tearing the country apart and pushed to have Kansas admitted to the Union as a slave state (his attempts stalled in Congress, and Kansas became a free state in 1861 once Buchanan was out of office and Southern states had seceded from the Union). He managed to anger both Northern and Southern states and clearly saw the South planning to secede but had no taste in trying to use federal resources to stop them as Jackson had, setting up the Civil War that was to come. He lived his last years consistently arguing that "history will vindicate my memory," although it has not.

All these elements come to play in *Raising Buchanan*, which focuses on Ruth (Amanda Melby), a ne'er-do-well who gains access to President Buchanan's body when it arrives for DNA testing by a rich socialite in present-day Arizona. Needing quick cash, Ruth and her friends decide to steal Buchanan's body from his coffin and hold it for ransom. The only problem is most everyone thinks she is lying, and those who do believe her simply aren't interested in getting back the body of someone viewed as the worst US president. As she deals with the situation and reads up on the dead president, Ruth begins to have imaginary conversations with Buchanan (Rene Auberjonois), where they discuss his career in more detail than one would expect in such a movie and how it reflects on her own shattered prospects.

The movie is remarkable in being one of the few attempts to present a president not as a conquering god or imperious political leader but as simply human. Reminiscing on his glowing career before achieving the presidency, the stubborn Buchanan comes to realize that he aimed too high and if he had admitted and worked to fix his errors while in office, there would have been more reverence for his presidency. Of course, these discussions are all inside Ruth's head, where she is examining her own foul-ups in life in comparison to Buchanan, but the framework makes for an excellent history lesson and a breezy comedy that shows we all have struggles that cannot be remedied by a few words or even pages of text. David Donald in his preface to his book *Lincoln* recalls a conversation with John F. Kennedy where the president dismissed polls and reviews of previous presidents as unfeeling and unknowing. "No one," he told Donald, "has a right to grade a President—not even poor James Buchanan—who has not sat in his chair, examined the mailing and information that came across his desk, and learned why he made his decisions." *Raising Buchanan* is the embodiment of that statement and the need to be in the shoes of another before really understanding them.

Not until nearly 150 years after Buchanan's death did a movie examine his life, and then it was only within a comedy where he is repeatedly referred to as the country's "shittiest president." Nevertheless, *Raising Buchanan* at least gives him a chance to be brought back by way of the movie screen to present him as a breathing person. That's more than what many presidents between him and Andrew Jackson got, even if some appeared in more movies over the years.

Film appearances by Martin Van Buren, who replaced Andrew Jackson, are discussed earlier, totaling three cameo appearances in various films and in only one case—*Amistad*—as president. That is better than William Henry Harrison (1773–1841), who battled the Shawnee chief Tecumseh at the Battle of Tippecanoe, leading to the famous campaign slogan "Tippecanoe and Tyler too!" when Harrison ran for president with John Tyler as his vice-presidential pick. A general in the War of 1812, representative, and later a senator from Ohio, Harrison is best remembered today for the unfortunate distinction of being the first president to die in office, which occurred just thirty-one days after his inauguration. Harrison appears in only one Hollywood film, *Ten Gentlemen from West Point*, which stars George Montgomery and Maureen O'Hara and features Douglass Dumbrille as General William Henry Harrison. If Dumbrille's name rings a bell, it's because he's already appeared twice here, first as Governor Claiborne in *The Buccaneer* (1938) and later in 1946 as George Washington in *Monsieur Beaucaire*. The film is a fictional portrayal of the first class at West Point, with the graduates taking part in the Battle of Tippecanoe and Harrison appearing just long enough to ground the importance of the battle before disappearing from the film.

Even that is better than John Tyler (1790–1862), Harrison's vice president who finished his four-year term and is covered in more detail in chapter 2 (due to how he became president). Tyler faced turmoil in his presidency, with his cabinet quitting and his frequent use of the veto resulting in the first override of a president's veto by Congress as well as the first attempt to impeach a president. He was also the first president to get married in office, raising eyebrows by marrying a woman thirty years younger than he was. He was openly in support of states' rights over federal, and after leaving office, he sided with the Confederacy.

But you won't see any of that information about Tyler in the movies. To make up for that, Hollywood invested more time in James Polk (1795–1849), featured in the short *The Monroe Doctrine* discussed in chapter 1. Polk, sometimes referred to as "Young Hickory" due to his association with Andrew Jackson (once again showing Jackson's influence after he left office), began as a lawyer in Tennessee and then rose to become governor of Tennessee in 1839. In 1844, he ran on annexing Texas and Oregon (Texas became a state in December 1845), with his

stance on Oregon being the popular slogan "54-40 or Fight!" This referred to an ongoing clash with the British at the time about where the
US boundary lay in the Northwest, with the British wanting the line at
the 42° parallel and Polk campaigning on annexing the entire area up
to what was then Russian America at the 54°40' parallel (an area that
reached up to the tip of what is now Alaska and east to the Continental
Divide). The discussion finally landed on the 49° parallel as the border
between the US and the British sides. Polk also landed a treaty in 1847
that allowed the United States the right of passage through Panama,
which later led to the building of the Panama Canal.

Polk's expansion of the country is a primary source of his appearances
in movies over the years. In the musical western *Can't Help Singing*
(1944), starring Deanna Durbin as Caroline Frost and Robert Paige as
Johnny Lawlor, Polk is seen at the beginning giving a speech. Take a
quick look, though, because after a minute of his speech, the camera
gets bored and pans over to the parents of Durbin's character. From
that point onward, aside from Caroline's father talking Polk into assigning her beau to California and thus setting up her adventure out West,
we never see Polk again in the film. Edward Earle, who plays Polk,
doesn't even get a screen credit in the movie. Polk has even less to do in
the 1947 western *California*, with an uncredited Ian Wolfe in the role.

*The Oregon Trail* (1959) with Fred MacMurray allows Polk more
screen time, even though the actor playing Polk, Addison Richards, is
once again uncredited. The plot deals with the government's concerns
over attacks from British North America against settlers heading along
the Oregon Trail. As events play out in the West, the movie twice returns to Washington to show Polk, but he is little more than an envoy.
His first scene is exposition to set up the border dispute and his need
for agents to protect the settlers, as seen in *Can't Help Singing* before
it, and the second scene shows him continuing treaty discussions with a
British ambassador, which allows for an awkward insertion of his campaign slogan "54-40 or Fight" into the conversation. Like *Can't Help
Singing* and *California*, Polk's presence has no impact on the story, but
having him send people on missions creates a sense of importance for
the proceedings.

It is this common theme of the president as a celebrated messenger
that repeatedly turns up in films, especially those that are action ori-

ented. Films with the Founding Fathers feature a bit of this, but typically it's films with the presidents pressed into service to do something related to that action, especially with Washington during the Revolutionary War. In an era when presidents were accustomed to sitting in Washington, being advised and giving advice, Hollywood instead settled into showing them rounding up agents or sending off others on adventures, transferring national importance to these movie heroes. Andrew Jackson may have fancier cameos in the two *Buccaneer* movies, but even he can't quite get out from this duty, and it remains common.

For example, Zachary Taylor (1784–1850) pops up at several intervals in the 1951 movie *Distant Drums*, which features Gary Cooper as a captain in the Second Seminole War, where Taylor took part in major battles between 1837 and 1840. Taylor orders Cooper's character, Captain Wyatt, to destroy a fort and save hostages, with the film occasionally cutting back to Taylor (Robert Barrat) sitting at an outpost far from the action, looking concerned and fearing for Wyatt's life, until they meet up for a short scene at the end of the film. Zachary Taylor spent forty years in the military before becoming president, fighting in the Black Hawk War, the Second Seminole War, and the Mexican-American War, but he is in *Distant Drum* for no reason other than to introduce the real hero and look concerned because the audience knew that if the president is worried, then it is probably a big deal. An earlier film, *Rebellion* (1936), uses Taylor for an even shorter amount of time as a messenger when President Taylor (Allan Cavan) sends Captain John Carroll (Tom Keene) to California to stop the exploitation of Mexicans by American landowners. His appearance in the two-reeler *The Fall of Blackhawk* (1912), with George Cole as Taylor, is even shorter and nothing more than a setup for a fictional adventure story about how Jefferson Davis met Zachary Taylor's daughter Sarah and saved her from the Blackhawks. Then again, for a man who was president for less than a year and a half, being the second president to die in office, he at least got two movies and a short. That's more than his successor, Milliard Fillmore (1800–1874), whose only appearance is in *The Monroe Doctrine* mentioned many times before.

The last president before James Buchanan was Franklin Pierce (1804–1869), who makes one appearance in the Preston Sturges movie *The Great Moment* (1944), portrayed by Porter Hall as a buffoon. The consensus among historians is that Pierce was a remarkably ineffectual president who tried so hard to create balance between political parties that he ended up making no one happy, leading to his political party abandoning him for a second term. He also pushed the Kansas-Nebraska Act of 1854 and the Fugitive Slave Act of 1850 (which forced federal agents to track down runaway slaves and disavowed evidence of those accused of being an enslaved individual, thus possibly forcing free people into slavery), intensifying the fight between free and slave states and helping solidify Abraham Lincoln's platform against slavery in the 1860 campaign that won him the presidency. *The Great Moment* deals with William T. G. Morton, a physician who claimed to have discovered anesthesia for surgery by having patients breathe in ether; he looked for some type of patent or monetary payment for the invention, even though some suspected he was not the creator and did not think he should be paid for usage of such a common product as ether. In the film, Congress plans to give Morton $100,000 for his discovery, but Pierce refuses to pay due to criticism from the public and the press. He suggests Morton place a claim on the usage by suing a doctor using ether and laughingly sends him on his way. The lawsuit, however, only fuels resentment toward Morton and shows Pierce to be a bad negotiator. Nevertheless, even as the role indicts Pierce, he is simply a messenger who pushes the movie plot along and nothing more.

The presidents of this chapter created policy for better or worse in the White House that affected the course of the country. Some were more impactful than others, but they always acted with an eye not to history but to tranquility—or at least some semblance of it for the White settlers in the nation. The deference of dealing with slavery and the disposition of powers between state and federal rights were left over from the Founding Fathers, who never could agree and hoped future generations would resolve those issues. They preferred to kick things down the road for someone else to handle, and it shows in our interest in their worth. Even the handful of movies that depict the most famous, Andrew Jackson, tends to focus on one battle before his presidency and skims over the rest, dealing only with the righteous gossip (*The Gorgeous Hussy*, *The President's Wife*) and not with his frequent dismissal of rights for people of color, which rightly darkens our view of his administration today. The rest are presented as cookie cutters to merely push the narrative, even John Quincy Adams in *Amistad*.

They and others that come later are relegated to a second tier in our eyes and in our movies because history demands it. They limited the risks and thus limited their exposure to providence. Then again, when it all came to a head after Franklin Pierce, destiny found the next president to be the most remembered in the history of the country, in exchange for his life.

# 4

## ABE LINCOLN

### The Praeses ex Machina

As the preacher once said, I could write shorter sermons, but once I
start, I get too lazy to stop.

—Abraham Lincoln in *Lincoln* (2012)

**A**braham Lincoln (1809–1865), who has appeared as a historical figure
in more movies than any other president, experienced a fate different
from the messenger presidents of the previous chapter. Instead, as already seen in *Man without a Country* mentioned previously, he comes
in to save someone in their hour of desperation and at the last possible
moment, like a praeses ex machina.

Lincoln was born in Kentucky and had little schooling, although he
was known as a voracious reader of books. His mother, Nancy, died
when he was nine, and his relationship with his father, Thomas, turned
tense as Abraham got older and leaned toward books and away from
physical labor. Abraham, however, got along well with his stepmother,
Sarah, whom Thomas married a year after the death of Nancy. Abraham
moved to New Salem, Illinois, at the age of twenty-one and met Jack
Armstrong, who picked a fight with Lincoln that, whether he won or
lost, initiated Lincoln into the good graces of the townspeople and with
Armstrong. This friendship led to Lincoln becoming the captain of the

militia that went to help fight in the Black Hawk War for several months in 1832.

He also met Ann Rutledge, the daughter of a tavern owner. Historians have argued for years whether she was Lincoln's first love or simply a friend, as there are no records of any affectionate relationship between the two for the two years they knew each other. Nevertheless, when she died in 1835 from typhoid, Lincoln reportedly became depressed and later told a friend after becoming president that he often thought of Ann. Contrary to what is commonly shown in biographical films, Abraham remained in New Salem for a time and became engaged to Mary Owens, an engagement that both later regretted. In 1837, Lincoln broke up with Owens, left the general store he ran in New Salem, and moved to Springfield, Illinois.

Once there, Lincoln began studying law. In his autobiography, Lincoln mentions discovering *Commentaries on the Laws of England*, a four-volume dissertation on common law by Sir William Blackstone, in the bottom of a barrel left to him by passing settlers at the New Salem general store where he worked. However, this appears to be merely a tale made up by Lincoln, and there is evidence he purchased it in 1834 while visiting Springfield. Either way, he devoured the series and recommended it to others wishing to learn law. Lincoln spent time bouncing between the state legislature and a law practice until making it to the House of Representatives in 1847. His time there lasted only two years, however, when he refused to simply follow party lines and endorse the Mexican-American War (1846–1848), although he readily backed financing the military in the cause.

In 1840, Abe met Mary Todd, the daughter of a rich family out of Kentucky. Family members saw Lincoln as unfit to be part of the Todd family, which led to the pair breaking up for a year, only to begin dating again in secret and eventually marrying in 1842. Mary and Abraham had four sons, of which only one, Robert Todd Lincoln, lived into adulthood. Edward Lincoln died at the age of three from tuberculosis in 1850. William Lincoln died at the age of eleven during Lincoln's presidency from what is assumed to be typhoid fever, which also affected his younger brother Thomas "Tad" Lincoln, although he recovered and lived until the age of eighteen. Mary had issues with depression, compounded by the death of her sons, the periods when Abraham was away on business (and his later violent death), and a carriage accident that resulted in crippling migraines. She passed away in 1882.

Lincoln was doing well with his law career, with consensus showing him to be a fine trial lawyer, and in 1857, he was involved in his most famous case, involving the *Farmer's Almanac*. On August 29, 1857, James Preston Metzker died in a drunken fight with James Norton and William "Duff" Armstrong. Armstrong was the son of Jack Armstrong, a man who had been friends with Abraham in New Salem, and when Duff's mother asked Lincoln to defend her son in the trial, Lincoln agreed to do so for no fee. At the trial, the lead witness was Charles Allen, who swore he saw Duff from 150 feet away clobber Metzker around midnight with a slungshot (a form of blackjack) in the back of the head, killing him. Lincoln had Allen repeat the story in court several times and verify that he saw this due to the moonlight that evening, after which Lincoln produced a copy of the *Farmer's Almanac* that showed at midnight on the date, there was a low-setting new moon, meaning that there would have been no moonlight for Allen to see the crime. It was enough to lead to Duff Armstrong's freedom and showed the type of clever reasoning skills Lincoln used.

Even as a career trial lawyer, Lincoln never quite removed himself from politics. The Kansas-Nebraska Act of 1854, which nullified the Missouri Compromise (which was to stop slavery in any new states above the 36°30' parallel, except for Missouri), infuriated Lincoln and led him back into politics by running against Stephen A. Douglas in the 1958 Illinois senatorial race. Douglas, who sponsored the bill, ironically enough at one time was a possible suitor to Mary Todd. Lincoln accepted the nomination of the Republican Party with a speech about how the country could not be sustained if slavery split it apart, including the famous statement, "A house divided against itself cannot stand." Lincoln lost the race, but fame followed, and soon enough came the chance to run for president in 1860. He arrived at the White House with seven states having already seceded and more to come, and then April 1861 saw Fort Sumter attacked by Southern forces.

The American Civil War began, with the Union suffering defeats to the Confederacy due to a variety of issues, including discord between the leader of the Union Army, General George McClellan, and Lincoln, which led to Lincoln dismissing McClellan in 1862. Also in 1862, he produced the Emancipation Proclamation, which guaranteed the freedom of enslaved people who made it to the Union from one of the rebel states. By 1863 and with the victory of Union forces at the Battle of Gettysburg, there was hope for the Northern states, and the war drew rapidly to a close after General Robert E. Lee surrendered to Ulysses S. Grant at Appomattox Courthouse on April 9, 1865. On April 14, 1865, John Wilkes Booth killed Abraham Lincoln by shooting him at Ford's Theatre during a play, thus making Lincoln the first president assassinated.

The earliest films with Lincoln as a dramatic character depict him in small but pivotal cameos that set him up as a savior to men in uniform. The most common version of such a story depicts court-martialed Union soldier William Scott, a sentry during the Civil War who received a death sentence for falling asleep at his post, which inspired a famous poem by Francis De Haes Janvier called "The Sleeping Sentinel." Newspapers and Scott's superiors were disputing the severity of the punishment, while the register of the treasury, Lucius E. Chittenden, informed President Lincoln of Scott's sentence. Lincoln passed a request on to Major General George McClellan to pardon Scott, and Scott went on to fight for the Union, dying in battle in 1862.

*The Reprieve: An Episode in the Life of Abraham Lincoln* (1908); *Abraham Lincoln's Clemency* (1910, with Leopold Wharton as Lincoln); and *The Sleeping Sentinel* (1914) are derived from Scott's story, with some minor revisions: *The Reprieve* features Scott's wife pleading with Lincoln, while *Abraham Lincoln's Clemency* has Scott's mother begging and allows Lincoln to personally pardon the soldier. Of course, having a poor, crying woman on her knees to Lincoln certainly is more dramatic than the register of the treasury merely bringing it to Abe's attention, even if the real-life details found Scott facing the firing squad when the order came to release him. Lincoln gets the dramatic opportunity to stop the execution in progress in *The Sleeping Sentinel*, as the short has Lincoln (credited as being played by George Steele) whisking the sentinel's mother in a carriage to the firing squad and stopping the execution in progress. Lincoln also provides a similar last-minute stay in the one-reel Edison Films drama *The Blue and the Grey; or The Days of '61* (1908), when the girlfriend of a Union soldier unjustly accused of treason begs Lincoln to save him (the girlfriend arrives just in time with the pardon after jumping a wall on her horse). *The Seventh Son*

(1912) has Lincoln (Ralph Ince) pardoning a deserter when his mother pleads that he is the only son out of seven she has left. *When Lincoln Paid* (1913, with director Francis Ford as Lincoln) has a mother begging Lincoln to save a Confederate soldier in payment for an old IOU he had given to her many years before.

There are several other shorts with Lincoln as the same praeses ex machina, and it didn't just stop there. The famous/infamous D. W. Griffith movie *The Birth of a Nation* (1915) starring Lillian Gish is based on Thomas Dixon's novel *The Clansman*, and with a title like that and its praise for the creation of the Klan, it is easy to surmise that the film may be rough going when it comes to heavy racism. None of that deals with the president, however, as the movie has Lincoln (Joseph Henabery) appearing near the end of the first half of the film to perform his frequent pardoning act of the movies. Oddly, even for what is considered an epic movie dealing directly with the Civil War, Henabery as Lincoln has only two major scenes before his exit at Ford's Theatre: one where he dismisses retribution against the South after the end of the war and another where the mother of a captured Confederate soldier pleads for her son's life and Lincoln finally relents and writes one for her on the spot.

It doesn't end with silent films, either. At the end of the 1940 movie *Virginia City*, with Errol Flynn as Union captain Bradford, who is to be executed for refusing to disclose where gold he captured that belongs to the Confederacy is hidden (he wants it to be used to help the South rebuild instead of it being used by the North, thus allowing Flynn's hero to be both a Southern sympathizer and Northern hero). Miriam Hopkins as Bradford's girlfriend, Julia, manages to meet with Lincoln and plead for Bradford's release. As seen in *The Birth of a Nation*, a woman runs to plead for a loved one, and once again the praeses ex machina gives her a Hollywood happy ending, leaving us with the idea that Lincoln had a daily line of grieving mothers and girlfriends outside his office and a blank book of pardons to pass around. As a side note, Lincoln (Victor Kilian, who later played the Fernwood Flasher on the television series *Mary Hartman, Mary Hartman*) is seen only in the shadows and facing away from the camera, a common way to show presidents in films after FDR was elected, which is discussed in more detail in a subsequent chapter.

*The Littlest Rebel* (1935) also has a court-martialed man pardoned by Lincoln (Frank McGlynn Sr.) at the last minute, this time with the pleas of Shirley Temple. McGlynn had a tendency to hold his head up so high as Lincoln, with his nose in the air, that it would come off as comical, but audiences felt he fit the role, and McGlynn started a tradition for actors: If the actor is any good in the role, he will play Lincoln a handful more times over the years. Such a situation may have occurred with actors playing other presidents but not as often as it occurred with those who took a crack at Lincoln. McGlynn first played Abraham in the 1915 movie from the Edison Studios *The Life of Abraham Lincoln*, which covers Lincoln's marriage to Mary, running for senator (including his "House Divided" speech), the 1860 election, the Civil War, and his assassination—all within fifteen minutes. He then returned to the role on Broadway in 1919 in the John Drinkwater play *Abraham Lincoln* and later starred in a road production for two years, before appearing in a condensed sound film in 1924, also titled *Abraham Lincoln*. Both the play and film center on Lincoln's career in the White House, with the William Scott story once again popping up. The year 1936 was big for McGlynn as Lincoln but in cameo roles: *The Plainsman* (1936), directed by Cecil B. DeMille and starring Gary Cooper, has Lincoln cameoing in the first scene to cheer on the ending of the Civil War before others question what will happen to all the guns left behind from the war, leading to the main movie plot; in *Hearts in Bondage* (1936), he consoles the sweethearts of the movie while strolling alone through a park before drifting off into the fog in the last scene; and in *Prisoner of Shark Island* (1936), about Samuel Mudd, the doctor sent to prison for treating John Wilkes Booth after Lincoln's assassination, we see a weary Lincoln enticing a crowd to play "Dixie" to show his leniency to the South, before being shown at Ford's Theatre and his assassination. In 1939, McGlynn was in another short film about the president, *Lincoln in the White House*, which was in Technicolor and once again covered strictly his time as president, from inauguration, the start of the Civil War, the Emancipation Proclamation, William Scott (it's his mother pleading this time), the Gettysburg Address, and even another version of the "Dixie" request story.

Cameos continued into 1937, including the introduction of Lincoln sending people out on mission to steal, save, or protect a shipment of gold (much like in the 1940 film *Virginia City*), with McGlynn as Lincoln asking Joel McCrea as Ramsay MacKay to save a $2 million gold shipment before disappearing from the movie. *Western Gold*, released the same year, has McGlynn sending Smith Ballew as Bill Gibson to go out West and stop holdups on gold shipments there, as well. The most interesting aspect of McGlynn's lone appearance in *Western Gold* is Lincoln setting up a story to make a point with his cabinet and his secretary of war, Edwin Stanton (Gordon De Main), pleading with him to stop with the unnecessary funny stories at such a serious time. Steven Spielberg's *Lincoln* seventy-five years later has a scene very much like it between Stanton (Bruce McGill) and Lincoln (Daniel Day-Lewis), although in that case, Stanton walks out rather than hearing the story. McGlynn's final appearance as Lincoln is also a cameo in the 1939 picture *The Mad Empress*. Lincoln appears briefly with his cabinet to discuss how to deal with the seating of Maximilian I, Austrian royalty, as the emperor of the Second Mexican Empire (1864–1867).

Frank McGlynn Sr. was not alone. George Billings was an actor who used his striking resemblance to Lincoln to his advantage, playing the role in amateur productions and reciting Lincoln's speeches in vaudeville. Al and Ray Rockett approached him in 1924 to appear in their biographical film about the president, *Abraham Lincoln* (1924, also known as *The Life of Abraham Lincoln*, *The Adventures of Abraham Lincoln*, and *The Dramatic Life of Abraham Lincoln*), with Phil Rosen directing and Billings in the lead. Surprisingly, it is one of only two full-length movie biographies showing Lincoln's life from birth to death (and once again featuring the William Scott pardon), albeit Abraham's time before moving to New Salem as an adult is only quickly reviewed. The 1908 film *Life of Abraham Lincoln*, released by Essanay Film on October 7, 1908, and featuring Ralph Ince as Lincoln, is also a full biography, but as a one-reeler, it was reviewed by *The Moving Picture World* as "well-staged and fairly well acted, but the story is told in such a disconnected manner that it fails to carry the interest it should."

Billings continued his association with the role onstage, giving recitations of Lincoln's famous speeches at showings of the movie from 1924 through 1926. He also collaborated on a vaudevillian act between 1926 and 1927 with an up-and-coming young actor name Henry Fonda, where Fonda played Lincoln's secretary and set up various speeches and moments for Billings to play out. Known for strolling in full Lincoln garb from hotels to make his appearances, newspapers by 1929 were stating, "That guy won't be satisfied until he's assassinated" (a gag commonly linked to writer George S. Kaufman about Raymond Massey's various Lincoln appearances more than a decade later). Billings returned in front of the camera as Lincoln for cameos in *Barbara Frietchie* (1924) and *The Man without a Country* (1925). A slightly larger role for Billings in the Raymond Griffith comedy *Hands Up!* (1926) has Lincoln sending out a Union captain (played by future George Washington Montagu Love) to get a gold shipment (it was a popular mission, it appears). His final appearance in the role came with him reciting the Gettysburg Address in the 1929 short *Lincoln*. He died in 1934 and was virtually forgotten beyond his work as Lincoln.

In August 1929 came news that D. W. Griffith planned to direct a biography about Lincoln, with Billings at the top of the list to play the role, along with repeat offenders Frank McGlynn, Joseph Henabery, and Charles Edward Bull, who had played Lincoln in the 1924 John Ford movie *The Iron Horse*. Bull appears in the first twenty minutes of *The Iron Horse* for two scenes. The first scene shows him sending off the hero, Davey, as a boy from Springfield with his father to follow his father's dream of setting up a railroad out West, leaving his friend Miriam behind. We next see Lincoln in 1863 meeting up with Miriam and her fiancé just as he is about to sign the bill for the transcontinental railroad, thus setting up the mission of every character in the movie after that. Bull, a justice of the peace picked for the role due to his likeness, is stiff in the role (even for a silent movie), although he looks physically younger than many other actors around that time attempting to do Lincoln for the camera. He made one more short appearance in the 1927 movie *The Heart of Maryland*.

In early January 1930, the press announced that Walter Huston would play the role of Abraham Lincoln in Griffith's movie. It was Griffith's first all-talking movie and next-to-last film that he directed (his final one, *The Struggle*, made in 1931, was not a success). Griffith sought out Carl Sandburg to write the script after reading his two-volume biographical study of Lincoln's life before becoming president, *Abraham Lincoln: The Prairie Years* (1926), but Sandburg's asking price was too high. Griffith, looking for prestige when it came to a scriptwriter, instead turned to Stephen Vincent Benet, who had won a Pulitzer Prize in 1929 for his blank-verse poem, "John Brown's Body." United Artists, the studio making the film, along with Griffith reworked the resulting script, but it's easy to see Benet's input from the very first scene, which shows enslavers on a ship dumping a body over the side, resonating the prelude to Benet's poem, even as it has little impact on the rest of the film. Lincoln wandering the White House in a nightgown and carpet slippers from book 2 of the poem appears in the movie, as well.

As with the 1924 movie starring George Billings, the film professes to be a full biographical study of Lincoln's life, but his years as a child are fleeting. In fact, only one movie spends any time discussing Lincoln's childhood years, the little-seen 2014 movie by A. J. Edwards, *Better Angels*, which solely focuses on Abraham's life from the ages of eight to eleven and the transition from the death of his mother, Nancy, to his father's marriage to Lincoln's stepmother, Sarah. As a movie dealing with a child's loss of one parent and acceptance of another, it is of interest, although it must be seen as speculative because so little is known of those years. Of course, with information pertaining to Lincoln's childhood coming from Abraham himself, who tended to give only sparse answers to questions about those years, it is understandable that other historical adaptations tend to leave things as in Griffith's *Abraham Lincoln*, with a few minutes taken up with a baby being born in a log cabin and given the name Abraham before moving on to Lincoln as an adult.

As briefly mentioned previously, however, Griffith's *Abraham Lincoln* begins with no focus on Abraham at all. Instead, the first scene shows the pain of those in chains on a slave ship and men onboard tossing a body over the side. Two comparative scenes follow of men in the South and in the North both complaining and refusing to support the opposite states while saluting George Washington for bringing them all together. It is only after setting up the damage done to the country by slavery and talk of secession that we arrive at 1809 and the birth of Abraham. That moment is all we see of Lincoln's mother and father, however, as the next scene has Walter Huston as Lincoln being folksy at the general store in New Salem and then wrestling Jack Armstrong (Edgar Deering), gaining the acceptance of other men in the town.

The still-argued but often touched-upon relationship between Abraham and Ann Rutledge (Una Merkel) is the next focus of the film,

showing Ann as Abraham's teacher and then love interest, with no
mention of her real-life fiancé to detour the storyline. After agreeing to
marry, Ann gets sick and dies, leaving Abraham near suicidal and throwing himself on Ann's grave in the rain. Such emotions are quickly over
by the next scene, as a bemused Abraham leaves New Salem in debt, out
of luck, and on to Springfield, where he courts Mary Todd (Kay Hammond). As is typical in many other films, Mary is shown to be aggressive
and controlling, pushing Abraham forward in his career, although Abraham disappearing on their wedding day because of some misery over
Ann is featured for dramatic effect and is not based on any real event.

Romantic issues get more time in the film than Lincoln's political
climb, as Stephen Douglas debates Lincoln, Lincoln runs for president,
and he wins in less time than Abraham courts Ann. With the presidency
comes the Civil War, and the film slows with Lincoln having little to
do beyond shuffling around in his socks at night in the White House or
darting to the telegraph office at the War Department to find out new
communications about ongoing battles. Next, out in the fields, Lincoln
dashes into a court-martial just in time to appear as the praeses ex
machina and pardon a soldier who threw down his gun in fear after seeing a childhood friend dead in battle. The Emancipation Proclamation
is next, followed by getting Grant to command the army. Battle scenes
showing the demise of the Confederate Army and Robert E. Lee's ad-
mittance to the same concludes with the war ending. John Wilkes Booth
plots Lincoln's death with other conspirators, while Lincoln conflates a
couple famous speeches to talk to the audience before the play at Ford's
Theatre. After Booth's shooting of Lincoln, a model shot of the Lincoln
Memorial appears, and a heavenly light shines from behind Lincoln's
statue as the movie draws to a close.

The movie covers the main events of Lincoln's life in a fanciful way
that only Hollywood can provide (Ann looking like Little Bo Peep in
nineteenth-century rural Illinois is difficult to ignore, for example).
Huston, forty-seven at the time of filming, isn't much older than any of
the previous (or at least one future) Lincolns in movies but is so heavily made up to look younger in the New Salem scenes with Ann that he
shifts between looking comical and looking ghoulish. Once Ann is gone
and Mary becomes a minor character, the film settles on Civil War
sequences—where Griffith has been before with *The Birth of a Nation*.

Griffith is in his element, and the second half of the movie breezes along, even if Lincoln fixates on saying "Preserve the Union!" far too often. Griffith, a gifted filmmaker of the silent era, tends to fall back on the overly dramatic when it comes to the emotions of his actors, in a script that may have been lyrical on the page but hard to pull off as speech. These two elements led to some unfair criticism of the performances over time, especially that of Una Merkel, who is given little to do beyond being a "sweet young thing" for Lincoln to go all "gosh shucks" over (that's not exaggeration, as it is close to their level of dialogue when they are together).

There is such a fixation on shoving so many events of Lincoln's life into the film that the movie becomes unfocused. A sequence shows Abraham being born, only for him to be an adult ten seconds later. Jack Armstrong wrestles Abraham in New Salem, with no further relevance to the film. Lincoln is devastated by Ann's death, and then the next scene (sometimes cut or covered by music to eliminate dialogue) has Lincoln joyfully leaving New Salem after some time in the legislature and losing his business. Lincoln breaks up his engagement with Mary (which is true) on their wedding day (which is false), only for him to rush back to her in the next scene (and her willingness to take him back, which seems unlike the character). Lincoln goes from losing to Stephen Douglas to being president like a turbo–Peter Principle rise in power. The Union looks to be winning the war via telegraph; two minutes later, they are losing and then winning again a few minutes later. The best example appears when Lincoln gives an impromptu speech (which didn't happen) at Ford's Theatre that is a mash-up of at least two other famous speeches by the president not heard earlier in the film, as if the filmmakers suddenly realized at the end of filming that they needed to cram those in somehow.

The episodic nature of the film, which is unavoidable in trying to sequentially tells a person's life story, works against the movie. There has also been some critical reanalysis of the movie for its lack of discussion about slavery, but then again, there's little talk about secession beyond Abraham's constant lament about "preserving the Union." It is clear Griffith dropped in elements dealing with the brutality of slavery in the first scene and a later one showing men struggling with moving equipment over a bridge, perhaps even in light of criticism he faced with *The*

*Birth of a Nation*, but once again, it seems to be information that simply sits as a fragment without really connecting with the rest of the movie in a relevant manner as it should. The movie had some praise from critics who were fans of Griffith's work, but there were mixed reviews as well, and ticket sales were not very good for the feature at a time where there were still plenty of other Lincoln shorts and films floating around at the local Bijous.

Yet what Griffith's film brings to the fore, even more so than the 1924 biopic with George Billings, is something new to the world of Hollywood's portrayal of presidents in the movies: their humanity. Earlier films play it safe by showing us presidents who have no internal emotions, even in the multiple portrayals of George Washington and President Lincoln of the silent days. Washington or Lincoln (such as in John Ford's *The Iron Horse*) may smile at the hero kissing the girl, but that is only evidence of a divine acceptance by these superheroes of their love and tells us nothing of the men. Understandable, as public common knowledge of the individuals beyond their professional careers in the military or in politics was sparse. As the press continued to grow in power during the second half of the nineteenth century and after Lincoln's death, people wanted to know more of the man they saw as saving the Union. It helped that Lincoln, even if he did have what some see as clinical depression, had a public persona of cheer and humor, making him seem approachable. That breakthrough resonates into later movies about Lincoln and into films about other presidents after this point.

Walter Huston managed to avoid the curse of other actors in the role in that he never played Lincoln again after making Griffith's film, although he did play two fictional presidents after this in *Gabriel over the White House* (1933) and *Trans-Atlantic Tunnel* (1935) as well as made appearances in several films with connections to Franklin Delano Roosevelt (see chapter 7). Not that he wouldn't get roped into another movie with Lincoln again.

In 1938, Huston appeared in *Of Human Hearts* (1938) from MGM Studios and based on a novel by Honoré Willsie Morrow called *Benefits Forgot*, which centered on a piece of lore about Lincoln lecturing a soldier for not writing home. Huston plays Reverend Ethan Wilkins, a minister arriving in a small town in Ohio with his wife and young son, Jason (played in the first half of the film by Gene Reynolds). The minister has a strained and abusive relationship with Jason, pushing the boy away from him and to the town's doctor, who is like a second father to him. Midway through the film, ten years pass, and Jason has grown into an adult (now played by James Stewart). After a physical altercation with his father, Jason leaves for medical school, and when the reverend dies, Jason pushes his mother to sell off all her personal belongings and their beloved horse to help pay for his education.

The pain over his relationship with his father drives Jason from responding to his mother's letters as the Civil War begins, and he works in the field hospitals, gaining a reputation as a brilliant surgeon who avoids amputations. Called from the fields to appear at the White House, Jason arrives to talk with President Lincoln (John Carradine). After a discussion about his rising career, Lincoln asks about Jason's family, leading to Jason discussing his mother's willingness to sell her things, only to brush that off as worthless items, little realizing how much sacrifice she had endured for him. Lincoln then comes to the real reason he brought Jason there: Jason's mother had not heard from him in two years and had assumed he died in the war, with her letter to the president asking where to find his grave. Lincoln, furious with Jason's disregard and ingratitude for his mother after all her sacrifice, commands him to sit at his desk and write a letter to her. In tears over the realization of the anguish he caused her, Jason requests a furlough, returns to his mother, and receives her forgiveness in the last moments of the film. Carradine, an actor known for chewing scenery whole when given the chance, is remarkable as Lincoln, looking and sounding nothing like the John Carradine so often seen in movies. His Lincoln has a low, calming voice, with minimal physical movements, which may have something to do with the makeup, which slightly immobilizes Carradine's face, but makes for a brilliant performance in a pivotal but small role.

The next actor featured in a biographical film about Lincoln, Henry Fonda, found himself in a position similar to Huston, who saw no recurrence of the Lincoln role but plenty of chances to play a fictional president again. *Young Mr. Lincoln* (1939), directed by John Ford and written by Lamar Trotti (*Drums along the Mohawk*, *The Ox-Bow Incident*), begins in 1832 with an adult Lincoln in New Salem, Illinois, running for the state legislature. It then immediately jumps into the famous but discredited story of Lincoln buying the barrel containing *Blackstone's*

*Commentaries*, which leads right into the questionable tale of Lincoln's relationship with Ann Rutledge (Pauline Moore). Rutledge's presence is much shorter than in D. W. Griffith's *Abraham Lincoln*, however, with Lincoln visiting her grave in the scene immediately following her introduction to the film.

**Young Mr. Lincoln (1939), with Henry Fonda as Abraham Lincoln, seen here with Pauline Moore as Ann Rutledge in an often-visualized romance that probably did not happen to the real Lincoln.** *Official press still, author's collection, © 1939 by Twentieth Century-Fox Film Corp.*

The film next turns to Lincoln setting up as a lawyer in Springfield, Illinois, and meeting Mary Todd (Marjorie Weaver), skipping over his relationship with Mary Owens in New Salem before his move (Griffith's film also skips over Mary Owens). The implication in the movie is that Mary Todd was spending a good amount of time with Stephen Douglas, and while he was a suitor, there appears never to have been a clash between Douglas and Lincoln over Mary. After this and for the remainder of the film, the plot deals specifically with the *Farmer's Almanac* case of 1857, although the film implies it occurred before Mary and Abraham married. The movie also wildly exaggerates the case, changing the names of the Armstrongs to the Clays and showing that the witness (whose name is changed to Cass) must have killed the man with a knife, leading to a confession in court. The movie ends with Lincoln getting the admiration of Mary Todd and Stephen Douglas and the thanks of the Clays, before heading off alone into a storm.

Knowing his past association with George Billings, one wonders how much of that performance came through in Fonda's take on the role. His version of Lincoln is not quite as folksy as Houston's, thus giving his Lincoln a slight edge as being more knowledgeable than his appearance may present. There are attempts to bring in some elements of Abraham's life, such as the barrel story, being part of the legislature, Ann Rutledge, and the Mary Todd–Stephen Douglas dynamics, but Ford and Trotti make the wise choice to concentrate on Lincoln's growing career as a lawyer and his meticulous manners to resolve cases. The early moment when Lincoln quickly sews up a legal fight between two men and gets a fee out of it is a good example of this, leading to the eventual presentation of the *Farmer's Almanac* trial. Dramatic license is sprinkled earlier in the film, only to really flow during the trial, which is presented as having taken place years before it occurred, along with name changes for those involved. Lincoln stopping a near lynching of the men is fictional, as are the various apparatuses attempted by others to sway confessions from the Clays. Most importantly, the outcome of the trial, with Lincoln badgering a witness into a courtroom confession, is a brilliant, dramatic ending to the movie, but it has nothing to do with reality, where the witness was laughed out of court, and the case was dismissed. Even with these differences, the essence of Lincoln comes through in Fonda's performance, and the audience readily believes this man could shrewdly win cases and move on to higher goals. It's certainly very easy to watch Fonda confront the real killer in court and see Fonda's later juror in *Twelve Angry Men* (1957).

*Young Mr. Lincoln* did fine at the box office, managing to squeeze in right before the anticipated release of *Abe Lincoln in Illinois* in 1940. *Abe Lincoln in Illinois* began as a play written by Robert E. Sherwood (*Waterloo Bridge, The Petrified Forest*; he was also a speechwriter for Franklin D. Roosevelt) and based on Carl Sandburg's *Abraham Lincoln: The Prairie Years* (1926). The play won a Pulitzer Prize in 1939 and ran for more than a year on Broadway, with Raymond Massey in the title role, before RKO Pictures released a movie adaptation in April 1940. As with *Young Mr. Lincoln*, the focus is on Abraham as an adult in Illinois, starting in 1831, with Abraham agreeing to join a riverboat to prove his worth. It is on this journey that he meets Ann Rutledge (Mary Howard) in the town of New Salem and decides to move there to help run a store. A wrestling match with Jack Armstrong (Howard Da Silva) leads to Abraham's acceptance into the town, and eventually, he is asked to be the captain of the local militia.

**Raymond Massey, who appeared as Lincoln on Broadway, in *Abe Lincoln in Illinois* (1940). *Official press still, author's collection,* © *1940 by RKO Radio Pictures, Inc.***

A run for the state legislature coincides with Ann's death (Abraham was a representative for nearly a year before her passing in 1835). Overlooking Abraham's relationship with Mary Owens once again, Abe is next seen in Springfield, being wooed by Mary Todd (Ruth Gordon). Her determination to push him to greatness fatigues him, and he leaves her. He finally returns to her, and she accepts his marriage proposal. The film montages progress in the country and in Lincoln's career, but issues with slavery—including the arrest of radical abolitionist John Brown—increasingly appear. Lincoln runs for the senate against Stephen Douglas, with a good stretch of the film given over to their speeches in their legendary debates. The movie then focuses on the political apparatus that led to Lincoln's popularity and pushed him to run for the presidency, even if Lincoln himself isn't particularly sure of the idea. On the night of the election, Mary has an episode in front of others, leading to Lincoln chiding her for such a public display, before apologizing to her for upsetting her. Soon after, the word comes that he has been elected president, and the movie concludes with him getting ready to head to Washington.

The movie finds a middle ground between Griffith's *Abraham Lincoln* and Ford's *Young Mr. Lincoln*, showing Abraham's rise through New Salem and Springfield, his relationship with Ann and Mary, and finally the election to the presidency. The Jack Armstrong story gives the film a humorous anchor by making Armstrong a constant strong-arm attachment to Lincoln's political aspirations, which works better than in earlier films, where Jack turns up to wrestle and disappears (he doesn't even turn up in *Young Mr. Lincoln*, where his appearance would have helped set up the murder trial later in the movie). Ann Rutledge's story is better fleshed out, and while it's not completely accurate, her reasons for putting Abraham at a distance due to her relationship with another man are truer here than in other films. Ruth Gordon as Mary Todd demonstrates the shrewdness of the character without becoming charmless, like in some other interpretations, and their mid-engagement breakup and reconciliation are closer to the facts than in the Griffith movie.

Raymond Massey was in his early forties at the time of the film and looks much older than the twenty-two-year-old Lincoln in the beginning of the film. Charles Middleton, the Lincoln of several cameos discussed in various chapters, plays Abraham's father, Tom, and looks younger than Massey, which is slightly unsettling and a good reason to avoid too many close-ups in the first scene of the movie. Beyond that, Massey physically looks the role and is rousing when given a chance to perform one of Lincoln's speeches (an element that Fonda manages to avoid in *Young Mr. Lincoln* and Huston slams through in *Abraham Lincoln*), making it clear why he got the role on Broadway and for the film. Massey received a nomination for the Academy Award for Best Actor and played Lincoln several times again on television, stage, and a final theatrical outing with a cameo in the Cinerama feature *How the West Was Won* (1962). Surprisingly, although the film had strong critical favor, it did not do well at the box office, and the call for another biography film about Lincoln would have to wait close to seventy-five years.

Not that Lincoln didn't pop up in other films in between. *The Story of Mankind* (1957) was an Irwin Allen production based around the concept of world history through the lens of Hollywood and with a cast of famous names. Austin Green, who played Lincoln on the television series *Medic* and *Twilight Zone* (in the classic episode "The Passersby") recites the Emancipation Proclamation in the movie. After that, many films that even hint at a Lincoln connection deal mainly with assassination attempts, unsuccessful and successful.

The year 2013 saw the limited release of *Saving Lincoln*, a film by Salvador Litvak and starring Tom Amandes as Abraham Lincoln and Lea Coco as Ward Lee Lamon (the title obviously is a play on the 2011 Bill O'Reilly and Martin Dugard drama-infused book on the assassination of Lincoln, *Killing Lincoln*, which became a television documentary). The film is from Lamon's point of view as an old friend of Lincoln's who became Lincoln's bodyguard. Lamon was involved as a US marshal in protecting Lincoln's life, including what became known as the Baltimore plot, a rumored attempt on Lincoln as he was traveling to Washington, DC, for his inauguration in February 1861, leading to Lincoln secretly traveling through Baltimore to Washington, DC. The movie uses green-screen effects to place the actors within photos of the time, which is simultaneously both intriguing and jarring and plays better on the small screen than on the large. Contemporaries also viewed Lamon as a bit paranoid about Lincoln's safety and a dunderhead, which is not the direction the movie takes with Lamon, presenting him as an action hero. Nevertheless, Amandes does an appropriate job showing Lincoln during a close-to-twenty-year period, and telling Lincoln's story from the viewpoint of a friend, along with the visual effects, makes it a unique take on Lincoln.

The Baltimore plot covered in *Saving Lincoln* is the focus of the 1951 Dick Powell movie *The Tall Target*. The movie has Powell as John Kennedy, a police sergeant who uncovers the plot, which his boss dismisses as being unbelievable. On his own initiative, Kennedy tries to telegraph Lincoln and boards a train in hopes of intercepting the new president to alert him of the possible attempt on his life, only to find that the cabal is planning to stop him from reaching his destination one way or another. Kennedy manages to stop the final hidden conspirator in the plot, and in the last minute of *The Tall Target*, we see Lincoln (Leslie Kimmell) had been hidden away on the train due to Kennedy's concerns. As the train approaches Washington, we hear Lincoln comment with regret over coming into his role "like a thief in the night." While the character of John Kennedy is fiction, Lincoln's secret entry into Washington did occur and, once discovered by the press, was overwhelmingly ridiculed, leaving Lincoln to regret having taken the advice to do so. Thus, Lincoln's brief cameo does hint at the reality he faced due to the rumored Baltimore plot.

A conspiracy theory was also at the center of the Sunn Classic Pictures movie *The Lincoln Conspiracy*, based on a book released the same year by David Balsiger and Charles E. Sellier Jr. The film and book go back to a long-discredited notion that Secretary of War Edwin Stanton and some Republican senators conspired with Booth and others to have the president kidnapped to stop the Reconstruction plans for the South, only for Booth to assassinate the president instead, leading to a massive cover-up. Lincoln is played by John Anderson, who also played Lincoln in *The Fortune Cookie* (1966) and in an episode of the fantasy television series *Voyagers!* (1982). The 2003 film *Gods and Generals*, dealing with the Civil War career of Stonewall Jackson (Stephen Lang), at one point contains a subplot about John Wilkes Booth (Chris Conner) and his rising determination to do something about Lincoln (Christian Kauffman), including one point when he eyes Lincoln in the balcony during a performance of *MacBeth* and directs some of the speech his way, suggesting what is to come. Elsewhere, *Conspirators* (2011)

features Lincoln briefly at Ford's Theatre during the assassination in a
film dealing with those who may or may not have worked with Booth.

The last major film to feature Lincoln is Steven Spielberg's 2012 film
starring Daniel Day-Lewis in the role. The movie is the longest film,
at two and a half hours, and covers the shortest span of time, less than
four months, of any of the movies dealing specifically with Lincoln.
Based on the book *Team of Rivals: The Political Genius of Abraham
Lincoln*, by Doris Kearns Goodwin, the script was by Tony Kushner
(*Angels in America*, *Munich*) and deals with Lincoln trying to position
the House of Representatives to pass the Thirteenth Amendment abol-
ishing slavery in the United States, between January and April 1865,
before the end of the Civil War. Lincoln's concerns were that if the war
ended before the amendment passed, then returning Southern states
would not vote for its passage, and it would fail. Expecting changes to
or dismissal of the Emancipation Proclamation after the war, Lincoln
knew that without the amendment, the country could splinter again,
and slavery would be reaffirmed in a number of states, making the war
meaningless. Many members in Congress lean toward the amendment,
but there is foot-dragging, with some politicians hoping that the war will
end and afford them the chance to not even be forced to vote. The film
follows various members of the cabinet and agents working for Lincoln,
while he holds a neutral position, attempting to draw enough members
in favor of the amendment to get it passed. Lincoln must also deal his
son Robert (Joseph Gordon-Levitt) wishing to join the forces in the war,
while Mary (Sally Field) objects in fear of losing another son.

Spielberg initially went into the project in 2001 with a script from
John Logan (*Aviator*, *Hugo*, *Gladiator*) that focuses on Lincoln's years
as president, but the project moved to Kushner to write, with the focus on the Thirteenth Amendment. Liam Neeson was to play Lincoln,
only for him to back out in 2010, and Daniel Day-Lewis replaced him.
Released in November 2012, the film earned high critical acclaim and
a successful box office, with Day-Lewis winning Best Actor at the Academy Awards, among many others winning awards for the film.

*Lincoln* is uncommon as a presidential movie, as it deals much more
with the political process than is typical for a Hollywood movie and certainly for a historical film. In an age when the public comes to expect
Congress to spend months and years doing little for progress, the film

Daniel Day-Lewis in the iconic movie poster image of Abraham Lincoln from *Lincoln* (2012). *Poster, author's collection.*

shows that this is nothing new. Everyone has an agenda; the objective is to find enough people who benefit together to move the amendment forward, whether for noble reasons or otherwise. Lincoln also knows that there is a real possibility that he may have to hold off meeting representatives of the Confederacy who wish to end the war to make sure Congress has no choice but to vote on the measure, which leaves the possibility of unnecessary battles—a position that could create outrage if balance is not found. Historical review has found issues with some of the actions made in the film for dramatic purposes, such as putting Lincoln in a position where he directly must make decisions that would have been made by others, but there is agreement that for every wrong thing, there are ten other things that are right in the film. The sets, costumes, and (perhaps a weird element to notice) even the hair is remarkable to look at and feels correct for the time.

Daniel Day-Lewis's performance is extraordinary from the first scene, showing a man weary with the burdens of the war but ready to be the commander the soldiers need as he sits on what appears to be a throne, as if looking down on his creation. There are moments when the Lincoln we are used to seeing in the movies shines through, especially as he tells humorous stories to motivate those around him, but it is clear there is a seriousness behind the lines spoken and a sense of dread within the quiet between them. The movie also doesn't shy away from Mary and Abraham's issues, with Lincoln's depression being clear and Mary's near collapse over their son driving him near the edge. Yet the feeling is that each has their reasons for pushing as they do and not with malice in mind. Even so, when the cabinet argues over what to do and Lincoln slams his hand on the table to get their silence, it feels honest and as important as any words possible at the time. The country needs the amendment, and he needs to see that it is done, without excuses. In lesser hands, that moment could have been less impactful, but Day-Lewis makes us believe he is this man who understands who we are and how human the process is.

The movie draws slowly to a close with the amendment passing and Lincoln getting ready for a night at the theater on April 14, 1865. At that point in the film, as he walks toward the light out of the White House, we expect the film to end. That is not the case. We feel the dread in what we know will come next and then see his body being taken to a home near the theater and then his death. The movie concludes with a flashback to his second inaugural speech, allowing us to see his efforts living on after death.

Still, at the time of first watching the film, I recall feeling that the movie was playing itself out too long by going past that traditional moment when Lincoln grabs his hat and walks out the door into the light. In hindsight, it was incorrect to think that way. That's actually the Hollywood ending we expect. That destiny we know to come is still waiting for him outside, but by closing the film before it happens, we keep Lincoln alive in a sense. It's how other films fade out: Massey fades off on a train as it pulls away from the camera; Fonda walks off into the growing storm; McGlynn disappears into the fog. Lincoln leaves us behind and becomes something greater after he is gone. Instead, we witness not the violence of his death but the sadness of our loss as we look at him on his deathbed. We have no power but to watch as we kill another messenger. With his role, the president has but one curse: The praeses ex machina cannot save himself. And it's what makes him ultimately human like the rest of us.

# 5

# THE PRESIDENT IN JEST

## The President in Traditional Comedies and Dramas

A house divided against itself would be better than this.

—LEGO Lincoln in *The LEGO Movie* (2014)

One well-remembered trait of Abraham Lincoln is his good-natured humor. As Robert Mankoff points out in the 2012 *New Yorker* article "Lincoln's Smile," Lincoln avoided using that humor to taunt others and instead loved to tell humorous stories that led to points he wanted to make, including self-deprecating humor. (Once in the Lincoln-Douglas debates, when Stephen Douglas accused Lincoln of being two-faced, Lincoln replied, "Honestly, if I were two-faced, would I be showing you this one?") With that in mind, one wonders how he would feel about some of his more jokey appearances in comedy movies over the years. In a movie like *Mr. Peabody and Sherman* (2014) or *The Phantom President* (1931), the joke is typically Lincoln being presidential in an inane situation. But for every innocent gag like that, there are the pot-smoking ghost of Lincoln (Keven Sorbo) in *FDR: American Badass!* (2012) and the antagonistic LEGO Lincoln with his space chair in *The LEGO Movie* (2014). If he saw them, then he would probably let most of it roll off his back, although secretly he would favor the "Party on, dudes!" fun that his movie self exerts in *Bill and Ted's Excellent Adventure*. After all, he not only gets to wrestle someone, but he also leaves telling everyone to "be excellent to each other." Lincoln, in a roundabout way, easily could have endorsed that message.

It's interesting to see how often presidents are presented in a serious light in movies. Even in biographical portraits of real presidents, their faces are typically stern as they deal with a crisis of some sort, rather than given a chance to relax and be personable. The Lincoln biographies of the 1930s and 1940s open that up a bit with an insight into his family and past (such as showing the uncertainty he had marrying Mary Todd), which hadn't been investigated in Hollywood before with other presidents. Yet the fate of the fictional presidents doesn't change much. Over the years, there have been only a small number of movies that feature even a fictional president in a situation that doesn't involve them facing terrorists, criminals, natural disasters, or space invasions. When we have drifted down to a more a domestic drama, dealing with interpersonal relationships, it has usually been for the sake of comedy, although there are a handful of dramas dealing with the presidency, as well.

One of the first films out of Hollywood dealing with fictional presidents (although not the actual first, as commonly reported) is the Fleischer Studios cartoon for Paramount *Betty Boop for President* (1932), released to theaters within weeks of the election. Along with the fantasy setup showing how Betty would run the country while singing "If I Were President," Betty imitates Herbert Hoover, the Republican candidate, and Al Smith, the assumed Democratic candidate when the cartoon was produced (the Democratic National Convention nominated Franklin D. Roosevelt in July; more about the two in chapter 7). The concept of the cartoon and many of the gags later turned up in the cartoon made by Famous Studio (Paramount's subsequent animation studio after Fleischer Studios) called *Olive Oyl for President* in 1948. Of the films that would run before main features at theaters, there's also the early Warner Brothers Vitaphone short *Rufus Jones for President* (1933) about a seven-year-old Sammy Davis Jr. who dreams of becoming president, with Ethel Waters as his mother. All three shorts here deal with the same silly, dreamlike world of what changes a person would make if they were president, to the cheers of everyone. It's all merely a fantasy over the space of seven to twenty minutes and all about setting up songs and gags.

The first full-length movie comedy to deal with the presidency, *The Phantom President*, was released in September 1932, six months before the better-known, fantasy-tinged *Gabriel over the White House* and nineteen years after the futuristic *The Sons of a Soldier* from 1913 (covered in more detail in chapter 10). Directed by Norman Taurog (known for his later work with Jerry Lewis and Elvis Presley) and written by Walter DeLeon and Harlan Thompson (*Ruggles of Red Gap*), *The Phantom President* is based on a novel by adventure writer George F. Worts, with some reworking of the plot to give the story a twist ending. More importantly, it is the first talking film with Broadway king George M. Cohan, later immortalized in *Yankee Doodle Dandy* and having a connection with Franklin D. Roosevelt, covered more in chapter 7. Cohan, fifty-four at the time, plays dual roles in the movie. The first is a dull banker named Theodore K. Blair running for president, with a campaign being financed by his political party. Blair has all the credentials for the job and will be a good yes-man for the group, but his personality is so boring that it is clear he has no chance of getting the public interested in his campaign. Cohan's second role is "Doc" Varney, a huckster who has the needed personality and looks exactly like Blair. The campaigners send Varney out as Blair to win votes, and it works but too well. Blair's girlfriend, Felicia Hammond (Claudette Colbert), falls in love with the energetic, for-the-working-man fake Blair, as his success with the public begins to convince Varney into believing what he's selling. Meanwhile, the real Blair is jealous of his twin's success and hires goons to kidnap Varney and ship him off to the Artic. Felicia, who has figured out the man she loves is not really Blair, foils the kidnapping by convincing the goons that the conman is Blair, so they pack up the real Blair instead. The film ends with Varney as Blair being elected president, the real Blair freezing by an igloo and listening to the news on a radio, and a bright tomorrow on the horizon for everyone in the country.

The film was heavily promoted, received good notices, and released to coincide with the heated 1932 presidential campaign (with reviewers noting a similarity of the dull businessman Blair and President Hoover, who was running for reelection). Yet it was not a success, and Cohan did only one more movie before heading back to Broadway. The issue really is that the movie does not gel, as Cohan shows a remarkable lack of charisma in both roles, making it hard to root for either character,

**George M. Cohan as Theodore K. Blair in *The Phantom President* (1932). Or is it? *Official press still, author's collection, © 1932 by Paramount Pictures Corp.***

although you're supposed to be instantly drawn to Varney. It is only during a medicine man number early in the film when Cohan comes alive (and, unfortunately, in blackface for no reason that supports the number). Interviews after the release of the picture reveal that he didn't like working on the picture or having to sing tunes by Richard Rodgers and Lorenz Hart (who ironically worked with him a few years later; again, check out chapter 7), and that resentment bleeds through on the screen. One can just imagine how an up-and-coming star like Bing Crosby would have been magical in the dual roles.

Claudette Colbert, who was on a rise that soon saw her in *It Happened One Night* and *Cleopatra* (both 1934), is excellent as the girlfriend who falls for Varney, while Jimmy Durante as Varney's friend tears up the screen in an early, manic role but to little overall effect. The movie's premise is an early example of the accidental president, however, with Varney pushed to take on the role of a presidential nominee who does what he's told, only to eventually choose to be his own man, leading him to become a better person and most probably a better president.

The setup must have made an impression, as author Charles G. Booth (*The General Died at Dawn, The House on 92nd Street*) wrote a short story, "Caviar for His Excellency," with a similar premise that became the 1939 movie *The Magnificent Fraud*. This film deals with an actor who is forced into replacing his look-alike, the president of a Latin American country, after he is assassinated. A drama, this movie was remade in 1988 as the Paul Mazursky comedy *Moon over Parador*. In that version, American actor Jack Noah (Richard Dreyfuss) is threatened by people in the government into taking the place of the president of Parador, a fictional country in Latin America, when the real president dies of a heart attack. The charade works, although the president's mistress (Sonia Braga) easily sees through the disguise, much like in *The Phantom President*. The two then conspire to use the opportunity to work around their puppeteers and help the country get back on its feet.

*Moon over Parador* failed at the box office, but the idea popped up again five years later and came full circle with *Dave* (1998). In this variation, the president of the United States (Kevin Kline) has a charming public persona hiding a cold, snide hustler underneath, which drives him away from the First Lady (Sigourney Weaver). Elsewhere in Washington is a man named Dave who supplements his income running an employment agency by jokingly impersonating the president at various events. It's convincing enough that Dave is asked to be a decoy for the president at an event, apparently for security reasons but is actually a means for the president to have a tryst with a staffer (played by Laura Linney, who went on to play Abigail Adams in the HBO series *John Adams* and a mistress to the president in the 2013 film *Hyde Park on Hudson*). When he suffers a stroke that puts him into an unresponsive coma, Chief of Staff Bob Alexander (Frank Langella) and Communications Director Alan Reed (Kevin Dunn) have the president kept alive in secret and convince Dave to continue playing the role. Unknown to Dave, Bob plans to insinuate the innocent vice president (Ben Kingsley) into a financial scandal, thus forcing his resignation, whereupon Dave will nominate Bob to replace him as vice president. Thereafter, Bob can have the president's unresponsive body found, leading him to become president, per the Twenty-Fifth Amendment (yes, the scheme is way too elaborate, but stick with the fantasy of the film for now).

With resentment toward her husband, the First Lady ignores Dave, allowing the pretense to continue for a time, but Dave's gentle nature and concern for others grows on her until Bob signs a veto in the president's name that defunds a shelter. When angrily confronted with the news by the First Lady, Dave is stunned and stages a public review of the budget with his cabinet, forcing various cuts to help restore the badly needed money. It is with this that the First Lady realizes Dave is an imposter but is happy to go along with the idea, when not only is it clear that he will make a better president but also that she discovers she is falling in love with him.

Feeling Dave is getting in the way of his plans, Bob threatens to expose him, only for Dave as the president to demand Bob's resignation. Bob does so but implicates the president and vice president in the financial scandal as retaliation. Dave, with the help of Alan and the First Lady, proves the innocence of the vice president while also exposing both the president's and Bob's involvement in the scandal, leaving Bob's career in tatters. Dave then fakes a heart attack during a televised event, with the real president's body replacing him in the ambulance and Dave able to walk away. After the death of the comatose president, the vice president becomes the president, and Dave is back in his office working to win a seat on the city council. Then the now former First Lady appears in disguise to rekindle their relationship.

*Dave* was a success with audiences and reviewers. What may have helped is that the character of Dave is not coerced into the situation, like in *The Magnificent Fraud* or *Moon over Parador*, nor is he trying to scam everyone, like the main character in *The Phantom President*. Only once he is involved does he realize Bob and Alan lied to him and are forcing him to do their bidding, resulting in a return to the concept of the accidental president. This isn't a case of lazy writing as much as setting up a traditional three-act story arc found in many of these movies, with the end of its second act being a crisis resulting from the protagonist's misguided faith in the system. When Dave gets the job, he is happy to act the role with no repercussions for whatever actions Bob and Alan take on the part of the president. Once the funding is denied to the shelter, however, just as other presidents in movies before him, he realizes his mistake and takes action to make amends.

Interestingly, in *Dave*, cameos of real politicians are peppered throughout the movie, such as Senators Paul Simon and Howard Metzenbaum as well as Speaker of the House Tip O'Neill, plus individuals from the media, like John McLaughlin, Larry King, and Jay Leno. It was unusual at the time to see real politicians and media commentators injecting real-world political debate into a dramatic film; in the past, it was seen as beneath the dignity of individuals in Washington to do so unless under strict control. It is still very infrequent for politicians, although people from the media have been more accepting of the idea in recent years. Of course, all such individuals appear in positive cameos, always in favor of the things that are good for people and then questioning the president when he does something wrong (the emergence of the financial scandal is an example of this, with television coverage showing everyone turning on the president for sliding back to his old ways).

Getting elected, as seen in *The Phantom President*, was and remains a popular setting for movies about the presidency, such as in the 1948 movie *State of the Union*, starring Spencer Tracy and Katharine Hepburn. Coincidentally, Claudette Colbert from *The Phantom President* was set to costar with Tracy but bowed out after creative differences with director Frank Capra, so Hepburn took her place. Grant Matthews (Spencer Tracy), a successful manufacturer of airplanes, is offered by his girlfriend, newspaper magnate Kay Thorndyke (Angela Lansbury), and political strategist Jim Conover (Adolphe Menjou) to run for the Republican nomination for president. To help with the campaign, they want Grant to tour with his estranged wife, Mary (Katharine Hepburn), to help his image. Grant begins making speeches that go over well with people in the streets but rankle the money spenders, and as time progresses, he shifts to prepared speeches and agrees to deals that open the purse strings, only to drive away the common man. When Mary discovers how much control Kay has over her husband, she initially refuses to participate in the hypocrisy but is talked into giving a speech that Grant immediately notices is not her own thoughts. Realizing that he had lost his values in pursuit of becoming president, Grant stops her midspeech and announces on radio and television that he will not run for office, exposing a union leader who promised to give him 700,000 votes in exchange for favors and daring any other big spender there to try to stop him. With the campaign lost and Grant reunited with Mary after his on-air speech, Kay decides to search elsewhere for her bid to have power in the White House.

If the film sounds like it has some similarities with the previously discussed *The Candidate* (1972) in chapter 2, that's because it's a common theme in many of these films dealing with the campaign—a person who has strong views but is naïve about the ways of politics is handpicked by a campaigner and/or other people in a political party to run for office. In *The Candidate*, we first see Marvin Lucas (Peter Boyle), whose career is looking for campaigns to run, pull Bill McKay (Robert Redford) into the senatorial race with the promise that he can say anything he wants. As time goes by, Lucas wields more influence until McKay wins the election, but McKay isn't sure what his own point of view is anymore. When McKay asks what comes next, Lucas has no answer and moves along, just as Kay in *State of the Union* does (and it isn't hard to see Angela Lansbury's manipulative "person behind the throne" in *State of the Union* someday becoming the crazed mother of Raymond Shaw in the 1962 movie *The Manchurian Candidate*). The job is over with the win or loss, not anything that affects people once in office. *State of the Union* heads down this same road, only for Grant to pull back when he sees someone whose judgment he trusts soiled by dirty politics.

This same theme appears in the 2003 movie *Head of State*, produced by, directed by, written by, and starring Chris Rock, although with more positive results. The idea for the film came to Rock as he thought about the 1984 election and how Geraldine Ferraro became the first female Democratic nominee for vice president as a last-gasp attempt to win over voters (Sarah Palin's position for the Republicans in the 2008 election was seen similarly). In the movie, Rock plays Mays Gilliam, a local council member who receives favorable press after saving a woman's life and is offered a chance to run for president by campaigners after their original candidate died. They figure he will lose to the Republican candidate, but nominating a Black man will look good to voters. At first, Gilliam allows the campaigners to dictate his moves and speeches, but (as in *The Man* and *State of the Union*) he finally decides to go off script and talk directly to the people. In doing so, he wins the election and becomes president.

*Long Shot* from 2019 stars Seth Rogen as Fred Flarsky, a reporter who becomes a speechwriter for presidential candidate Charlotte Field (Charlize Theron). At one point, she is asked to tone down a speech that would be sure to upset some of the money people, but Fred convinces her to stick to her guns, saving her campaign in the process. A later incident leads to her being extorted into supporting an antienvironmental position in order to avoid the release of damaging information about Fred, ending the budding romantic relationship between the two. In the end, she exposes the blackmail, earning the public's trust and becoming the first female president, with Fred as her husband.

The 2011 movie *The Ides of March*, produced by, directed by, written by, and starring George Clooney, also deals with extortion playing into the corruption of a candidate. In this case, Clooney plays Mike Morris, who is running for the Democratic nomination against Ted Pullman (Michael Mantell). Both candidates need the large number of delegates that a senator has to offer, but while Pullman is ready to dangle a cabinet position at the senator, Morris refuses, as the senator's policies conflict with his own. Yet by the end of the film, Morris finds himself blackmailed by his own junior campaign manager into offering the vice presidency to the senator to get the delegates and win the nomination. Morris is not happy with the idea, but he is coerced into it by his handlers, losing his integrity in the process.

The 2006 Robin Williams movie *Man of the Year* is a mixed bag of comedy and political paranoia action-adventure from director Barry Levinson (*Diner, Avalon*) that deals with winning the election but from another angle. In *Man of the Year*, our presidential candidate is host Tom Dobbs (Robin Williams) of a late-night comedy show that pokes fun at politics. As typically occurs around presidential elections, humorists like Will Rogers or Pat Paulsen announce their intent to run for president, with the known objective to make fun of the process over the months into the election. In the case of Dobbs, he manages to get on the ballot in thirteen states as an independent, and suddenly, the joke campaign is a serious endeavor for him. The campaign is thrown into chaos, however, when Dobbs begins to make fun of the process in the middle of a presidential debate with the Republican and Democratic candidates. It's an incident that realistically would have probably killed

Dobbs's chances and driven him out of the race, but here—because it is Robin Williams—it earns him more support.

The political intrigue begins after the election, when it turns out that Dobbs has won in all thirteen states where he appeared on the ballots, giving him enough electoral votes to win the race. Eleanor Green (Laura Linney once again) works for the company that supplies the voting machines used across the country and realizes Dobbs did not win the election based on votes but due to a glitch with the machines. Wanting to expose the truth, Green is soon on the run from the company's goons, and only Dobbs can save her. Once Dobbs exposes the truth on an episode of *Saturday Night Live*, the bad guys are arrested, Dobbs resigns, and Green naturally (okay, Hollywood "naturally") ends up in a relationship with Dobbs.

The film starts off with the promising idea of someone who gains a career mocking the political system now having to serve that very system, possibly even suggesting a story yet again of someone losing their internal judgment when a brass ring like the presidency is dangled in front of them. Unfortunately, this premise is swept under the rug midway through the film for the political thriller happening on the side. The other issue is that recent events in politics show that the premise would be unlikely, due to the country's acknowledged multiple counting systems when it comes to votes. Also, the 100 percent loss for a major party candidate (as all states outside the thirteen went to the incumbent Republican candidate, leaving the Democratic candidate with no votes at all) would send up so many red flags—even without any tinfoil conspiracy theorists—that investigations would be immediate, and the truth would be exposed without all the running around and car chases.

Problems with the voting machines play a major part in the Touchstone family film *Swing Vote* (2008), written and directed by Joshua Michael Stern and starring Kevin Costner. Logically, things get off on the wrong foot when young Molly (Madeline Carroll) votes for her father, Bud (Kevin Costner), which is of course fraud, no matter how innocent a twelve-year-old's intention may be. The voting machine doesn't pick up a winner, which means the vote would be discarded and the election that ends in a tie for the state of New Mexico (as in the movie) would end with a coin flip. In other words, the incident would be over before the movie really begins. Instead, it is decided that the entire country-wide election will be stalled to have Bud decide within ten days on the winning vote for New Mexico, which will swing the election to either the Republican candidate (Kelsey Grammar) or the Democratic one (Dennis Hopper). The focus of the film really is how Bud, a slacker who refuses to help his daughter, turns his life around with the attention he receives thanks to his daughter's dedication. The political commentary, meanwhile, is the previously seen notion of candidates ready to sell out at the drop of a hat. In this movie, they back agendas that they think will get the final vote from Bud, until (shades of the mistake of the accidental president once again) they finally ignore their campaigners and speak truthfully to the American people. The film also depicts a certain number of media stars commenting on the events, such as Bill Maher, James Carville, and Tucker Carlson, in a continuation of efforts to ground the story in some form of reality, like in *Dave*.

The voting process related to a president comes into play in *Advise and Consent* (1962), based on a novel by Allen Drury and directed by Otto Preminger (*Anatomy of a Murder, Exodus*), although not in the election process for the presidency. Instead, in this drama, the president (Franchot Tone) is at the heart of a vote in Congress for his choice of secretary of state, Robert Leffingwell (Henry Fonda). Leffingwell is a likeable man with a family, but his liberal leanings rub some the wrong way, including the vice president, Harley Hudson (Lew Ayres). The president, knowing he will die soon, wants to swiftly push Leffingwell's nomination through as his legacy, before the vice president gets a chance to take over and pick someone else. The nomination leads to young Senator Brigham Anderson (Don Murray) heading a senatorial subcommittee to investigate Leffingwell, who admits to the president a short-lived Communist affiliation in his youth, only to perjure himself when asked about it in the committee. The president refuses a request from Leffingwell to pull his nomination and stalls any investigation into the claims. Another senator, Van Ackerman (George Grizzard), is so eager to win the president's favor that he threatens Senator Anderson with exposure of a same-sex affair he had in Hawaii during the war if Anderson does not approve Leffingwell. The possibility of scandal compels Anderson to commit suicide, closing the investigation, and a vote proceeds on Leffingwell's nomination. The Senate evenly splits, and the vice president is about to cast his vote when he receives word that the president has died. The vice president declines to vote as he plans to nominate someone else for the job, concluding the film.

As Thomas Mallon points out in his fiftieth-anniversary review of the Allen Drury novel, *Advise and Consent*'s suicide due to a gay scandal has basis in real-life going-ons in the Senate. In the early 1950s, Senator Lester Hunt of Wyoming picked a fight with Senator Joseph McCarthy over McCarthy's continuous bullying of various congressional members by slandering them with gossip of being Communist sympathizers. In 1953, two senators working with McCarthy told Hunt that they would tell the press about his son's recent arrest for soliciting a male police officer if he did not immediately resign from the Senate. Hunt refused to do so and even announced his intention to run again in 1954, when he committed suicide in his office on June 19, 1954. The death would be one more element to tilt Congress away from McCarthy and the red baiting that occupied Washington and most of America in the 1950s.

A scandal dealing with a gay affair also is used in the film *The Best Man* (discussed in chapter 2) to extort a politician, and it pops up again in the movie *Primary Colors* (1998), and it leads to a suicide, as in *Advise and Consent*. The film, based on a novel written by Joe Klein under the name of Anonymous in 1996, tells the story of a young political advisor helping with the presidential campaign of a candidate who has some hidden issues and is clearly a fictionalized review of Bill Clinton's 1992 campaign for president, with made-up details added. The film adaptation has John Travolta as Jack Stanton, a Southern governor running for president, with Emma Thomson as his wife, Susan. It follows the familiar grounds of *The Candidate* and *State of the Union* although from the viewpoint of an advisor for Stanton, Henry Burton (Adrian Lester). Burton joins the campaign with high regard for Stanton, only to realize that the candidate is not as perfect as his image makes him out to be, with his affairs being outed—including one with an underage girl—and his instant willingness to change policies if it will help win campaign support. When former governor Fred Picker (Larry Hagman) starts to gain on Stanton, Burton and another advisor, Libby (Kathy Bates), find evidence of Picker having a same-sex affair with his cocaine supplier. When Stanton confirms he'll use the "dirty linen" to take down Picker, Libby is so distraught over shattering her image of Stanton that she commits suicide. This forces Stanton to reevaluate his plan and not go public with the evidence. He instead passes it on to Picker, who agrees to drop out of the race and support Stanton. Burton also threatens to quit after the suicide, but Stanton convinces him that needing to adapt and play dirty isn't great but winning the election is for a greater good. Although the book was a best-seller, partially due to its anonymous authorship, the movie did poorly with critics and at the box office. After all, with the Clintons' escalating tribulations readily playing out 24/7 on the news channels at the time, there was little need to pay ticket prices to see more of it in the theaters.

Beyond retreading the same-sex-affair plotline, the movie takes us down a very familiar road at this point, where politicians say and do anything to make it, and only those who decide to bail or ignore temptation get to keep their integrity. Stanton nearly loses his in *Primary Colors*, but the suicide of a staffer brings him to his senses. And as in previous films listed here, once he does so, he is rewarded. The same thread runs through *The Contender* from 2000, written and directed by Rod Lurie. In *The Contender*, President Evans (Jeff Bridges) is looking to replace the vice president after his death in office. The film has an *Advise and Consent* vibe, as the president wants Senator Laine Hanson (Joan Allen) as the vice president, while his Republican opponent in Congress, Sheldon Runyon (Gary Oldman, who also produced the movie), wants Virginia governor Jack Hathaway (William Petersen), who saved a woman's life from a car accident. Runyon is given photos of what appears to be an orgy with Hanson from her college days, and he leaks the information to the press, demanding she respond to his accusations. She refuses, and as time drags on, President Evans agrees to drop Hanson for Hathaway if Runyon drops his crusade against her. Just as he is about to make that announcement to Congress, Hanson reveals an FBI report showing that Hathaway faked the car accident to boost his image, ruining Hathaway's chances for the vice presidency. Later, in private with the president, Hanson makes clear that she did attend the party in the photos but left before anything happened. Even so, she refuses to go public with the information, as to do so would validate questioning her participation as acceptable in the first place. President Evans, upset with himself for doubting Hanson and bending to Runyon's demands, goes before Congress and asks them to commence with an immediate vote for her confirmation.

Insinuating evidence also comes into play with the earlier 1995 movie *The American President*, directed by Rob Reiner and written by Aaron Sorkin (*A Few Good Men, Moneyball*). Michael Douglas plays President Andrew Shepherd, who is running for reelection with a 63 percent approval rating, but he has two bills that could give him blowback: a crime bill that has been gutted of its gun-control emphasis in order to get it passed in Congress and an environmental bill to cut emissions by 20 percent. Shepherd, a widower, is attracted to Sydney Ellen Wade (Annette Bening), a lobbyist for an environmental group, and most of the comedy in the film comes from the complications of this very important world leader trying to build anything like a normal relationship while in office. The drama comes from the same source, as political rival Senator Bob Rumson (Richard Dreyfuss) tries to use Wade's past against the president, including a photo of her at an anti-Apartheid event where an American flag is burned as well as innuendo from "sources" that Wade performed sexual acts for political favors in the past. After nearly ruining his chance to be with a woman he loves and recognizing that he has watered down policies to the point that nothing is accomplished, Shepherd goes to the press to denounce Rumson's attacks and state that he plans to reintroduce his crime bill, with the handgun legislation put back, and the environmental bill, with a full 20 percent emissions reducation, to the applause of the press and Congress at the State of the Union.

Both *The American President* and *The Contender* deal with how people manipulate the narrative against others and when it is right to stand up to accusations. Shepherd, just as Hanson in *The Contender*, feels any response helps only the opponent, but the ultimate message of *The American President* is to meet such comments head on. Shepherd realizes that by trying to avoid such obstacles, he is losing his path as a good person and as a politician and counters his actions just in time to save his relationship with Wade and—it appears at least—his two bills by strongly voicing his opposition to the attacks.

Shepherd's final speech to the press is a powerful bit of writing, with the president dressing down his attacker and our reliance on game playing in politics instead of risking votes to do the right thing. For some, it was too good to pass up. More than ten years later, a snit occurred on Twitter between two Republican candidates in the 2016 election cycle involving *The American President*. At one point during the Republican nomination process, Donald Trump insulted the wife of his opponent Senator Ted Cruz. Cruz responded by commenting on CNN's *New Day*, "If Donald wants to get in a character fight, he's better off sticking with me, because Heidi is way out of his league." It is a good line, but the problem is that it was so obviously a quote from *The American President* that Trump merely turned it around to mock Cruz, responding in a Tweet, "Lyin' Ted Cruz steals foreign policy from me and lines from Michael Douglas—just another dishonest politician." The line that worked so well in a movie made Cruz look inept, and within a year, he saw Trump in office and having to help push his agenda. At least Cruz wasn't quoting from the movie within a prepared speech as if they were his own words, which occurred in 2012 to Anthony Albanese, at the time a leader in the Australian House of Representatives. In discussing opponent Tony Abbott, Albanese paraphrased a portion of Shepherd's final speech to the press about needing "serious people to solve serious challenges" and that Abbott was interested "in two things: making Australians afraid of it and telling them who's to blame for it." It just goes to show how too good a speech it was not to use in real life and perhaps why it works so much better in a Hollywood ending.

The president having to deal with family members is a common start point in presidential comedies, sometimes with the president taking a backseat to the action. When Chelsea Clinton, President Bill Clinton's daughter, decided to go to college, security had to be beefed up around the college campus for her. This drove the narrative for two comedies from 2004, *Chasing Liberty* (with Mark Harmon as the president) and *The First Daughter* (with Michael Keaton as the president), both of which deal with the daughter of a fictional president graduating high school and leaving the nest, only to fall in love with a man who turns out to be an incognito Secret Service agent assigned to protect her, creating headaches for all involved. Both *Dr. Dolittle: Tail to the Chief* (2008, with Peter Coyote) and *Max 2: White House Hero* (2017, with Andrew Kavadas) deal with dogs in the White House that end up causing political chaos for the president. *American Dreamz* (2006) has the First Lady talking the president (Dennis Quaid) into being on her favorite game show, only to lead to an assassination attempt by a contestant. The 2004 movie *Welcome to Mooseport* has Gene Hackman as a former president who decides to run for mayor of a small town to avoid having his house taken away in a divorce settlement with the First Lady.

*Kisses for My President* from 1964 is an early example that shows how such an emphasis on another character can work against the story. The film deals with the first female president, Leslie Harrison McCloud (Polly Bergen), who has won in a fair election with no weird shenanigans, sudden deaths of other politicians, or hocus pocus (like Popeye's dreamworld where Olive Oyl is president). Yet for such an innovative concept of the time that would be revisited over the years in multiple films and television, very little is done with it beyond the noted irritating tendency of every man to try to diminish her by complimenting her beauty and not her work.

The thrust of the president's story in the film has to do with a senator (Edward Andrews) trying to intimidate the president into financing Central American dictator Valdez (Eli Wallach). Bergen is good as a serious president dealing with her treatment at the hands of the senator and

**Polly Bergen is the first female president in *Kisses for My President* (1964), although she gets little to do in the movie.** *Official press still, author's collection,* © *1964 by Warner Brothers.*

with the foolish dictator, but that thread pretty much peters out halfway through the film. Instead, the movie spends most of its time following Thad McCloud, the president's husband, and his frustrations of no longer dominating in a traditional "male" role. Attempts to get him involved land him in hot water with the press, while an old female friend tries to use his influence for her business. Meanwhile, their teenage daughter and young son are out of control, but the insinuation is that this is more due to the mother being too busy being president than the father wandering off because he isn't in control any longer. Worse yet, Thad solves the issue with the senator and the dictator for his wife, and when the president finds out she is pregnant, she resigns. Thus, while *Kisses for My President* has its brief progressive moment, the overall theme is sadly that it's a man's job.

In other circumstances, having the president be the linchpin to the comedy can pay off. *The President's Analyst* (1967), written and directed by Theodore J. Flicker (*Barney Miller*), never actually shows us the president, but there would be no movie without him. The film stars James Coburn as Dr. Sidney Schaefer, a psychiatrist who is picked to help the president with stress and anxieties facing him in his position. (Oddly enough, 1967 saw another James Coburn action comedy featuring a never-seen president, *In Like Flint*.) The problem is that due to security measures, Dr. Schaefer carries the president's emotional weight with no one to turn to himself, and with constant surveillance on him, he becomes paranoid. And rightly so, as it turns out everyone, including his girlfriend, is spying on him. Cracking under the strain, Schaefer goes on the run, which allows multiple government agents to try to kidnap him for his knowledge about the president, while US spies are ordered to either catch him or kill him. An alliance between two of his patients, one old and one new, work to save Schaefer but not before he is captured by the most ruthless power in the world, the Phone Company. They have created a wireless device that allows people to instantly communicate with anyone in the world, which also gives the company control over the people, but they need the president to help push through their plans in Congress and Schaefer to help convince the president to do so. Schaefer, with the help of his friends, manages to stop the threat to the world by making everyone hate the Phone Company, and the world is saved from

James Coburn as the psychiatrist who is losing his mind once he becomes
*The President's Analyst (1967). Original movie poster, author's collection.*

a technology we depend on night and day feeding information about us to a powerful company. At least that's what my cell phone tells me.

But *The President's Analyst* is an excellent example of how the presidency can lead to satire, with the ultimate villain not being another government but a company that at the time was pretty much a monopoly in the country. Satire also allows for poignant moments in drama, which is seen with Agent Masters (Godfrey Cambridge) in an early session with Schaefer. Masters reflects on how learning the N-word as a kid led to internal hate he feels when killing opposing foreign agents in the field. The dialogue and emotion shown by the actor is so haunting that it is a mystery Cambridge did not end up with one or more awards for that scene alone. The 1979 movie *Being There*, directed by Hal Ashby (*Harold and Maude*, *Shampoo*) and written by Jerzy Kosinski (who also wrote the novel on which it is based), stars Peter Sellers as Chance, a quiet, simple man who suffers from a disorder (never named) where his perception of life is based on two things: the gardening he has done his entire life for an old rich man living in Washington, DC, and anything said on television. Outside of those two windows, Chance has no understanding. When the man he works for dies, Chance is kicked out into the streets, where he coincidently meets up with the wife (Shirley MacLaine) of a businessman (Melvyn Douglas) who is friends with the president (Jack Warden). Chance is thrown into the world of business and politics, which means a narcissistic world of people, where no one plainly speaks and everything is in code. Thus when Chance gives nonsensical responses to questions based on his limited perception of the world, everyone assumes he is being purposefully cryptic and interprets them any way they want. Because he appeases them and without any intentions to do so, he becomes the ultimate yes-man and rapidly moves up the ladder, leading to more and more people thinking he's important. The president, meanwhile, is struggling to do the right thing in his position but is professionally (and personally) impotent because he can't speak in a manner that wins people over like Chance does. By the end of the movie, the president's handlers are discussing putting Chance up for the presidency. It is clear Chance has no interest in or understanding of the job, but because he gives people the answers they want to hear instead of what they need to hear, they think Chance will win—a common theme in politics before then and certainly now.

Three films turn a skewed eye on how war can shape public perception of a president by way of satire: *Wrong Is Right* (1982), *Canadian Bacon* (1995), and *Wag the Dog* (1997). Only the most recent one was successful at the box office. *Wrong Is Right* was written and directed by Richard Brooks (*Elmer Gantry, In Cold Blood, Looking for Mr. Goodbar*) and was the most serious of the three. Based on the novel *Better Angels* by Charles McCarry, the story is set in the near future, when television is everything, and Patrick Hale (Sean Connery) is an adventurer-newscaster who uncovers a plot by an Arabian king to help a terrorist named Rafeeq (Henry Silva) threaten to nuke New York City unless President Lockwood (George Grizzard) resigns. The president is up for reelection and running against a former president, Franklin Mallory (Leslie Nielsen), who is advocating for war in the Middle East, while Lockwood is trying to avoid it. Lockwood keeps seeking advice from those around him. Everyone is working for someone else (or maybe two others), and we even get a Black female vice president (the always underused Rosalind Cash, sadly underused here, as well) in the mix, but the film is a mishmash with little humor and missing narrative to explain some things to the audience as we move along. Connery is also surprisingly bland in the movie, drifting along with the story instead of really coming off as the necessary television-created action hero for the script to work, while Katharine Ross looks to be the costar as a journalist working for the US government, only to be killed off unexpectedly early in the film. Meanwhile, Robert Conrad, Leslie Nielsen, Robert Webber, and Dean Stockwell all look prepared to be funny, only for nothing to happen to allow them that chance. When the movie failed to do well in the United States, it was retitled *The Man with the Deadly Lens* to try to tie it into Connery's James Bond past, but it still failed to do well in sales.

The movie ends with nuclear bombs set to go off on top of one of the World Trade Center buildings, only to be stopped in the nick of time by the CIA, with an agent slyly admitting to Hale that maybe it wasn't just by chance they found the bombs there. Soon after, Lockwood declares war on the country in the Middle East, earning him praise from Americans, an assured reelection, and even a pat on the back from his opponent Mallory as Lockwood joins the troops in the new war in order to televise it to all the happy people back home. Obviously, it is now not easy to watch a movie dealing with the World Trade Center being bombed by terrorists and leading to a war in the Middle East without wondering how much fiction can influence reality.

This setup of the president working to stage a war in order to help his chances with the public in an election cycle or even to divert from other scandals occurs in both *Canadian Bacon* and *Wrong Is Right*. *Canadian Bacon* (which shares G. D. Spradlin from *Wrong Is Right* in the cast) was directed and written by Michael Moore, the documentary filmmaker known for *Roger and Me* (1989) and *Bowling for Columbine* (2002). While his other films have satirical edges, *Canadian Bacon* is so far the only full comedy film he has done, although it still deals with politics on an international stage. In the movie, the president (Alan Alda) needs to improve his poll numbers and figures a conflict of some kind with another country will do it. With Russia uninterested, the president is convinced to stage a propaganda war against Canada, which works too well, with some Americans attempting to stage riots and even acts of terrorism in Canada. During all this, a military supplier who had his plant shut down by the president activates codes in Canada to set missile silos in the United States to attack Russia unless the president agrees to buy his weapon systems for $1 trillion. The president pleads with the Canadians to stop the codes, only for them to be ultimately stopped by one of the misguided Americans thinking the launch site is part of a Canadian plot. Even though the president arguably prevents World War III, it is explained at the end of the movie that he loses the next election to Oliver North in the "largest landslide in US history" and goes on to host a talk show on Cleveland television.

The movie is really a softball attack on how manipulative the political process can be, especially from such a filmmaker as Moore, who usually can go for the jugular when calling out politicians in his documentaries. *Canadian Bacon* has a good cast, including John Candy, Rhea Perlman, Kevin Pollak, and Rip Torn (who plays an authoritative figure so often in movies you'd think he had a set of military uniforms at home to pull out for any role), and Alan Alda looks to be enjoying the chance to poke some fun at his own image in the role of an ineffectual president who can't quite get on the right wavelength with anyone. The main problem is that it is just too nice, and the promising idea of an actual war with modern Canada is discarded in the final third of the film for the subplot of the businessman ending another missile silo countdown. *South Park:*

*Bigger, Longer and Uncut* does a better job with a Canadian-US war four years later. The film is also very static in its production value, giving everything a TV-movie look that doesn't support the needed massive look to put over the "let's go to war" parody here. The film ended up with a number of poor reviews (Canadian reviewers were more positive, strangely enough) and made very little money at the box office.

*Wag the Dog* came out two years after *Canadian Bacon* but was a big success at the box office, no doubt due to being directed by Barry Levinson, written by Hilary Henkin and David Mamet, and starring Dustin Hoffman and Robert De Niro. Much like *The President's Analyst*, we never see the president, nor is he ever named, but everything revolves around him. In the movie, the president is running for reelection when news breaks that he attacked a Girl Scout in the Oval Office. To distract the public from that story, an advisor named Conrad Brean (Robert De Niro) suggests staging a war—not a real one but one that will grab the public's interest and hopefully bring them back to supporting the president. The war is supposed to be in Albania, a country in Europe far enough away for people in the United States to not really know of it beyond the name, and footage is shot with the help of film producer Stanley Motss (Dustin Hoffman) to create the visual. Thing spiral out of control, but ultimately the story is contained, with those involved who know too much taken care of and the president being reelected. Unfortunately, it also creates the opportunity for a true terrorist organization to be created in Albania based on the legend of the war.

The presidency as a sight gag has been used a few times in the movies, as well. For example, the president in Robert Downey Sr.'s *Putney Swope* (1969) is played by Pepi Heimine (*Even Dwarfs Started Small*) as a German-accented little person for no other reason than because it's bizarre to see the president in such a manner. The gag in *Jane Austen's Mafia!* (1998) is that the protagonist's girlfriend (Christina Applegate) goes off on her own midway through the film and comes back near the end as the president of the United States, ready to announce world peace, thus setting up the joke that all the protagonist's actions in the movie seem pointless in comparison to her off-screen story. *Jane Austen's Mafia!* was written and directed by Jim Abrahams, who was part of the team that made the classic parody film *Airplane!* (1980). Abrahams also wrote and directed *Hot Shots! Part Deux* (1993), a sequel to the earlier *Hot Shots!* movie, both being parodies of 1980s action films. In *Hot Shots! Part Deux*, Lloyd Bridges from *Airplane!* is the dimwitted president of the United States who takes an action-president role in the movie by fighting the bad guy in the climax of the movie. Bridges's *Airplane!* costar Leslie Nielsen appears as the president in *Scary Movie 3* and *Scary Movie 4*, with the role being much like his Frank Drebin character from the *Police Squad!* series of films. Bridges and Nielsen obviously played off past screwball characters in other movies as payoff to gags.

There's been only one film where the presidency is mocked as the basis of the entire movie (rather than as a one-off gag): Buck Henry's 1980 movie *First Family*. Bob Newhart stars as President Manfred Link, another president out for reelection who is struggling in the polls (a newscast early in the film notes that Link was elected after his opponent died in a freak accident, and still 30 million voted for the dead candidate). The First Lady (Madeline Kahn) does a bad job hiding her constant alcohol consumption, while their twenty-eight-year-old daughter is so sex crazed after being forced to stay a virgin for the family's image that she is constantly trying to break out of the White House to attack men. Needing the UN vote of a newly recognized African nation called Upper Gorm, Link inadvertently agrees to visit the nation and meet with its leader. The nation's leader is happy to help the president out with the vote but only if the president agrees to send thousands of White Americans to the country to be an oppressed minority. Link balks at that idea but then is shown that the naturally radioactive fertilizer found in the country causes fruits and vegetables to grow to abnormally large sizes. Wanting to surprise the nation, the president is about to announce his trade deal when his cabinet discovers that Link has agreed to send people to Upper Gorm in exchange for fertilizer. Fearing for their jobs, the cabinet stages a car crash that makes it appear the president is dead. Using the Twenty-Fifth Amendment, the idiot vice president (Bob Dishy) is put into office, but Dishy dies of a heart attack while being sworn in. Meanwhile, the vegetation the president plants around Washington using the fertilizer appears, shocking the nation. The cabinet goes to the president and asks him to return to office. Although reported as dead, they announce to the public that Link has returned like a "second coming" to save the nation. Link and his family smile and wave to the cheering crowds on their way back to the White House, which now has giant watermelons growing on the Great Lawn.

Newhart, known for playing mild-mannered nice guys on television, got a rare chance to play a bit of a jerk as President Link. In fact, as with *Canadian Bacon*, the cast is excellent, with Fred Willard, Richard Benjamin, Harvey Korman, and even Rip Torn again as part of the military. The problem is the script, which is not outlandish or energetic enough to really pay off as the parody it wants to be and comes off as trying too hard (a costume party is done for no reason other than to have a serious cabinet meeting with the president and others in funny outfits in the Oval Office). This is the surprising shame with the movie, considering Buck Henry's work as a writer, including on *The Graduate* (1967), *What's Up Doc?* (1972), and *Heaven Can Wait* (1980); yet even with all this talent within one movie, the results do not pay off.

The film at least shows us a vice president in action, even if he is an idiot. Beyond *Dave*, which has a vital vice president part, many movies here have the interesting tendency to simply discard the vice president with no mention whatsoever. *Wrong Is Right* and *Kisses for My President* also feature vice presidents, but they get little more than an acknowledgment in one scene and then pretty much fade to the background. The vice president gets a little more to do in the final movie under review here, however: *My Fellow Americans* (1996).

The movie was directed by Peter Segal; written by E. Jack Kaplan, Richard Chapman, and Peter Tolan; and starring Jack Lemmon as former Republican president Russell Kramer (in an obvious wink at George Bush) and James Garner as former Democratic president Matt Douglas (acting like a Bill Clinton clone). They had been opponents in two elections, with Kramer winning the first time and Douglas beating him four years later. Douglas then lost the most recent election three years ago to William Haney (Dan Aykroyd), Kramer's former vice president. Haney was no dummy as vice president, but he was on the take with a contractor named Charlie Reynolds (James Rebhorn) while in office, and the deal, nicknamed Olympia, is threatening to become public. Haney, looking to distance himself, has his chief of staff change records so it appears that Kramer had done the deal, leaving Haney to appear innocent as a new election is just around the corner.

Jack Lemmon and James Garner play former presidents at each other's throats and on the run in *My Fellow Americans* (1996). *Official press still, author's collection,* © *1996 by Warner Brothers.*

Kramer begins to hear rumors of the plot against him, as does Douglas, who is asked by his party to see what he can find out so they can use it in the next election; the party also dangles a carrot in front of Douglas that they may even give him another chance at the nomination if his investigation turns up anything. Both Kramer and Douglas narrow the rumor to Reynolds, but when they individually go to meet him, they find him dead in his car. They are then put on Marine One to head to Camp David. Realizing they are headed in the wrong direction, the pair manages to be dropped off in the middle of nowhere, only to then see Marine One explode, suggesting that it was probably intended for them to be on the transport when it did so.

Fearing for their lives, they end up on a road trip to try to track down evidence that shows Haney is trying to incriminate Kramer. After many adventures, meeting up with common Americans along the way, many of whom recognize them, they manage to make their way back to the White House to confront Haney at a press conference set up to announce the deaths of Kramer and Douglas in the Marine One mishap.

Threatening to expose Haney over his deal, especially after he swears to the pair that he didn't know what happened to Marine One, Haney announces his resignation due to "health reasons." With his departure, the presidency is to move on to the moronic vice president Ted Matthews (John Heard), but Kramer and Douglas realize that the only one to benefit from this plan is not Haney but Matthews. Confronting him, the pair discover that Matthews had been playing the fool in order to set up his chances to take over the presidency, in a script twist that draws on movies in chapter 2 about evil vice presidents trying to get the president out of the way for their own rise in power. In this case, the vice president accomplishes his goal but only for a time, as it is revealed that Douglas was able to get a recording of Matthews confessing to the plot. Soon after, the vice president is arrested and goes to prison, while Douglas and Kramer decide to run together in a bipartisan team for the presidency. The pair are ready to make the announcement but are still unsure who should be president, when Douglas pulls one final trick on Kramer to divert his attention long enough for Douglas quickly to announce he is running for president.

The movie's charm is solely in seeing Lemmon and Garner together in a movie, bouncing off each other, and the final plot twist of the vice president works well, as do some of the gags in the script. Yet once again, the script doesn't quite match up to the potential with such a cast; it feels as if it were three rewrites merged into one, with plotlines that go nowhere (such as Sela Ward's reporter character, who is given a bit to do but no payoff for her character's actions) and characters who really have little more to do than pop up and then disappear, such as those for Wilford Brimley, Lauren Bacall, and Esther Rolle. Nor does the film find any definite tone to take when it comes to a political statement. Yes, there is the notion of both the Republican and Democrat bonding and perhaps becoming a strong presidential unit to vote for by the end of the film, but that merely becomes a throwaway ending gag to the film and is not built on during the movie. The only moment that does try to speak to politics is when both Douglas and Kramer are verbally tearing into a family who are woefully ignorant of American history and politics, displaying a chance for the film to give the former presidents an opportunity to state their own frustrations about public perception of their work, but this is thrown away for a simple sight gag of them being kicked out of the family car and then ignored for the rest of the film. Both Lemmon and Garner went on to do other films for a few more years, but this film was considered a miss, not quite making its money back on the box office and with mixed reviews from the critics, who rallied around the cast but not the film overall.

Admittedly, placing a comedy in the White House is not easy. The position of the presidency is difficult and many expect it to be taken seriously and carefully, which is hardly the basis for getting laughs. In the decades since the first presidential comedy in 1932, there have been only a few dozen presidential movies trying to find humor, and some of those, like *The American President*, are more of a drama with moments of humor than specifically a comedy. In light of how many action films, thrillers, and even horror and science fiction movies have been made with presidents, those with presidents simply doing their job are few indeed. It's as if the presidents without drama get little notice.

Which brings us to the topic of the next chapter, as we return to the presidents who came after the nearly impossible-to-top Abraham Lincoln.

# 6

# JOHNSON TO HOOVER

## Our Cameo Presidents

We are citizens of the world. The tragedy of our times is that we do not know this.

—Woodrow Wilson

Chapter 3 shows the dwindling return of movies about presidents working to deal with the recovery of the Revolutionary War and subsequent ripples of battles to settle the country into a new nation. With the scattered focus and tendency to push larger issues down the road, necessitating the Lincoln administration to deal with them, the presidency seemed smaller in a way, no matter how much work may have been going on in Washington.

If Franklin Pierce had presided over the Civil War, maybe he'd be remembered more, for better or worse, than he is today. Lincoln was there, dealt with it, lost his life to it, and is bound to our history in much the same way as Washington and Jefferson were to our beginnings. Seventy years after him, Franklin Delano Roosevelt was remembered not for the many policies created in his administration that are still felt today but because he was there to handle our involvement in World War II. It begs the question if big events in our history promote our glowing legacy of our presidents more than their leadership. We certainly concentrate a vast amount of our historical relevance to those events, much like the Revolutionary War.

In that gap between Lincoln and FDR are fourteen presidents. They saw the expansion of the country West and North, the slow restructuring of government after the Civil War, the attempts to both thwart and elevate civil rights, two assassinations, the Spanish-American War, and what was thought at the time to be the war to end all wars. Hollywood has produced more than seventy movies featuring these presidents. Only two films focus on any of the fourteen. The remaining presidents (and even the two who got major films made about them) appear in movies either as cameos to bring importance to the events of the film or as characters seen in previous chapters: messengers to activate plots or praeses ex machina to finish them.

Andrew Johnson (1808–1875) was vice president at the time Lincoln was assassinated. He missed out on being killed when he ignored a message from John Wilkes Booth asking if he would be at the hotel where he resided, and his would-be assassin, George Atzerodt, ducked out of the job. Johnson was picked for vice president due to his link to the Southern states and as a Democrat to help balance Lincoln's Republican and Northern heritage (making the final plot twist of *My Fellow Americans* in the previous chapter not a complete fantasy). No one really wanted him to be president. Even Booth and his fellow assassins wanted him dead, as Johnson represented a traitor to them for his role in staying with the Union, even as all other Southern congressmen left when their states seceded from the Union in 1861.

Andrew Johnson was born in Raleigh, North Carolina, and was apprenticed to a tailor. Apprenticeship had a different meaning at the time than it does today, where it simply means learning to do a job from an expert in the field. In the nineteenth century, it was typical for youngsters to be hired to work until their twenty-first birthdays for someone as part of a contract of indenture; breaking that contract could lead to imprisonment. Johnson learned to be a tailor in the years he worked as an apprentice alongside his brother William, but the pair ran away when Andrew was fifteen. He eventually settled in Tennessee, where he became a successful tailor in Greenville, which led to becoming a landowner and marrying a local girl, Eliza McCardle. Johnson's education had been limited to lessons he received from others while an apprentice and then later through his wife, who had received a formal education growing up, but he was known as having an appetite for reading, which benefited him in later years.

Having come from a poor background and forced to work as a child in the service of others, Andrew Johnson was drawn to politics in support of working people. He eventually was elected to the House of Representatives four times before being gerrymandered out by an opposing political party, whereupon he was elected governor of Tennessee and then became a senator for the state in 1857. It was there that he found himself stuck between two sides, as Jefferson Davis and others agreed to remove themselves from Congress when the secession began in 1861. But he remained, thus becoming the only Southern senator in Congress during the Civil War.

Johnson, who had enslaved people working on his land in Tennessee, had no love for the abolitionists and had once taken to the Senate floor to argue that slavery was human nature, but he liked the idea of leaving the Union even less than secession. He found the concept of seceding the worst thing the South could do at a time when Southern representation in the Democratic Party could outstrip support for the Republicans in Congress but only if they stayed (a realization that Lincoln used to good effect when passing the Thirteenth Amendment a few years later). He was considered a traitor by those in the South for remaining in Washington but seen as a patriot by many in Tennessee as well as by President Lincoln, who named Johnson a military governor of Tennessee in 1862, when most of the state had been returned to the Union in battle. Johnson convinced Lincoln to exempt Tennessee from the Emancipation Proclamation (Lincoln also did so with other border states in the Union: Missouri, Kentucky, Delaware, and Maryland) so that slavery could continue, but he soon concluded that if slavery was to divide the nation, then it needed to go. Johnson freed the people personally enslaved by him in 1863 and called for the end of slavery in the state, which was written into the state constitution in early 1865.

Johnson was named as the vice-presidential pick for the ticket in Lincoln's reelection due to his work in Tennessee, which helped Lincoln draw Democratic support away from the former commander of the Union Army, George McClellan, who was running against Lincoln in the 1864 election. After Lincoln's death, the assumption was that Johnson would be easily talked into siding with certain Republicans who wanted to come down hard on the Southern states after the war (there were even rumors, especially after the botched assassination attempt on him, that Johnson was part of the conspiracy to rid the North of Lincoln). Johnson, however, felt further penalties against the Southern states did nothing to address issues of the nation. He announced a return of civil governments to the area and amnesty to most Confederate soldiers, among other things. His approach helped the South quickly rebound but was seen by many in Congress as too laid back and allowed many Southern states to find other means to suppress the formerly enslaved population, such as the creation of the Black Code, which restricted the rights and liberties of such individuals. Johnson, seeing these actions as a state issue and one that had preoccupied the nation for too long, attempted to turn a blind eye, which only infuriated Northerners, who felt that there was little point in the Civil War if those enslaved merely ended up enslaved under a different name. Johnson's image was further hurt by his stance against expanding the Freedmen's Bureau, set up in 1865 to help freed people, for the reason that Congress was not doing anything to help "our own people," along with vetoing the Civil Rights Act of 1866 giving Black people American citizenship (a veto overridden by Congress).

Republicans in Congress, known as the radical Republicans and led by Congressman Thaddeus Stevens (horrendously dramatized as the villain in Griffith's *The Birth of a Nation* and given a hero's treatment by Tommy Lee Jones in Spielberg's *Lincoln*), wanted quick and drastic changes made in the South to ensure the liberties of Black individuals and punish the secessionists. They soon gained power in Congress and began to pass bills that Johnson could not override with a veto in order to have what they viewed as proper reform in the South. When Johnson fired Secretary of War Edwin Stanton, whom he felt was working against him, Johnson knowingly violated the recently passed Tenure of Office Act of 1867, which forbade the president from dismissing a member of his cabinet without congressional okay (it would later be rejected as unconstitutional by the Supreme Court in 1926; President Dillman in *The Man*—see chapter 2—faced a similar bill to restrict his ability to fire cabinet members in that film, which was based on Johnson's presidency). The sacking led to the first full impeachment trial of a president. Johnson, under the advice of his representation, refused to appear at the trial and instead agreed to certain Reconstruction efforts from the states in order to gain acquittal. Several senators were also reluctant to vote for impeachment, as it would mean Senator Benjamin Wade of Ohio, a radical Republican who was too radical even for the Republicans, would become president. The final vote was one less than the two-thirds majority needed.

Johnson served out his term, with a legacy of the Homestead Act of 1862 passed while he was senator, which helped poor individuals to claim ownership of land out West. He was also known for purchasing Alaska from Russia in 1867 and getting the eight-hour workday law passed. Yet Johnson is best remembered for two things in particular: his attempt to gently reinstate the Southern states into the Union after the Civil War and his dismissal of ensuring the rights and liberties of Black people in those same states. Surprisingly for a man who could foresee that splitting the country by secession would do no good, he orchestrated tension in Congress that is seen as causing many issues with state and civil rights more than a hundred years after his death.

The perception of Andrew Johnson has blown both ways over the years, depending on how one views his accomplishments. Straight out of the presidency, Johnson was seen as an obstructionist, hurting the country due to personal issues with Congress. Later, the pendulum swung, as in *The Birth of a Nation*, where those who opposed Johnson were seen as wanting to destroy the country by "conquering" the South and placing individuals there by force who would hurt the White people living there. More time away from such racial stirrings have placed Johnson near the bottom of the list of presidents of the country. Presidents before him, like Buchanan and Pierce, at least had the luxury of trying to avoid pushing for civil rights and federal rights due to the fear of "what ifs." Johnson had the cards to transform the country after the war and instead tried to fall back on where we were before, stagnating the country's progress for many years to follow.

In 1942, MGM released a full-length movie about Johnson, with Van Heflin in the title role, *Tennessee Johnson*. The movie begins with Johnson arriving in Greenville as a runaway teenager with an iron around his ankle. Heflin looks youngish but nothing like the teenager he is playing, nor was Johnson swinging around a leg iron by the time he got to Greenville, years after leaving his apprenticeship. There he meets Eliza

McCardle and settles in as a tailor in town. A meeting of people to discuss land rights ends with the death of a close friend and Johnson's resolve not to resort to violence in the future.

Johnson steps into politics to help others, and the movie briskly skips to his becoming a senator, where he is giving a speech about secession right before Jefferson Davis arrives to announce he and others will be leaving with the election of Lincoln. (In reality, Johnson made his speech after Davis in hopes of persuading others to stay.) Staying in Washington for a time, Johnson returns to Tennessee to fight the Confederacy and save Nashville from being taken. The film then cuts to his being asked to run for vice president (Lincoln is seen only in a long shot at one point and in a photo) and his inauguration, which shows him being incapacitated. The film suggests that Lincoln then wrote to Johnson to play down the embarrassment of the drunken moment, which Johnson refers to again on the Senate floor later in the movie. The letter is fiction and never occurred.

With Johnson becoming president, Thaddeus Stevens (Lionel Barrymore) suggests a deal for Johnson's involvement in the Reconstruction of the South. Johnson refuses to go along with the plan, and after Stanton is kick out of the cabinet, Stevens works to begin the impeachment trial. At the end of the trial, one of the senators is rushed from the room in illness, while Johnson appears, soon followed by Eliza in the gallery, to make his stance to Congress. It's a rousing speech, and it didn't happen, as Johnson never appeared, per the advice of his counsel. The vote is taken with one vote less than needed for impeachment, when the ill senator staggers into the room and collapses at his desk, raising his head only long enough to vote against impeachment. Again, this is another moment that didn't happen, as in reality it all came down to Senator Edmund Ross, who refused to state before the count how he would vote and then was the last to do so, voting against impeachment. Stevens is carried away in defeat. The movie then skips ahead to show an older Johnson eventually being elected senator again, and he appears back in the Senate as the film ends.

The film was directed by William Dieterle and written by John Balderston and Wells Root based on a story from Milton Gunzburg and Alvin Meyers. Filming completed in the summer of 1942 but then had to go to extensive reshoots requested by the Office of War Information (see the next chapter for more details on how this department came about) after NAACP protests over rumors of the villainous depiction of Thaddeus Stevens in the film (this explains an early scene where Stevens gets cozy with Johnson's grandchildren in order to make him more likable). Additional petitions and national protests from various groups about the film's portrayal of Johnson as the hero and Stevens as the villain further caused headaches for MGM. Producer James McGuinness stated that the film was reshot not due to demands but because scenes "were overacted by Lionel Barrymore," which is hardly the way to keep the talent happy with decisions. When actor Zero Mostel signed a petition along with other actors against the movie, he was informed that MGM was cutting several of his scenes in the musical *Du Barry Was a Lady*.

Heflin playing a heavily romanticized version of Johnson is fine. Barrymore is even more cantankerous than normal, just a smidge less than his soon-to-be-famous Potter of *It's a Wonderful Life*, being carried around by others in a seat that is based on history but used to make him appear as a conquering emperor. The film gets certain details correct, but there is so much candy-coating to Johnson's story to gloss over his stance on slavery that what little he did to help doesn't get a mention worth noting. After all the brouhaha about the movie, it amounted to little, as the film received only so-so reviews and did not make back its money at the box office.

Even in a fairy-tale reckoning of his story, Johnson at least was awarded an entire film dedicated to him. Ulysses S. Grant (1822–1885), Rutherford B. Hayes (1822–1893), James Garfield (1831–1881), Chester A. Arthur (1830–1886), Grover Cleveland (1837–1908), Benjamin Harrison (1833–1901), William McKinley (1843–1901), Theodore Roosevelt (1858–1919), William Howard Taft (1857–1930), Woodrow Wilson (1856–1924), Warren Harding (1865–1923), Calvin Coolidge (1872–1933), and Herbert Hoover (1874–1964) have their places in Hollywood—and almost all of them are in cameo form.

This can be hard to conceptualize when it comes to someone like Ulysses S. Grant. After all, he was the commander of the Union Army in the Civil War, and we have the stubborn image of him in his military uniform, with usually a bottle of alcohol in front of him, full beard, and slouching slightly. And that caricature of him is what we get in the movies, with Grant commonly discussing war efforts with Lincoln or other soldiers, if he's seen before the presidency. Once president, he is commonly seen sending people out on missions—*Secret Service* (1930); *Drum Beat* (1954); *From the Earth to the Moon* (1958); *Wild, Wild West* (1999); *Jonah Hex* (2010)—or as the praeses ex machina, like in *Sitting Bull* (1954). Grant (Jason Robards) at least gets to do a bit of action-president work in *The Legend of the Lone Ranger* (1981) when he is kidnapped. That's better than in *Silver Dollar* (1932), where Walter Rodgers as Grant only gets to nod in agreement with Edward G. Robinson's character several times at the opera.

It helps that many of the movies for these presidents are westerns, leaving the action out West and the president back East and therefore limiting the president's use beyond popping up to move the plot along. Sometimes that can lead to awkward ways of inserting them into the action, as well. James Garfield, the second president to be assassinated, was killed in 1881 at a railroad station in the Washington area by a man who felt slighted by the president. Garfield's assassination made its way into the Italian western *The Price of Power* (1969), with Van Johnson as Garfield (and looking nothing like Garfield and everything like Van Johnson). In the case of that movie, President Garfield goes to Dallas, represented as a stereotypical western town with a saloon, a hotel, and a handful of settlers, where he is assassinated while riding with his wife in a carriage in a parade. The would-be assassin is captured from a nearby second-story window, while the real culprit nearly gets away if not from the help of the hero, played by Giuliano Gemma. Van Johnson gets a bit of a stretch in the film to look worried before being killed off, but the film really is just a setup for an analogy of the JFK assassination in Dallas in 1963, even if it means moving Garfield's death from Washington to Dallas and changing a lone crazed gunman into a conspiracy. Obviously, the thought was that most people wouldn't remember how Garfield died anyway.

Chester Arthur at least gets to brush off Edward G. Robinson in *Silver Dollar* (probably because of the way he treated Grant before him in the movie; no, seriously, it's to show a president willing to take part in a ceremony but not wanting to be friends with the protagonist). Grover Cleveland, the only president to have two nonconsecutive terms in office, helps set up the plot to *The Oklahoma Kid* (1939) by being shown signing the sale of the Cherokee Outlet, leading to the land run in 1897. Cleveland gets a slightly larger part in *Buffalo Bill and the Indians; or*

*Sitting Bull's History Lesson* (1976), with Pat McCormick looking more like Chester Arthur than Cleveland, but even here it's to show the president's disinterest in events happening around him (Cleveland's wife, played by Shelley Duvall, has more to do in the Robert Altman movie than McCormick does). Benjamin Harrison (Roy Gordon), meanwhile, at least has a fun little bit in the John Philip Sousa biography *Stars and Stripes Forever* (1952), where he requests Sousa play something up-tempo at a presidential ball to speed up the reception line.

William McKinley was the first president to be filmed staging a moment to be seen by an audience in 1896, after he won the Republican nomination for president. It was filmed weeks after McKinley was informed of his winning the nomination, recreated for American Mutoscope and Biograph Company's camera to show McKinley receiving the news from his secretary, George Cortelyou. Footage of his inauguration in 1897 and 1901 exists as well as film of McKinley giving a speech on September 5, 1901, just a day before he was assassinated. Ironically, the longest footage for McKinley would be that of his funeral. In some ways, McKinley may have been aware of how the power of movies could affect his presidency, but he doesn't get much love in Hollywood, where he appears to set up the plot in *A Message to Garcia* (1936) and *This Is My Affair* (1937) as well as briefly in *Teddy the Rough Rider* (1940), a two-reeler from Warner Brothers that gives us a very condensed version of Theodore Roosevelt's career. *Teddy the Rough Rider* stars Sidney Blackmer (who appeared as Roosevelt in the previously discussed *The Monroe Doctrine* and *This Is My Affair*) and shows him squinting his eyes and sharply jabbering as Roosevelt through the main events of Roosevelt's career. The Oscar-winning short swiftly moves through Roosevelt working as president of the board of police commissioners in 1895, as a colonel of the "Rough Riders" during the Spanish-American War, coining the phrase "speak softly and carry a bit stick," becoming president, and retiring, with Blackmer scowling all the way. Well, you only have twenty minutes to tell a life story, after all.

Which is a shame, as Theodore Roosevelt has this amazing life story. A political outsider within his own party, Roosevelt came from wealth but supported reform to stop corruption and policy to help the poor by working against financial giants of what was rapidly becoming an oligopoly. Roosevelt seemed not so much destined for greatness but blasted to it,

*This Is My Affair* (1937) has Sidney Blackmer in one of his many appearances as President Theodore Roosevelt, while also featuring Frank Conroy as the rarely seen President William McKinley. *Courtesy of PhotoFest.*

ready to make a mark to prove himself. Before he was forty, he was the assistant secretary of the navy. The short-lived Spanish-American War of 1898 led to Roosevelt forming a group of men as the Volunteer First Cavalry to go help fight and leading a charge up San Juan Hill while in battle. The United States won the war to help Cuba gain independence from Spain, and Roosevelt came back a hero, forging the way to his selection as vice president for McKinley's 1901 run for office. When McKinley was assassinated in 1901, Roosevelt became president and was reelected in 1904. Roosevelt regulated the railroads, pushed the Interstate Commerce Commission, regulated the food industry, and helped negotiate the Russo-Japanese War, becoming the first American to win the Nobel Peace Prize. He was known for his massive and heavily publicized hunting trips, leading to Roosevelt being one of the first presidents parodied in the movies. The Edison Manufacturing Company release of *Terrible Teddy, the Grizzly King* in 1901 shows Roosevelt being closely followed by his press agent and photographer as he "heroically" kills what appears to be a house cat stuck in a tree. His later expedition trips led to another parody in 1909 called *Teddy in Jungleland*, with Roosevelt dealing with several men dressed up as apes. Even with hunting, however, he became known for establishing national parks and preserving other resources throughout the country. Roosevelt tried to run one more time in 1912 and beat William Taft (who was running for reelection) but lost to Woodrow Wilson. He went on a dangerous expedition in South America in 1913 with his son Kermit, and when America finally declared war against Germany in 1917 during World War I, Roosevelt tried to put together a division to lead into battle (Wilson denied sending the nearly sixty-year-old out to the fields of war).

It's a life full of adventures, with just the 1913 expedition alone making for a worthy and dramatic film. Roosevelt was also keenly aware of how the movies could help promote his work, and he certainly loved the publicity, being filmed from 1898 up to the time of his death in 1919. For all that, Hollywood's treatment of Teddy Roosevelt amounts to a twenty-minute short and several cameos to represent Roosevelt's life in the movies. (One could argue for the very popular portrayal by Robin Williams in the *Night at the Museum* franchise [2006–2014], but his part is that of a wax figure of Teddy Roosevelt and not really of the president himself.) Rarely do such appearances give us any insight into Roosevelt; instead, most of the appearances establish the time period of the film or the importance of other characters by being in proximity to the president than giving us a proper character within the context of the movie, such as *Take Me Out to the Ballgame* from 1949 (with Ed Cassidy), *Citizen Kane* (Thomas A. Curran) in 1941, and *The Curious Case of Benjamin Button* (Ed Metzger) in 2008. Roosevelt also acts as the praeses ex machina in *This Is My Affair* (Sidney Blackmer) and *My Girl Tisa* (1948, with Sidney Blackmer) and as a messenger in movies like *Newsies* (1992, with David James Alexander); *The Wind and the Lion* (1975, with Brian Keith); and *In Old Oklahoma* (1943, once again with Sidney Blackmer).

Roosevelt is allowed more space in *Fancy Pants* (1950), a Bob Hope comedy based on *Ruggles of Red Gap*. Bob Hope plays an actor hired to play a butler as part of a prank, only to end up being sent to America to work as a butler for a western family who struck it rich and is trying to shed their backwoods persona for the upper class. His arrival gets off on the wrong foot when people in the town think he's an earl, but the family sees how it elevates their image in town and tells him to act the role (thus being an actor playing a butler playing an earl). Things get out of hand when President Teddy Roosevelt comes to visit and takes the "earl" on a foxhunt, with the actor having no clue how to ride a horse and a suitor for the family's daughter (Lucille Ball) who is determined to expose the actor as a fake. The movie features John Alexander, who played Teddy Brewster, a man who thinks he is Theodore Roosevelt, in the 1944 comedy *Arsenic and Old Lace*. He really doesn't have much to do beyond being president-like, but it helps set up the third act, with the various contrivances created to keep the president from finding out about the deception. A similar although more tragic third-act use of Roosevelt is in *Ragtime* (1981), where he is played by Robert Boyd. One of the main characters, Sarah (Debbie Allen) tries to get Roosevelt's attention and is beaten down by security for trying to get too close. She ends up dying, which leads Coalhouse Walker Jr. (Howard E. Rollins Jr.) to initiate the violence of the final portion of the film. Roosevelt has no real contribution to the story as a character, but because of his presence as a type of McGuffin, the plot continues onward.

If Teddy Roosevelt couldn't get far in the movies, then Taft, Coolidge, Harding, and Hoover certainly were not going to get much further. Coolidge briefly turns up in *The Court-Martial of Billy Mitchell* (1955, played by Ian Wolfe) and in *For Greater Glory: The True Story of Cristiada* (2012, played by Bruce McGill), and Taft is seen in *The Greatest Game Ever Played* (2005), performed by Walter Massey. Harding and Hoover don't get even that much of a notice in theatrical movies beyond mentions or some stock footage. Woodrow Wilson, though, got a full-length film in 1944.

In some ways, Wilson was the flip side of Andrew Johnson, at least when it came to education. Johnson was self-educated, learning to read and write with the help of his wife and others as he grew up, rather than receiving a formal education. Wilson, however, had written several books, earned multiple college degrees, and was the president of Princeton University before being asked to run for governor of New Jersey in 1910. As typical for the time, party bosses decided who would run for office, and they picked Wilson, figuring him to be (like Johnson and

**Alexander Knox as President Woodrow Wilson in the biopic *Wilson* (1944).**
*Courtesy of PhotoFest.*

others before him) a weakling who would be easily pushed to do what the party wanted. Instead, Governor Wilson called for various reforms affecting political rule by the bosses. In 1912, Wilson ran for president and found himself the winner when Teddy Roosevelt split the Republican vote with Taft.

Wilson helped create the Federal Trade Commission (FTC), the Federal Reserve System, and what we know today as the yearly income tax system. He spent time in office trying to keep the United States out of World War I, but ultimately, he agreed to have the country join the fight after Germany announced they would continue to sink American ships. His wife died in 1914, but in 1915, Wilson remarried while still in office. He spent much time late in his second term trying to establish the League of Nations, which later was replaced by the United Nations. He also saw the Nineteenth Amendment giving women the right to vote passed, as well as the Eighteenth Amendment, creating Prohibition. Wilson's history of liberal reform unfortunately was tarnished by his views on segregation, his discrimination against African Americans for federal jobs (a practice that started under Roosevelt and Taft), his racist jokes in office, and his screening of *The Birth of a Nation* as the first dramatic full-length film ever shown in the White House. In working to get the public on his side for the League of Nations, Wilson ended up having a major stroke. He finished his second term but had no further political career and died three years later.

Darryl Zanuck, producer of films like *Young Mr. Lincoln, The Grapes of Wrath, 42nd Street,* and *How Green Was My Valley,* was a fan of Wilson and got Henry King (*The Song of Bernadette, Twelve O'Clock High*) as director and Lamar Trotti (*Young Mr. Lincoln, The Ox-Bow Incident*) as scriptwriter for what was to be a lavish production about the president. Alexander Knox, who later found trouble with the McCarthy era of looking for communists, played Wilson, with Ruth Nelson as Ellen Wilson (his first wife) and Geraldine Fitzgerald as Edith Wilson (his second wife). Ignoring anything about his segregationist past, the movie focuses on Wilson's career from near the end of his tenure as Princeton president until his leaving the White House after his second term. The film covers everything in crisp segments—governor, president, war, League of Nations—with Knox always prepared, rigid, and ready to say the right thing. The issue is that there is no energy to the storytelling. Things happen, Wilson comments, time moves on. Even when Wilson gets angry, his voice rarely rises. There's nothing quite wrong with the story being told as it is, but with no insight into why Wilson is like he is, there's no connection for the audience.

Audiences made it clear that it wasn't enough to see expensive sets and a large cast. *Wilson,* like *Tennessee Johnson* before it, was an expensive, lavish production that failed to produce much momentum among critics and failed at the box office. Rumors were that Darryl Zanuck felt so wounded after it failed that he enforced a rule that no one speak of the film when around him. Also like *Tennessee Johnson,* the film tried to entice audiences by tying into wartime patriotism, which was completely understandable, as everyone was doing their best to stay positive during the ongoing war in the years these two films were released. It was World War II, and the president in office, Franklin Delano Roosevelt, was present for the most radical changes to come when depicting the president on the silver screen. It would never be the same after him nor as abundant and yet restricted at the same time.

# 7

## AMERICAN BADASS

### Franklin Delano Roosevelt

*If Mr. Roosevelt were alive today, he would turn over in his grave.*

—Sam Goldwyn, on how FDR would feel
about being portrayed by actors in movies

**T**here is a certain sense of irony in seeing Franklin Delano Roosevelt's public image being put through the wringer of Hollywood over the past few decades. It didn't start that way; most of the early results were flowery, overprotective work that seemed to find virtually no flaws with the man, beyond a sly wink here and there. Even so, FDR and his family were never quite content with such portrayals and took deliberate aim to rectify any grievances they had. Such safeguards have disappeared in more recent works, with scandalous depictions of the man that would have embarrassed Roosevelt. For someone who knew how to put pressure on the media to control the public's perception of him even years after his death, the tables have substantially turned.

Born January 30, 1882, to devoted parents James and Sara Delano Roosevelt, Franklin was part of what some considered to be New York royalty, thanks to his father's fortune and business accomplishments. It didn't hurt, either, that the name Roosevelt had a certain prestige (or notoriety, depending on who was speaking), thanks to Franklin's fifth cousin, Theodore Roosevelt, and his rise in power to the presidency (see chapter 6 for more details on Teddy). The families of the two Roosevelt clans were well acquainted, often meeting in formal social gatherings as well as family events. They were, however, far apart in distance (Franklin's family lived in Hyde Park, seventy miles to the north of Teddy's family in Oyster Bay, New York) and in politics (the Hyde Park Roosevelts were long-time Democrats who financially supported various campaigns, while the Oyster Bay Roosevelts were Republicans).

The occasional meetings between the two clans were how Franklin met Teddy's niece Anna Eleanor Roosevelt in 1902. The two had vastly different personalities that somehow clicked when together. Franklin was eager to be involved and always with a smile, albeit with an air of being above it all, especially in moments of stress. Such a cheery disposition was developed when Franklin was a child, after his father suffered a heart attack, and he and his mother were advised by his father's doctor to avoid emotional strain around James. This façade of cheerfulness became a trademark of FDR's personality that was beneficial to his work as president during the Great Depression and World War II, although some took it as dismissive. Add in his tendency to hold back his head with his chin out, his natural almost-mid-Atlantic accent that spoke of his station in life, the weathered fedora, and a cigarette holder clenched between his teeth, and we have the image of FDR most famously conveyed by impressionists and actors through the years.

His father's heart attack also led to Franklin bonding with his mother, and he would continue to look to her for council, even after reaching the White House and until her death in 1941. This, combined with FDR frequently allowing Sara to stay with them, contributed to the speculation that FDR was dominated by his strong-willed mother, a subject touched on for good and bad in later films. It is also perhaps a reason that Franklin often formed lasting, confiding relationships with women who held strong opinions, another aspect reflected in various examinations of FDR's life.

Eleanor, however, was reserved and quiet while also possessing a strong intellect developed through reading and an education in France as a teenager that propelled her to be proactive when pushed. This naturally would lead to Franklin's interest, although such independence and her physical looks eventually drew out more vicious caricatures of

Eleanor in the media over the years, overemphasizing her thinness, an obvious overbite, and the stiffness of her voice and posture, along with attempts to position her as manly due to her forthright nature or clueless due to her left-leaning political stance.

Eleanor and Franklin married in 1905 and had six children, one of whom died in infancy. Their marriage was shaken in 1918 when Eleanor discovered romantic letters written between Franklin and Eleanor's former social secretary Lucy Mercer (later Lucy Mercer Rutherfurd). Although some biographers still debate how intimate Franklin was with Lucy, it was a serious enough breach that divorce was discussed. However, Sara and Franklin's political advisor Louis Howe persuaded the pair that divorce was out of the question for personal and political reasons. Instead, the couple remained married until Franklin's death in April 1945, with the marriage becoming more of a personal and professional partnership, especially after Franklin's physical issues in the 1920s.

After an education that included Harvard and obtaining a law degree from Columbia University, Franklin started his career as a law clerk in New York, although his sights were on bigger things—namely following the path his cousin Teddy took to Washington and the White House. He wasn't alone there; several in the Democratic Party saw benefits in Franklin's family ties and name recognition, selecting him to run for the New York state legislature in 1910, which he won in a county dominated by Republicans. Many felt the win was due to his aggressive but jovial "get out the vote" nature, as he happily ventured out to meet voters when transportation was not the easiest.

Franklin liberally slathered his positive attitude on everyone, which sometimes infuriated his political enemies and friends alike. He dismissed wins and losses in the legislature as larks, going so far as to tell the *New York Times* after one such loss, "There is nothing I love as much as a good fight. I never had as much fun in my life as I am having right now." His tendency in his early political career to back away from hard fights in favor of ones that generated good press (at one point, he avoided attempts to reduce the workweek to fifty hours because he knew it would not be politically beneficial to him) made it easy for many to view Roosevelt at the time as a playboy politician rather than a concerned protector of the people.

In 1913, Franklin was appointed assistant secretary of the navy under President Wilson, the same position Teddy Roosevelt had before moving to the White House, and he remained in the post until 1920. Franklin's political aspirations were sidelined in August 1921, however, when one morning at the family summer home on Campobello Island in New Brunswick, Canada, Franklin had trouble standing. He quickly developed paralysis from the chest down and was eventually diagnosed with poliomyelitis, a disease that attacks the central nervous system and leads to various forms of paralysis. (It is believed today that FDR may have had Guillain-Barré syndrome, an immune disorder that attacks the nervous system in a similar manner, but even if this had been true, there would have been few alternatives for doctors to treat him.) Roosevelt eventually regained movement above the waist, and while he spent most of his remaining days in a wheelchair, steel braces, maneuvering his hips, a cane or crutch for one hand, and a strong assistant on the other arm allowed him to stand up and briefly move upright. On July 26, 1924, Franklin returned to the public eye by giving a nomination speech for New York governor Al Smith at the Democratic convention, where he referred to Smith as the "happy warrior of the political battlefield." And while that designation was meant for Smith, many listening by radio or watching in the hall felt the term *happy warrior* defined Roosevelt and his perseverance.

Even with this advancement, it took several more years before Roosevelt decided to fully submerge himself in politics. Remembering trips to Germany as a child to visit spas where his father swam to help his health after his heart attack, Franklin made periodic trips to swim in the warm waters of the Florida Keys between 1924 and 1926. Beginning in October 1924, he started visiting Warm Springs, Georgia, after hearing that the mineral water there would allow him to float upright and exercise his legs. The visits to Warm Springs impressed Franklin so much that he bought the property where the inn he visited was located and started what became the National Foundation for Infantile Paralysis at the location as well as the March of Dimes to help support the foundation. (Roosevelt became so synonymous with the dime that his face was added to the front of the coin in 1946.)

During this time, Franklin, along with his advisor Louis Howe, persuaded the typically shy Eleanor to help his image in the public eye by giving speeches to various group on his behalf. This training led Eleanor to become an advocate for various progressive causes and an outspoken critic who sometimes came off as abrasive to others, even Franklin, although they usually tried to collaborate on ideas to make sure they did not cancel each other out in the public eye. This further enhanced the partnership aspect of Eleanor and Franklin's marriage; they were often separated to deal with political goals, although they were always communicating and meeting. Before her death in 1962, Eleanor had become such a respected speaker and political thinker that it was not uncommon to see her beyond the role of a former First Lady. She eventually became an American delegate for the United Nations in the early 1960s and wrote several books on subjects she supported.

In 1928, Franklin returned to the political arena, first by again campaigning for Al Smith and then by running for governor of New York. Smith lost, but Roosevelt won, and FDR was the governor until 1932, when he was elected president. As president, he helped guide the country out of the Great Depression using several government programs under the umbrella title of the New Deal, which included many programs still with us today: the FDIC for banks, the SEC for securities, the Social Security Act, the National Labor Relations Act, the FCIC, and the Federal Communications Commission. He also reduced the workweek to forty-four hours and created a minimum wage. Such plans were not universally beloved due to concerns over spending and raising taxes, and he raised eyebrows by using loopholes to push through programs with little support from Congress and often earned pushback from the Supreme Court due to his methods (later joked about in FDR-related spoofs).

Creating more programs and nurturing others already in existence would take a backseat to World War II (to the disappointment of some liberals and Eleanor), as FDR maneuvered through early resistance to the war from the public and fellow politicians. Once the attack on Pearl Harbor occurred in December 1941, the public rallied with the president, as war efforts found the United States joining the Allies against the Axis powers. At the time of his death in April 1945 at the Little White House in Warm Springs, Roosevelt was still working on keeping support going for the war while also looking ahead to the future of the country.

In two films, *Sunrise at Campobello* (1960) and *Warm Springs* (2005), a scene occurs where Louis Howe sees Franklin interacting with citizens in a friendly manner and announces that Roosevelt is ready to return to politics. Each film views this discovery by Howe at different points in Roosevelt's life—1924 in *Sunrise* and 1928 in *Warm Springs*— and somewhat negates the fact that such behavior with strangers had always been an element of Franklin's personality, but the result is the same: It is suggested that Roosevelt's bout with polio grounded him, humanized him, and made him a better person who could now become president. Perhaps such an event did occur, but a bigger revelation no doubt came out of Roosevelt having to use a wheelchair. It was clear that public perception, especially at the time, of Franklin's physical limitations and having polio could have been career enders, but if the right positive message was directed to and reinforced by the press, then the public would accept it. Roosevelt knew this, and these two films (as well as the 1976 ABC miniseries) touched on Roosevelt establishing a congenial understanding with the press on how to cover his inability to walk unaided.

Of course, the public knew he had issues with his legs, and Roosevelt did not shy away from discussing the need for assistance at times and even joked about it; nevertheless, it was not common knowledge just how limited those abilities were, and that was thanks to the press. Roosevelt was cunning enough, perhaps lucky enough, in the early days of his physical issues that he avoided anyone using photos of him in a wheelchair, knowing that such a look could be harmful to his political career in that era. This agreement wasn't all one-sided, either. Although Roosevelt at times lashed out at what he saw as mistreatment from the media, the press was willing to help perpetuate this image for several reasons: The Secret Service would confiscate your film; FDR was typically willing to allow for prearranged photos and even quick questions from favored members of the press; and most importantly, the public did not want to see their president in what would have been a weakened light, certainly not during its initial love affair with FDR in the 1930s and especially during the war years of 1941–1945. This perpetuated the image of Roosevelt as a strong man. It also made clear to FDR that it was important to control his public image in a new era of communication, and he quickly took matters into his hands to do just that.

The world was changing quickly in the early 1930s as Roosevelt became president, not only due to world events but also with how popular communication media and technology were evolving around the globe. As discussed earlier, McKinley may have been the first to use the power of film to promote himself, but Warren Harding was the one to recognize radio as important as the earliest president heard on the radio and the one to install a radio in the White House. From his successor, Calvin Coolidge, onward, addressing the public via radio was an active part of delivering their administrations' objectives. Yet it was FDR who truly understood the power of radio, as he began what were referred to as regular "fireside chats" to the American public in March 1933. It was early in his presidency, and there were concerns that citizens were about to rush out to withdraw funds, fearing the banks would fold (commonly referred to as a run on the banks). His steady nerves in his speech helped calm the nation and avoid what could have been a financial disaster for the country.

Roosevelt knew that such talks could be an effective tool to communicate his ideas to the nation, but he also realized that he had to be selective about how his voice was heard on the medium. At issue was that several radio programs had used FDR impersonators on their shows, some for comedic effects, but a few used these actors in news programs, specifically in the popular show, *The March of Time*. The series, remembered more today as a theatrical news serial, was also a periodic fifteen- to thirty-minute program that ran on various national radio networks from 1931 through 1945 and covered world events through narration and public statements by those in the news. One problem for the program was that many events covered were not recorded. Thus, *The March of Time* used a handful of actors in regular rotation to mimic statements by public figures in the news, and FDR was no exception. Various performers, including a young Art Carney of *The Honeymooners* fame, was used until the program settled on William Perry Adams for the role. (Franklin wasn't alone; Eleanor was also impersonated by such actors as Jeanette Nolan and Agnes Moorehead.)

While other individuals in the news ignored the imitators, FDR did not take the effort so lightly. His "chats" were rare so they would stand out to the listeners as if from the voice of a prophet, and yet *The March of Time* used his voice so often that he worried it diluted his impact to that of a barker selling detergent. It was known, as well, that some viewers were writing to the show questioning how they could get the president to appear in person so often. And *The March of Time* was not alone in using such imitators; to not push to stop the practice would suggest that the White House had no issues with it, possibly allowing for questionable content coming out of the "president's mouth" on the radio in the future.

In 1933, the White House sent out a polite request to the radio programs that such impressions be curtailed, but by January 1934, strongly worded reminders were sent to *The March of Time* and other radio shows to "cease impersonation of President Roosevelt." At first, *The March of Time* resisted, but then came the creation of the Federal Communication Commission in June 1934 to regulate radio broadcasts. Although there were never any rules or laws made to stop such shows from doing imitations of the president, the pressure on the radio networks from an official commission made it clear that it was time to back off, and by fall 1934, *The March of Time* stop using FDR impressions.

The ramifications were swift, as radio networks began to walk on eggshells for fear of ruffling the feathers of a popular president. When a Columbus, Ohio, radio station featured a humorous FDR impression during a live talent competition in 1937, the station apologized in the local *Wilmington Daily Press Journal* the next day, as the "White House has a standing request that programs do not include mimicry of the chief executive's voice." There was no intended harm, but to the radio station in question, why look for trouble?

For the most part, radio and the press were in awe or at least wary of Roosevelt from the early days onward, but Hollywood was an elusive partner during the early 1930s, and with good reason. Public goodwill for the presidency and the US government tumbled with the start of the Depression in 1929, and this was reflected in the movies being released. Politicians were viewed as ignorant, weak-willed pencil pushers at their best or fat cats who did the duty of the rich and powerful with no concern for the poor at their worst, and Hollywood produced filmic fantasies that realized such ideals. *Washington Merry-Go-Round* (1932), based on a then ongoing and sometimes scandalous political newspaper column, depicts a squeaky-clean congressman having to fight a fraudulent recount of his election votes by other politicians who are in the back pockets of criminals. *The Phantom President* (1932, discussed in chapter 4) has political bosses pushing an inept candidate they can control to win power in the White House. As discussed in chapter 2, *The President Vanishes* (1934) has a major subplot about munitions dealers teaming with a weak-willed vice president to send the country into war simply to boost weapon sales.

That began to change in 1933, with Hollywood quickly falling into step to help promote the new president and his New Deal goals. *Footlight Parade* (1933), a classic musical featuring Dick Powell, Ruby Keeler, and James Cagney, includes a brief homage to FDR and the National Recovery Act (NRA) in its finale. It displays placards held up to present the US flag, which morphs into a painting of FDR and is then followed by dancers forming the NRA symbol of an eagle. The musical short *The Road Is Open Again* (also from 1933 and again with Dick Powell) has a musician using the ghosts of Lincoln, Washington, and Wilson to help him come up with a song to celebrate the NRA. All three former presidents are enthusiastic in their support for FDR and the NRA (and all long dead, thus not able to possibly decry their depictions in the short film).

*Gabriel over the White House* (1933) gives us a mix of the old and new views of Washington from the time. The movie features Walter Huston as Judd Hammond, a newly elected president who at first laughs at his duties, uses his position to give his friends cushy jobs, and then plays with his nephew while ignoring a radio speech describing the hardship of the unemployed hungry in the streets. Louis B. Mayer, a Republican whose studio produced the film, held back the movie in 1932 for fear that people would assume Hammond was a sly depiction of Republican president Herbert Hoover, and such a portrayal certainly would fall into line with earlier films mentioned here, like *Washington Merry-Go-Round*. However, the film then veers into the more hopeful view of Hammond after he awakens from a coma caused by a car crash. The president's behavior is radically changed, and Hammond takes control of the country by creating programs to put men back to work and cast out political bureaucracy. And while we today can view the film as setting up a dangerous despot who abolishes Congress and later threatens the world with military might to secure peace, in 1933, it was easy for those watching to delight in seeing a president who brings safety, jobs, and peace back to the nation.

Interestingly, although some viewers see the precrash Hammond as a harsh reflection of Hoover, it also mirrors the early political antics of Roosevelt himself, the FDR who dodged tricky political stances to avoid conflict and who looked to Washington as a fun lark not to be respected. Hammond's change may have been magical rather than the long-term evolution Roosevelt saw through a series of crises, but the similarities are certainly easy to pick up. Given that Hammond's hard choices bring world peace and prosperity, it is little wonder that the film quickly became a favorite of Roosevelt's and did well at the box office. The rays of hope seen at the time outshine the dark undertones we so readily see today in the film.

Yet all these sly winks were still a placeholder in Hollywood for Roosevelt himself. Referenced but not seen, seen but not heard, praised but not discussed. The movies of the 1930s flowed into the 1940s, with various nods to FDR but at arm's length, due to the studios being worried about the White House's reaction to portraying the sitting president, even if in good faith.

The most curious cinematic FDR connection in the 1930s came with the 1936 film *The President's Mystery*. The film was based on a mystery novel by the same name, which originated with Roosevelt in conversation at dinner on May 12, 1935, with Fulton Oursler, an editor at *Liberty* magazine. FDR, like Wilson before him and Kennedy and Clinton after, was a notorious reader of detective novels and had fiddled with the idea of writing one (the 2012 film *Hyde Park on Hudson* is one of the few films about FDR to mention this obsession). When Oursler asked Roosevelt if he had any ideas for a mystery novel, FDR replied, "I have carried the plot for a mystery story in my mind for years." The concept was simple in thought but complex in execution: A rich man, tired of his work, his life, and his wife, wants to take his money and begin a new life. Yet, as Roosevelt asked Oursler, "How can a man disappear with $5 million in any negotiable form and not be traced?"

It is easy in retrospect for some to wonder if Roosevelt's plot was wistful for his own yearnings for a different life, although such a suggestion seemed incredulous at the time. With Roosevelt's permission and assurances that royalties would go toward FDR's Georgia Warm Springs

Foundation, Oursler assembled a team of writers, Rupert Hughes, Samuel Hopkins Adams, Anthony Abbot, Rita Weirman, S. S. Van Dyne, and John Erskine, to create a round-robin serial based on the idea for the pages of *Liberty*. The chapters were then compiled into a book under the title *The President's Mystery* and published in 1936 (later to be reprinted in 1967 as *The President's Mystery Plot*, with an added ending chapter written by Erle Stanley Gardner that features a mention of his creation, Perry Mason). Reviews were tepid; Paul Jordan-Smith in the *Los Angeles Times* gave it a one-sentence review after describing the plot: "Something different—but not much good," and that was one of the more polite assessments.

Nevertheless, Republic Pictures announced they would make a film loosely based on the book, to be released in late 1936. The movie, written by Lester Cole and Nathanael West and directed by Phil Rosen (who directed a 1924 silent film about Abraham Lincoln), features Henry Wilcoxon (star of Cecil B. DeMille's *Cleopatra* and looking not unintentionally like a youngish FDR in droopy fedora and glasses) as lobbyist Jim Blake. Ashamed of helping to defeat a federal bill that would have put men to work (continuing Hollywood's negative view of Washington), Blake reads, of all things, *The President's Mystery* in the pages of *Liberty* magazine and devises a scheme to start a new life. Giving the appearance of being swindled from a bad investment in a phony company he secretly owns, he fakes his death and emerges as James Carter (yes, that would make him Jimmy Carter). Using his secreted money and his legal abilities, Carter reopens a cannery that was closed due to the loss of the bill he lobbied against, in hopes of revitalizing a small town, and winning the affections of the cannery's manager, Charlotte Brown (Betty Furness). Things are looking good until the accidental death of the wife (Ilka Blake, played by Evelyn Brent) he left behind leads to complications, but by the end of the film, Carter is proved innocent of his wife's death, as he kick-starts a cooperative after a rousing speech about people working together for a greater good.

The film, perhaps in part due to its legacy as a work generated by the president, got positive reviews. Frank Nugent of the *New York Times* called it a "well-constructed essay on one means of achieving a more abundant life, and it is an interesting picture as well." Herbert L. Monk of the *St. Louis Globe-Democrat* somewhat negatively suggested the movie "could almost be classed as propaganda . . . with a plot better than the picture turned out to be," but otherwise he had no qualms. The film is nothing more than a pleasant time waster, with Wilcoxon and Furness working well together and some nice early camera movements, but creaky plotting (no one questions how Blake obtains a cadaver to burn in a car crash for his fake suicide—a hack story device even in 1936—nor how a confession beaten out of a man proves Blake's innocence) and a preachy last-minute call for mankind to work together for a common good derails the film. Saying all that, the film did well at the box office (typically playing two to three days in spurts around the country). This was probably helped in part by plastering FDR's face in newspaper ads and in hype articles about the feature, which may have perplexed the White House because it looked as if the president endorsed the film. With profits from ticket sales given to Roosevelt's Georgia Warm Springs Foundation, however, such concerns were smoothed over.

Still, this could be seen as a sign of some openness from the White House for use of the sitting president's image, and by the time of the 1936 election, Bill Adams was back on *The March of Time* doing FDR's voice after nearly three years away. A further testing of the waters came in 1937, when Columbia added Roosevelt as a *praeses ex machina* to the plot of the Three Stooges short "Cash and Carry." The short has the Stooges, trying to raise money for a boy's operation so he can walk without a crutch, inadvertently breaking into the US Treasury. Things look bad, but the featurette ends with actor Al Richardson as FDR giving the Stooges amnesty and agreeing to help the boy get the surgery he needs. Albeit a short and not a feature film, it is worth noting for a few reasons: Richardson becomes the first actor to play FDR on-screen in a studio film; he is filmed in what becomes a traditional manner for FDR, with his back to the camera, sitting at a desk; and most interestingly, the plot deals with a boy unable to walk unassisted who gets help from Roosevelt. While there are no blatant parallels made, it is clear that the audience was expected to pick up on the fact that FDR would be sympathetic to the boy's plight, what with his own physical issues, reinforcing that the American public knew about Roosevelt's struggle with his legs but chose to ignore it.

Yet what worked for radio and less than a minute's worth of film in a two-reel comedy was not enough to prove to Hollywood that using FDR in their films would be a good idea. The movie studios knew to step gingerly, even more so as world politics began to heat up with World War II. Fortunately for one studio, Warner Brothers, a press occasion helped them in their quest to feature FDR in their movies.

Legislation was initiated in Congress in 1936 to give George M. Cohan, the popular musician mentioned earlier as the star of *The Phantom President*, a Congressional Gold Medal to honor his patriotic music over the years, such as "You're a Grand Old Flag" and the World War I–era song "Over There." The legislation eventually passed in January 1939, only for world events and the reluctance of Cohan, a conservative Republican who disliked Roosevelt's policies, to meet with FDR, thus pushing back the award ceremony until May 1, 1940. Contrary to what is suggested in the movie *Yankee Doodle Dandy* (1942), the award was unique and not a Congressional Medal of Honor, and the ceremony was presented in front of invited guests and the press, unlike the movie, where it suggests the award was secretly given to Cohan in the middle of the night in a darkened room like an act of espionage. Then again, considering how the pair felt about each other's politics, perhaps an incognito award ceremony would have been preferred.

Strangely enough, during the wait to get the award legislation passed, Cohan appeared on Broadway as Franklin D. Roosevelt in the musical comedy *I'd Rather Be Right*. The musical, produced by Sam Harris, written by George S. Kaufman and Moss Hart, and with music by Richard Rodgers and Lorenz Hart, gently targets FDR and his New Deal policies. The plot is a protracted, convoluted dream sequence about a young couple determined to get married only after Roosevelt has balanced the country's budget. Cohan plays Roosevelt as a singing, dancing, and somewhat devious man in charge, as the musical punctures Roosevelt's tendency to sidestep Congress (at one point telling a subordinate to put pen to paper and "take a law"), his fights with the Supreme Court (who periodically pop out of hiding to knock down his ideas), his ease at assigning new taxes to pay for programs, and even Sara as being dominating. While Cohan was not enthused by some of the material, especially the music, he was more than happy to punch at the Roosevelt myths.

At first, the National Democratic Council voiced displeasure with the lampooning of a sitting president, but the White House kept mum.

(Rumor was that Eleanor, who escaped mocking in the show, greatly enjoyed it when she went to see it.) The silence over the parody in comparison to disgruntled concerns over the serious *March of Time* imitations could be easily seen: *I'd Rather Be Right* was a short-lived Broadway show with a limited audience; Cohan was a nationally be-

**George M. Cohan (once again), this time as FDR in the Broadway show *I'd Rather Be Right* (1937). James Cagney later played Cohan as FDR in the 1939 film *Yankee Doodle Dandy*. Courtesy of PhotoFest.**

loved entertainer, and the jokes were mild jabs at best; and possibly, FDR not only comes off as the hero, but he also gets the best lines. To come out swinging against the musical would have made Roosevelt look like he couldn't take a joke, and FDR avoided such press. Besides, the White House and Roosevelt certainly had no problems with the idea of people associating the president with walking and dancing unaided. Anything to help perpetuate that notion to the public was probably appreciated. FDR would even quip in the award ceremony that Cohan was his double, to prove he was a good sport. (The "double" gag, which was reported by the press, popped up in the opening of *Yankee Doodle Dandy*, as well.)

Soon after the Congressional Gold Medal ceremony came news of the largely fictional biography about Cohan, *Yankee Doodle Dandy* (1942), that was planned by Warner Brothers. Reaching out to the White House, FDR agreed to be featured as a character in a dramatic motion picture, making him the first sitting president of the United States to be featured as a character in a full-length feature film (at three reels, Fred Truesdale's performance as Woodrow Wilson in the 1913 film *The Sons of a Soldier* just misses the mark). The film, directed by Michael Curtiz, stars James Cagney as George M. Cohan, with Walter Huston (*Abraham Lincoln, Gabriel over the White House*) as Cohan's father. The movie opens after a performance of *I'd Rather Be Right*, with Cagney as Cohan receiving a telegram requesting his appearance at the White House. We next see Cohan arriving there and being taken up a long staircase to meet Roosevelt in an office. Roosevelt is played by Jack Young, often credited as Captain Jack Young, sitting behind a desk, with his body away from the camera and face hidden from the view of the audience. Contrary to various sources then and now, it is not Jack Young's voice we hear as Roosevelt but that of actor Art Gilmore, who had previously done a brief imitation of FDR in the "Baby Weems" section of the Disney film *The Reluctant Dragon* (1941). Gilmore's FDR imitation is slightly exaggerated, but this is not unexpected in getting over to the audience that it is the president speaking. Gilmore continued as Warner's go-to voice for Roosevelt in two subsequent films, while he is probably best remembered today for his narration of newsreels, advertising (such as the movie trailers for *The Killing, Rodan,* and *To Kill a Mockingbird*), and for the television series *Highway Patrol.*

*Yankee Doodle Dandy* continues with Roosevelt discussing Cohan's vaudevillian past, leading to the core of the film: a flashback to Cohan's life story. The flashback ends with Cohan performing onstage as Roosevelt in the *I'd Rather Be Right* number "Off the Record," which jabs at Roosevelt's cozy relationship with the press and his tendency to comment on topics but then tell them to not print what he said. (*Gabriel over the White House* comments on this tendency, as well.) "Off the Record" concludes in the movie with Roosevelt suggesting that America would soon be going to war with Germany and Japan; lyrics added specifically for the film were not part of the original 1938 Broadway production (which would have been questioned at a time when America was heavily antiwar).

The film then shifts back to FDR and Cohan in the office at the White House as FDR gives Cohan the medal. They compliment each other and praise America in a brief stroke of war propaganda that Hollywood was building up in the early days of World War II. We finally get a full shot of Young as FDR as Cohan leaves the office, but the camera angle is high above the set, looking down, so there are no close-ups from the front of Young in the role. Still, with the White House approval of Young physically playing the role and Gilmore as the voice, they continued almost as official FDR impersonators for Warner Brothers through 1943, although not always together.

The next two films in 1943 needed Art Gilmore rather than Jack Young, however. *Edge of Darkness*, starring Errol Flynn and once again Walter Huston, is a story about a village resisting Nazis in occupied Norway. Although not credited, it is most likely Gilmore who recreates part of FDR's famous "Look to Norway" speech in the closing narrative to the film, as a group of new freedom fighters file from the village. *Action in the North Atlantic*, which came out a month after *Edge of Darkness* and stars Humphrey Bogart and Raymond Massey (Abe Lincoln in *Abe Lincoln in Illinois*) also features an ending narrative of Gilmore reading part of another speech FDR gave, this one dealing with the bravery of the Merchant Marines.

Young and Gilmore returned on the heels of *Action in the North Atlantic* with *Mission to Moscow*, a docudrama based on a biographical book from Joseph E. Davies about his experience as the US ambassador to the Soviet Union between 1936 and 1938. The film, considered whitewashed propaganda in praise of Stalin at a time when the Soviets were part of the Allies' war effort, features Walter Huston as Davies (and yes, Walter Huston certainly does seem to get mentioned a lot in connection with FDR in this chapter, including a supporting role in *Yankee Doodle Dandy*, almost as if Roosevelt made sure Huston would appear if he was going to allow use of his voice or image in a movie) and many famous historical figures, such as Joseph Stalin (Manart Kippen); Winston Churchill (Dudley Field Malone); and, naturally by this point for Warner, Young and Gilmore as FDR. There's another holdover from *Yankee Doodle Dandy* as well: the White House set, including the sprawling staircase to the second floor leading to FDR's office, seen as Roosevelt calls on Davies to become ambassador. As to Jack Young, the setup of the camera behind him is similar to his appearance in *Yankee Doodle Dandy*, with his Roosevelt sitting behind a desk in the Oval Office, his face away from the camera, and even some of the same ornaments on the desk. If some of the wall ornaments hadn't been changed, it would be easy to assume they chained Young to the desk and just kept shooting footage of him as FDR while different actors filed in to say their lines for each new film. Meanwhile, Art Gilmore supplies the voice of Roosevelt not only in the scene but also later on when recreating FDR's famous "Quarantine" speech from October 5, 1937, that suggested using economic measures to put aggressive nations in place (the speech is also used at the beginning of the 2019 remake of *Midway*).

Jack Young made a final appearance as Roosevelt later that year in *This Is the Army*, which features future president Ronald Reagan. There was no need for Art Gilmore for this role, as Young as Roosevelt appears only briefly and silently, leisurely strolling into a theater balcony high above the crowd for the stage show in the film and standing without assistance for a short time before sitting unaided (and far enough away from the camera to disguise any differences between Young and Roosevelt).

Roosevelt walks again in one final Warner picture from 1943, the comedy *Princess O'Rourke*, with an unnamed actor in the small but pivotal role of FDR. As with *I'd Rather Be Right*, FDR helps a couple with their romance, only this time it is a foreign princess (Olivia de Havilland) and a pilot (Bob Cummings) who end up being invited to stay at the White House when the princess's country is invaded. Even

Roosevelt's real-life dog of the White House, a Scottie named Fala, gets involved, as FDR helps the couple get married by a Supreme Court justice before they leave to start life anew. The White House set from *Yankee Doodle Dandy* makes a final appearance, although rumors persist that location shooting was done at the White House itself, with Roosevelt's permission. Roosevelt's dog Fala, who had been the subject of an MGM short film in 1943, *Fala: The President's Dog*, was rumored to appear as himself in *Princess O'Rourke*, although Warner heavily promoted the film as using a stand-in named Whiskers. As to FDR, he appears only as a figure partially blocked from view by a door in the final gag of the film, as Cummings's character gives a dollar to someone he mistakes for a guard (the gag being that FDR couldn't pass up a chance to take someone's money when offered).

*Princess O'Rourke* was filmed in 1942 but was delayed for a couple reasons. First, there were legal issues between Warner Brothers and Olivia de Havilland because she had grown tired of appearing in Warner movies that could be seen as minor, frothy comedies, leading to changes in long-term studio contracts with actors. Second, the US government was not happy with the way the White House and others involved with the ongoing war were portrayed. In 1942, Roosevelt created with an executive order the US Office of War Information (OWI), which was used to disseminate news and help develop programming to promote the war effort in all forms of media (creating the Voice of America for radio, as one example). For the film industry, the OWI had the Bureau of Motion Pictures (BMP) to advise and review films to make sure positive reinforcement about the Allies' war efforts was used. For *Princess O'Rourke*, the BMP raised objections to the comedic portrayal of Red Cross workers, Civil Defense, foreigners, and the Secret Service and suggested that the president's plan to help the couple made him out to be a busybody and a cheapskate who would steal a dollar, as in the final gag. Yet perhaps because Roosevelt was receptive to the film and allowed use of his dog as a character, nothing came of these concerns, and the film was released without changes.

Although FDR seemed to become a featured player at Warner Brothers in 1943, by 1944, the on-screen appearances of Roosevelt dissipated, although there were still occasional mentions, such as in *The Doughgirls* (1944), which features one of the lead couples in the film being invited to dine with the president and the First Lady. (One character, played by Jane Wyman, asks the couple to tell Roosevelt how good he was in *Yankee Doodle Dandy*.) Yet within a year of FDR's death, there was already talk of bringing him back to the silver screen and this time not by way of Warner Brothers.

The film was *The Beginning or the End* (1947), released through MGM Studios, which deals with the creation of the atomic bomb. The idea came by way of actor Donna Reed in 1945, when she received a letter from her old high school chemistry teacher, Edward R. Thompkins, who had been involved with the Manhattan Project, the government project that developed the weapon. Thompkins wrote to Reed, suggesting that a movie about the ethics faced by those involved would make for a fascinating movie. Reed passed on the idea to her husband and agent Tony Owens, who approached Sam Marx at MGM. The studio jumped on the idea, buying out a competing A-bomb movie planned at Paramount that was to be called *Top Secret*. Soon after, the newspapers began reporting the development of the film, with Norman Taurog (known mostly for comedies and musicals, including the previously mentioned 1932 film *The Phantom President*) directing and featuring Clark Gable, Van Johnson, Spencer Tracy, and Lionel Barrymore as FDR. Instead, the film ended up with Brian Donlevy, Robert Walker, and definitely not Lionel Barrymore as Roosevelt.

Gable, Tracy, and Johnson were pretty much pipe-dream names attached to the project for press reasons, but Barrymore was agreeable to the small, vital role of Roosevelt. The script featured two scenes with Roosevelt: The first, written by Ayn Rand (*The Fountainhead, Atlas Shrugged*), shows FDR discussing the merits and morals of creating such a weapon with his secretary, who tells him that the Germans would surely use the weapon if they had a chance; the second scene briefly shows FDR in his last hours at his Warm Springs home, about to inform Truman of the bomb in a memo before being escorted out of the room for his final portrait posing (and thus suggesting FDR meant to inform Truman, but didn't get the chance). Later in the film, after testing is completed, Truman is introduced as president, along with his dilemma in possibly using the bomb in the war. The depiction of Truman in the movie caused concerns at the White House, but that's a tale for chapter 9. The main concern from an FDR standpoint was that the Roosevelt family was not very happy with the script's depiction of Franklin or the idea of Barrymore playing the part.

Not that MGM had much risk if they had not involved the family, at least in legal terms. As pointed out in newspaper articles in June 1946, when controversy over Barrymore's casting became public, the studio could have gone ahead with the presentation of FDR as made in the script because the president was a public figure who "may be dramatically portrayed if the portray is historically accurate." There was, however, public opinion to consider about a president who many revered, a public that could be swayed to not buy tickets to a movie that the Roosevelts publicly denounced. The best option, therefore, was to get the okay before filming, which is what the studio did in early 1946, when a script was sent to Franklin's son James Roosevelt, who agreed to the script's portrayal.

At that point, press hype for Barrymore in the role kicked in mid-February 1946, including some dubious suggestions in the newspapers that Barrymore, being restricted to using a wheelchair in many of his later roles due to arthritis complicated by two hip fractures, was the "likely choice for the role because . . . he is also a wheelchair victim." Yet by April, some reporters noted a certain sense of irony that Barrymore was playing the role after being an aggressive campaigner for Roosevelt's opponent Tom Dewey in the 1944 election as well as a vocal opponent of FDR when he sought a third and then a fourth term. The script did little to help smooth over concerns about the actor; in its initial form, FDR is presented as a bit too giddy over the potential of the bomb and shrugs off the cost to the country for the Manhattan Project with, "What's $2 billion more or less to me since I'm so accustomed to tossing so many billions around?" Such dialogue may have been prepared as a sign of Roosevelt's good humor at dark times, but it easily could come off as uncaring, especially in the hands of an actor who was known to see the president as an ego-feeding spendthrift.

A screen test with Barrymore in the role to show the family was proposed, while James Roosevelt suggested the actor send a personal letter to Eleanor in hopes of soothing over feelings. Alas, the footage completed did not win over the Roosevelt children who viewed it, and Barrymore's letter did little to help. While the letter was ambitious and somewhat charming in trying to win over Eleanor, Barrymore could not help but attempt to lecture the former First Lady by stating, "It is true that during the 1944 presidential race I made two speeches on behalf of the candidacy of Thomas E. Dewey, which, I understand, is my constitutional privilege." While the public statements from the family were that the studio could do whatever they wish, the clear result was that they would be happier with someone else in the role.

Perhaps just as well, as some in the press had hinted that an older actor in a wheelchair was hardly the parameters in casting the role. Besides, Barrymore's stock, grumpy, and abrasive mannerisms that worked in his favor in many movies, including his turn as Andrew Jackson in *The Gorgeous Hussy* (1936), hardly did the same as FDR. Barrymore instead moved on to the film *It's a Wonderful Life* (1947), which cemented his status in movie history more than any other film he would do. Ironically, Donna Reed, the initial promoter for *The Beginning or the End*, ended up passing up a chance to appear in that movie, as she was already set to film *It's a Wonderful Life* at the same time.

*The Beginning or the End* still needed its FDR. Raymond Massey, former Lincoln actor and known Roosevelt supporter, was pursued, before he publicly announced his disinterest, feeling that the differences in physicality and voice between him and Roosevelt would "inadvertently hurt the memory of a man idolized by millions." Spencer Tracy, who had been suggested earlier for the role of General Groves, director of the Manhattan Project, was quickly broached for the role of FDR and then discarded as being too big of a star for such a cameo. Instead, the role went to Godfrey Tearle, best remembered as playing the main villain in Alfred Hitchcock's *The 39 Steps* (1935). Tearle looked remarkably like Roosevelt, even before makeup, and sounded more like FDR than Barrymore would have. He pulls in a fine performance of the president in the few minutes he appears on-screen, although not all were impressed after the film's release. Gita Bumpass of the *Forth Worth Star-Telegram* in her review of the film felt Tearle "looks like [FDR] in distant shots, but [his] voice fails to match the power of Roosevelt's."

The release of the film saw further complaints by Eleanor in the press. The second scene with FDR shows him clearly in a standard wheelchair, which would have been strongly frowned upon just two years earlier. The Roosevelts were also surprised seeing Tearle as Roosevelt filmed with the camera facing him in traditional lighting, as there had been an assumption that Tearle would be filmed as Jack Young had in the past: his back to the camera and perhaps in shadows, as in the Warner Brothers movies. Strangely enough, Art Baker as Truman appears in the movie shown only from behind and partially in shadows. Evidently the studio felt the "good taste" of hiding the president's features pertained only to those still alive.

With *The Beginning or the End* leaving a sour taste in the mouth and hearing rumors in mid-1946 that other studios were eyeing biographies about FDR, the Roosevelt family decided to take matters into their own hands. Truthfully, the Roosevelts would have been happier with no films being done about FDR for at least a generation, with James Roosevelt stating, "If it were possible in this day and age to eliminate all impersonations on the stage and in motion pictures of President Roosevelt, during the lifetime of those who knew him directly and/or indirectly, it would be a good thing." However, the family knew that was unlikely and thus felt it was better to "give full assistance to those in whose judgment, good taste, and integrity we have full confidences, rather than allow a multitude of inaccuracies and false impressions to be created." Thus, in February 1947, James Roosevelt announced that he would team with Jay Richard Kennedy, producer of the crime drama *To the Ends of the Earth* for Columbia Pictures and a former associate of the Federal Bureau of Narcotics, to create one or even multiple films about Franklin D. Roosevelt sometime in the next four years, with James as technical adviser and financial backer and Kennedy as writer and producer. No project ever came out of the deal, however, although attempts were made to create a new type of plastic makeup that would help convey the look of Franklin (thus suggesting that even the Roosevelts knew that hiding FDR in the shadows was not going to be possible in any future endeavors). What the deal did was cool the heels of the studios looking to make a biography, which was just fine by the family. Better no film at all than one that pictured FDR in a lesser light.

It would be another ten years before FDR would be portrayed again in a film and this time only briefly in one scene in the 1957 biopic *Beau James*, starring Bob Hope in one of his few dramatic roles as famous mayor of New York Jimmy Walker. Voice actor Dick Nelson plays Roosevelt in a scene taking place in 1932, when FDR was governor of the state and presiding over a committee investigating accusations of bribery and other dubious pursuits going on in New York City under Walker's watch. Unlike Jack Young, Nelson provides the voice for Roosevelt himself, with Nelson filmed from behind in the time-honored manner of the Warner Brothers films, but is given very little to do beyond a few waves of the hands as he delivers a few lines. Notably, the movie, a love letter to Walker, plays Roosevelt as calm and dignified during the committee scene, unlike how the press covered the real events, which showcase Roosevelt raising his voice in obvious frustration and often verbally sparring with Walker's defense. This impatient side of Roosevelt's personality, one rarely seen in public in his later years, along with concerns about how the hearings would have a negative impact on Roosevelt's ongoing presidential campaign in 1932, mounted pressure on Walker to resign for the sake of the Democratic Party, as suggested in the film. However, Walker was clearly no fan of Roosevelt and had personal reasons to resign. Still, to present Walker as "saving" Roosevelt was in line with the sympathetic portrayal presented in the movie.

The year 1957 also saw the start of the first full-length film about Roosevelt, one that had the official approval of the Roosevelts, although the movie did not go into production until 1960. Dore Schary (*Mr. Blandings Builds His Dream House, Bad Day at Black Rock, Designing Woman*), a writer-producer who at one time was the head of MGM Studios, wanted to do a movie dealing not with Roosevelt's politics but rather his struggle adjusting to and domination over his physical limitations brought on by polio in 1921. As Schary told Edwin Schallert in the *Los Angeles Times* when the project was announced, "I have a deep feeling that the story of President Roosevelt's ordeal during his illness can be a tribute and a dramatic record of importance, which is why I have long been interested in this unique undertaking." Schary's vision was to do the story first as a Broadway play for a time, building interest across the country, before finally bringing it to the big screen. The family agreed to officially stand behind the project based on it dealing with Franklin's personal story and the promise that the family would get $1 million upfront and possibly $5 million or more through profit sharing.

With their okay, Schary began writing the play for the Broadway show, which starts with a physically active FDR playing with his children at their Campobello home in 1921, before waking the following morning unable to properly walk. Although skipping over some physical

complications, the play follows the timeline of Roosevelt's illness, starting with the discovery of what was believed to be polio. While Franklin
deals with his physical limitations, the family must deal with Franklin's
mother, who believes he should retire and stay out of the public eye.
The play ends grandly, with FDR triumphantly walking with assistance
to the podium at the Democratic convention to give the "Happy Warrior" speech for Al Smith in 1924. Even though covering only a period
of less than four years, the play and the subsequent movie made based
on it were the first full biographical productions about Franklin and
introduced other major members of the FDR family, such as Eleanor,
Sara, the children, and even Louis Howe into the storytelling.

Vincent J. Donehue, who had directed *The Trip to Bountiful* in 1953
with Lillian Gish and went on to direct *The Sound of Music* on Broadway in 1959, was quickly added to do the same for *Sunrise at Campobello*. Mary Fickett, seen years later in several soap operas, including
*All My Children*, played Eleanor; Anne Seymour appeared as Sara; and
Henry Jones, a popular character actor in movies and television, played
Howe. By fall, all the pieces were in place for the play to go into tryouts
before moving to Broadway on January 30—FDR's birthday—in 1958.

The problem was finding the right FDR. In Schary's autobiography
*Heyday* (1979), he suggests that he envisioned the role with Anthony
Quayle, but if so, it was a pipe dream, as Quayle was bouncing between
film and stage work and was not available. If such a suggestion was
made, then it didn't make the papers at least, with the first announcement in July 1957 being that Schary was actively pursuing Henry Fonda
for the role. Fonda's response was to pass on the offer, and between July
and September 1957, there were a series of articles demonstrating the
slow-growing panic with the theater guild in finding a suitable actor to
take on the role. In mid-October, Leslie Nielsen (*Forbidden Planet, Airplane!*) was announced as being the number 1 choice "to play the role
of Franklin D. Roosevelt," but that was quickly superseded with news
on October 20 that Ralph Bellamy would be playing the part when the
tryouts began in Philadelphia on January 13, 1958.

Ralph Bellamy had typically played comedic roles in lighter films,
as in *The Awful Truth* (1937), which saw him nominated for a Best
Supporting Actor Oscar; *His Girl Friday* (1940); and even as detective
Ellery Queen in four films between 1940 and 1941. Today he's prob-

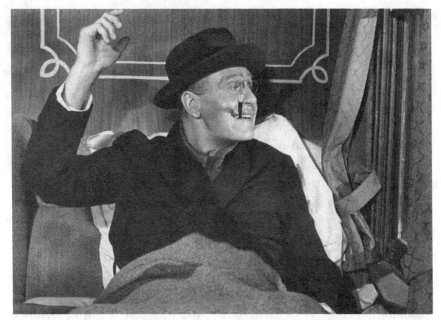

**Ralph Bellamy as FDR in the film adaptation of the Broadway play he starred in, *Sunrise at Campobello* (1960). *Official press still, author's collection,* © 1960 by Warner Brothers.**

ably best remembered for playing one of the Duke Brothers with Don Ameche in the comedy *Trading Places* (1983), but in 1957, he was mainly a panelist on the game show *To Tell the Truth*. According to Schary in his autobiography, it was his wife who suggested that Bellamy looked a bit like Roosevelt, and when Schary asked Bellamy to come to his place to discuss the role, Bellamy arrived dressed as much like FDR as possible. It was enough to convince Schary, who called Bellamy "Mr. President" upon seeing him.

The play opened on schedule at the Cort Theater on Broadway, with Eleanor Roosevelt in attendance, along with her four sons. Eleanor told the press afterward that she enjoyed the play, especially the performances of Bellamy and Fickett, but admitted that she had never read the play and felt no personal attachment to the proceedings played out onstage. "It has no more to do with me than the man in the moon," she said afterward. "I don't recognize myself onstage. I have no feelings of reality about it. It might just as well be about someone from Mars." The play, like the movie two years later, garnered some concerns from those

close to the family because Sara Delano Roosevelt is presented as a
negative influence on Franklin, but those in the production brushed off
such accusations, noting that every story needs an antagonist, and Sara
fit the bill. As to Eleanor's thoughts of the portrayal of Sara, whom she
admitted to sometimes clashing with over the years? She kept silent,
which may say more than if she had voiced an opinion.

Although Bellamy ended up winning a Best Dramatic Actor Tony
Award for his portrayal of the president, along with Henry Jones for
Featured Actor and Vincent Donehue for Director, critical reviews
were a bit mixed, suggesting that the outpouring of praise may have
been more for the play's protagonist than for the play itself. John Chapman of the *Daily News* the day after the premiere called it "much more
than a stirring drama; it is a very beautiful play . . . a living and moving
part of this country's life." T. H. Parker of *The Hartford Courant*, however, called the play "[e]mbarrassing. . . . As drama, it is mawkish." He
went so far as to state that Bellamy looked like Roosevelt only through
"assiduous apeing." A national tour of the play that began in October
1958, with Leif Erickson playing FDR, had "spotty" ticket sales and
folded in December, but once the Broadway show ended after 556
performances on May 30, 1959, most of the original cast successfully
toured the country, seeing its final performance in Atlanta, Georgia, on
the anniversary of FDR's birth in January 1960.

As planned, production on the promised movie adaptation began in
March 1960 at Warner Brothers. Casting began much earlier, however,
as the studio first pursued Doris Day in February 1959 to star as Eleanor. When she declined, Greer Garson (*Goodbye, Mr. Chips*; *Mrs.
Miniver*) accepted the role the same month. She immediately created a
mild ruckus by suggesting that her former *Julius Caesar* (1953) costar,
Marlon Brando, would make a perfect FDR in the film. To be fair, Bellamy suggested in the press the month before that the studio was looking to replace him with the younger Brando for the film version, as they
thought him too old to play the thirty-nine-year-old Roosevelt, so the
story was already out there, but it was Garson's remarks that the press
pushed. Upon hearing the idea, James Roosevelt told columnist Mike
Connolly, "My mother and I think it's the worst possible cast." Word
is that Brando thought so, too, feeling he was too busy, too young, and
not interested in another wheelchair role after having done one for *The

*Men* (1950). In the end, it was perhaps simply a method to get the studio firmly behind Bellamy, as he was officially announced to star in the film version soon afterward.

Garson also found herself under fire from both sides of the political spectrum for accepting the role of Eleanor because she was known to campaign for Republican candidates; yet if Eleanor had any objections like she had with Lionel Barrymore, she didn't make it public. Garson wore special dental appliances for the role to resemble Eleanor's well-remembered overbite, even though it gave audiences more the image of Greer Garson with an overbite. While not quite looking the role, Garson does better in the illusion of being Eleanor by replicating the physical stance and speaking voice of the First Lady in the film, thus understandably leading to an Academy Award nomination and a Golden Globe Award for her performance.

*Sunrise at Campobello* as a film is very much like the play, with most of the dialogue and actions intact and adding some exterior locations to spice up the scenery that is impossible for a stage-bound play. Location filming was done at the Roosevelt residences on Campobello Island and at Hyde Park, with Eleanor visiting the filming at the New York property for publicity photos with Bellamy and Garson, before transferring back to California for the remainder of the shoot. Besides Bellamy and Garson, included in the cast are Ann Shoemaker as Sara Delano Roosevelt (another holdover from the stage production, having taken over the role from Anne Seymour while on Broadway); Hume Cronyn (*Shadow of a Doubt, Lifeboat, Cocoon*) as Louis Howe; and Jean Hagen (*Singin' in the Rain, The Asphalt Jungle*) in the small role of Missy Le-Hand, Franklin's devoted secretary. While most reviews praise Garson's transformation for the role, even the *Daily News'* reviewer Kate Cameron, while very complimentary, couldn't help but point out that Garson "retains her own sweet ways" while playing Eleanor. Cronyn is good as Howe, demonstrating the humor and strategy of FDR's advisor in trying to keep Franklin's spirits up, while Shoemaker lends a sympathetic air to the "villain" of the piece as Franklin's mother.

Even so, the film really comes alive when Bellamy is on-screen as FDR, not only because he looks, acts, and sounds remarkably like the president, but also because the clockwork pace of the script following the known timeline of Franklin's ailment allows little creative exploration for any other character beyond FDR. This was reflected in critical reviews of the time, with admiration for the film's exploration of FDR's fight against his paralysis but noting that the other characters get lost in all the energy of humanizing Roosevelt's plight. The other issue is that being dependent on the stage play places most of the movie scenes in various rooms, with people talking for long stretches, which may be a necessity on a stage but tends to wear thin after a while in a movie theater, especially with the film at more two hours long and with an intermission.

It is easy to see this as one of Bellamy's best roles, allowing him to do more than be a second lead, as in many of his films, and he obviously revels in the chance—so much so that, at times, his take on FDR's sunny disposition can come across a bit thick, making one wonder if Bellamy was playing too broad after a year and a half of the role onstage and should have toned down the performance for the big screen. Yet any follower of Roosevelt's various talks and his history can see that Bellamy's performance is fairly accurate for how FDR behaved, especially in darker moments of adversity. Obviously, with the involvement of the family, the film and the play before it was not going to dig too deeply in the psyche of FDR, but it should be given credit for at least presenting a view of this period in Roosevelt's history when he was somewhat indecisive and even frustrated with himself, and Bellamy proves to be a good choice for the role. So strong is his performance that when it came time to present FDR in the 1980s television miniseries *The Winds of War* (1983) and *War and Remembrance* (1989), Ralph Bellamy was briefly brought back to play the role he had perfected so many years before (in a slight parallel, *Sunrise at Campobello* is set nearly twenty years before *The Winds of War*, while Bellamy's return to the role happens just a little over twenty years after the 1960 film, so his aging coincides with that of FDR in real time).

*Sunrise at Campobello* received positive feedback from audiences and critics alike but did not see huge returns at the box office, earning only $3 million in 1960. Not surprisingly, with the low financial return, Hollywood turned to other topics and gave FDR a good rest until 1976 and the production of the *Eleanor and Franklin* miniseries, followed by *Eleanor and Franklin: The White House Years* in 1977 for the ABC network. Although made for television, the two miniseries were important in the portrayal of FDR in a visual media for two reasons: It gave us Edward Herrmann as FDR, who, like Ralph Bellamy, returned to the role several times in the years to follow, and *Eleanor and Franklin* was the first biography about Roosevelt to depict the Lucy Mercer affair.

The affair cropped up several times over the years, going back to rumors from 1949 after Franklin's private secretary, Grace Tully, wrote a book about her time working with Roosevelt published as *FDR My Boss*. Tully's book was the first public mention of Lucy Mercer Rutherfurd being with the president at the time of his death at the Little White House in Warm Springs, and some reporters ran with it to question the nature of Roosevelt's relationship with Lucy. Over time, biographical studies made additional mentions of their possible affection for each other, but this was usually dismissed as nothing more than a mild flirtation—that is until Jonathan Daniels, admirative assistant and press secretary for Roosevelt, wrote a series of books in the late 1950s through the 1960s, most specifically *The Times between the Wars* (1966) and *Washington Quadrille* (1968), which hint at a more speculative romance between Lucy and Franklin. By this time, all three figures involved were dead—Franklin in 1945, Lucy in 1948, and Eleanor in 1962—and could not dispute the story. Libel laws had also toughened by 1964, with defamation of a public figure having to be proven with intended malice, leading the Roosevelt family to pull back from fighting such charges. As Elliott Roosevelt stated in an article by Inez Robb in 1968, "The family plans to take no actions in this obvious invasion of our family privacy. The Supreme Court has ruled that a man in public life is fair game and can be called anything, including a murderer. That precludes action."

More importantly, the family knew there were elements of truth in the stories told, as officially documented with the release of Joe Lash's book *Eleanor and Franklin* in 1971. Lash, a long-time friend of and researcher with Eleanor, had interviewed Eleanor extensively, as well as family members, and was given her papers after her death, leading to the publication of the book that allowed the public to learn of Eleanor's views on her years with Franklin (even more so than her own autobiographical work written while she was alive). While *Eleanor and Franklin* won a Pulitzer Prize in 1972, sales of the book were helped due to interest in the affair, which anchors the storyline of the first miniseries brought to television five years later.

In 1973, David Susskind, known for his intellectual television and film productions dating back to the 1950s (*Death of a Salesman, The Glass Menagerie, Requiem for a Heavyweight*), purchased the rights to the book in hopes of translating it to television. The initial idea was to create eight hour-long episodes, then three two-hour episodes, before finally settling on two two-hour episodes that eventually aired on January 11 and 12, 1976, on the ABC network. The series follows Eleanor as she arrives at the Little White House in Warm Springs after Franklin's death, only to be told that Lucy Mercer Rutherfurd was present before he died, and includes her journey with his body back to Washington, DC, by train. As she travels, she reminisces about growing up with a loving but undependable father, her courtship with Franklin, the discovery of his affair with Lucy, his battle with polio, and her emergence as a public speaker and advocate. The flashbacks end with Franklin agreeing to speak to the convention for Al Smith in 1921, as Eleanor arrives back in Washington.

James Costigan (*Love among the Ruins, F. Scott Fitzgerald in Hollywood*) was brought in to write the screenplay, with Daniel Petrie (who directed *A Raisin in the Sun* for Susskind in 1961 and directed *Kissinger and Nixon* in 1995 for the TNT cable network) as the director. Jane Alexander, who won a Tony Award and was nominated for a Best Actress Oscar for her role in *The Great White Hope* as well as appeared in *All the President's Men* (1976), was quickly cast as Eleanor Roosevelt. Rosemary Murphy, probably best remembered as the helpful neighbor in *To Kill a Mockingbird* (1962), played Sara Delano Roosevelt, and Ed Flanders (the series *St. Elsewhere*; he also played Truman in several productions, covered in chapter 9) played Louis Howe. But just like with *Sunrise at Campobello*, there were delays as the production went looking for its FDR.

What was needed was someone who could play Franklin as a young man, which would be a first and last for on-screen FDRs. All other productions have focused on Roosevelt between the ages of thirty-five and forty, up into his sixties during the war years, while *Eleanor and Franklin* sees the pair during their courtship when Franklin was twenty years old. Actor Edward Herrmann (who had appeared in such films as *The Paper Chase* in 1973 and *The Great Waldo Pepper* in 1975) benefited by looking much younger than his age of thirty-two and shared just enough of a resemblance that he was a good physical pick for the role. Much like Ralph Bellamy, he became so connected to the role of FDR with this program and its sequel *Eleanor and Franklin: The White House Years* (1977) that he returned to play Franklin several times afterward, such as briefly in the 1982 movie version of the musical *Annie* to sing "Tomorrow" with Little Orphan Annie and as Roosevelt's voice in the Ken Burns PBS documentary series *The Roosevelts: An Intimate History* (2014). The oddest recurrence was in a Washington, DC, concert performance of *I'd Rather Be Right* in March 1995, when Herrmann played the all-singing and somewhat-dancing FDR with members of the Senate, Congress, and Clinton cabinet in various other roles. Because of having played Roosevelt off and on for so many years, there is a tendency to think of Edward Herrmann as the "gold standard" of how the president should be played.

The forty-day production for the first miniseries went smoothly, although Petrie had some advice to give Alexander and Herrmann early on as they attempted to perfect their performances, as he told Bob Thoams for the Associated Press, "I became alarmed that Jane and Ed were imitating the vocal quality of the Roosevelts with little communication as human beings. Finally, I told them, 'The important thing is to reach for the soul of these characters, not to try for the trappings of voice and teeth.'" With this advice, Alexander and Herrmann convey the parts of the president and First Lady more subdued than Bellamy and Garson in *Sunrise at Campobello*, where it is difficult not to feel that the actors are playing to the back wall like in the theater to reinforce who their characters are. On the downside, the makeup used in the program to convey the couple in their elder years is not very successful and can take one out of the story (this was corrected by the time of *The White House Years* series in 1977). The miniseries was promoted as a limited-commercial special, with IBM sponsoring the entire production after seeing forty minutes of footage shot for the program (they were originally to pay only for the first half of the program, with another advertiser to pay for the second part). As a promotional tool, the full script for the miniseries was placed in the January 9, 1975, pages of the *Philadelphia Inquirer* so that students from the local school system would be able to use it as an aid while watching the program.

*Eleanor and Franklin* was a ratings success, leading to eleven Emmy Awards, including Best Television Movie, Supporting Actress for Rosemary Murphy, and Best Director for Daniel Petrie. A follow-up two-part miniseries was commissioned the following year, which deals with Eleanor and Franklin in Washington, during his presidency, allowing for some focus on the Depression and New Deal era, which is rarely touched on in film biographies of FDR.

The cast is excellent, and it has been noted as fairly historically accurate, which makes it and the sequel worth checking out for viewers interested in the Roosevelts' background. The issue for some, however, is that it is Eleanor's story even in the sequel series: her upbringing, her move to France as a teenager, her determination to get Franklin back to work after his illness, her travels to give speeches, and with a wraparound focus on her feelings after discovering that Lucy Mercer Rutherfurd was at the Little White House when Franklin died. Thus although Herrmann is excellent in the role, we never really see much character development in Franklin because the emphasis is on Eleanor. More importantly, because the emphasis is on the Lucy Mercer story, *Eleanor and Franklin* gave other productions the opportunity to follow that lead in later years.

It was again a few more years before there would come a film dealing solely with Roosevelt. Instead, the following years saw Franklin Roosevelt pop up for a few minutes to push along plot points in movies and then disappear. The next was *The Private Files of J. Edgar Hoover* from 1977, written and directed by Larry Cohen (*Q, It's Alive*) and featuring a couple scenes with Howard Da Silva (Benjamin Franklin in *1776*, Nikita Khrushchev in *The Missiles of October*) as a very foppish FDR, requesting Hoover to use wiretaps on individuals who might be Nazi supporters. The 1977 movie *MacArthur*, starring Gregory Peck and with an excellent Ed Flanders as President Truman, has a brief scene with Dan O'Herlihy as FDR questioning MacArthur about the war while at Pearl Harbor.

Several years passed with Roosevelt mostly regulated to television, with some hits and misses, such as Jason Robards as an excellent but solemn Roosevelt in *FDR: The Last Year*, a 1980 CBS network adaptation of Jim Bishop's biography after five years in development. Ten years later, however, Josef Sommer is so frantic in his good cheer as FDR in the miniseries *The Kennedys of Massachusetts* (1990) that he more resembles Batman's villain the Joker than Roosevelt. John Lithgow is respectful as Franklin in the NBC miniseries *World War II: When Lions Roared* (1994; also known as *Then There Were Giants*), which deals with Roosevelt, Churchill, and Stalin working together against the Axis powers during World War II. Roosevelt's appearance is so brief in the 1995 HBO biopic *Truman* that actor Lee Richardson goes uncredited. Also on HBO was a 1998 biography about influential newspaper columnist Walter Winchell, starring Stanley Tucci, with Christopher Plummer as an almost-menacing FDR lecturing Winchell on work ethics in two scenes and at one point delivering his Pearl Harbor speech. A remake of *Annie* (1999) by Disney for ABC features Dennis Howard as Franklin doing his part to find Annie's parents but avoiding singing with her this time around (the 2014 theatrical remake of *Annie* eliminates the part of the president completely, which is perhaps just as well—it always seemed to be shoehorned into the script in the earlier versions anyway). Elsewhere, a couple television films dealing with Winston Churchill during World War II appeared in the early part of the twenty-first century, each with Roosevelt popping up briefly to play his part in the narrative: Len Cariou in *Into the Storm* (2009) and David Strathairn in *Darkest Hour* (2017).

One more recent television movie dealing solely with Roosevelt is worthy of note: *Warm Springs*, which aired on HBO in the spring of 2005, twenty-five years after the last movie dealing solely with Roosevelt's life and the first since *Sunrise at Campobello* from forty-five years before that dealing mainly with Franklin's paralysis. The film, which won an Emmy Award for Best Movie, was written by Margaret Nagle; directed by Joseph Sargent (*MacArthur, World War II: When Lions Roared, The Man*); and stars Kenneth Branagh as Franklin, Cynthia Nixon as Eleanor, and a returning Jane Alexander (*Eleanor and Franklin*) as Sara Delano Roosevelt. The film depicts Franklin's recuperation in Warm Springs during the 1920s after being paralyzed from the waist down. In many ways, the film combines elements from the *Eleanor and Franklin* miniseries—specifically Eleanor's journey to become independent while working with Louis Howe—with Franklin's attempt to rebuild himself after his illness, seen in *Sunrise at Campo-*

*bello*, with a subplot dealing with the pair striving to come together again after drifting around in the early 1920s.

Branagh makes for a good Franklin although perhaps a bit too dashing, and early in the film, he is too emotionally dour, due more to the script than to his performance. For example, an early sequence where Franklin sarcastically dismisses the idea of going to Warm Springs as quackery seems inconsistent with someone who grew up believing the spas of Europe helped his father's health; also, Franklin was neither dismissive of nor afraid to interact with other polio sufferers in his early visits there, as seen in the film. Franklin's angry interactions with the train usher over Fred Botts being forced to travel in the baggage car is also a fantasy, as Botts actively sought the use of the baggage car for his wheelchair and arrived cheerful, healthy, and without incident.

The timeline has also been conflated, suggesting Franklin refused to deal with his affliction until he went to Warm Springs in 1924, when he had already made vast progress in adapting to his wheelchair and being able to move upright in his leg braces, as proven by his "Happy Warrior" appearance for Al Smith earlier that year (the final sequence in *Warm Springs* showing FDR arriving at the 1928 convention to once again nominate Al Smith plays very much like the ending to *Sunrise at Campobello*). This also makes Eleanor's concerns about Franklin seem trivial, as by the time he was visiting Warm Springs often, he was already beginning to look ahead to returning as a public figure, and the pair had adapted to their respective lifestyles, together and apart. Yet most of these quibbles come from too much research; the movie is fairly accurate in its depiction of what occurred, and to give the narrative a proper character arc, we must forgive the minor changes needed to create a dramatic film, as we've already witnessed in many films discussed here.

Interestingly, the movie demonstrates the distancing between Franklin and Eleanor by flashing back to Eleanor's discovery of Franklin's affair with Lucy Mercer. This discovery and the discussion of a possible divorce vetoed by Sara and Louis Howe are very similar to that seen in *Eleanor and Franklin*. That's not to suggest that it copies it verbatim but merely that there are only so many differences one can make with acknowledged events. In *Warm Springs*, the reasoning for these moments is to show why Eleanor is unemotional with Franklin and warms to him as events play out. It also suggests Franklin's earlier self-centeredness, with his time in Warm Springs being the breakthrough that would turn him by 1928 into the more personable man who could guide the country as president in the 1930s. *Sunrise at Campobello* makes a similar conclusion about Franklin, situating it only four years earlier in 1924, and it's not surprising. As mentioned at the beginning of the chapter, many saw Franklin as a wisp of a politician in his early career who grew into a powerhouse upon his return in 1928. To conclude that his efforts dealing with polio were when the switch flipped in Franklin's personality is a sensible, albeit perhaps too easy, conclusion to make, and it ends each film on an upbeat, with Franklin being cheered by many as he stands tall.

Ironically, some researchers have suggested that his affair with Lucy was the linchpin to this reversal in behavior that toughened him up, but such an idea has never been hinted at in the movies. Yet the film returns us again to the theme of Franklin as someone who cheated on his wife. We saw it before in *Eleanor and Franklin*, we see it again here, and we'll see it in the future in depictions of FDR, where sex is a defining factor of Franklin's personality—according to the movies at least.

Beyond television, the next theatrical appearance of Franklin Roosevelt comes with director Michael Bay's three-hour-long movie *Pearl Harbor* (2001). As one would expect, most of the film takes place at Pearl Harbor, with transitions to the Japanese invasion fleet moving in, like in *Tora, Tora, Tora* (1970), and much (some say too much) time is spent on a love-triangle storyline that has nothing to do with the battle that led to the United States entering World War II. At certain moments in the film, the scene shifts to Washington, DC, with Roosevelt, played by Jon Voight (*Midnight Cowboy, Deliverance, Coming Home*) being advised of the situation. Although Voight doesn't really capture the voice at all, he carries off the role, especially in a scene showing his stunned reaction to reading a report on how the navy was decimated by the Japanese in the December 7, 1941, attack. The scene is not wholly factual, but it does touch on Roosevelt's love for the navy, which has basis in fact. However, the actor is not served well by the script in a cringeworthy scene where Roosevelt, upon being told by his military advisors that retaliation against the attack can't be done, showboats by pulling himself out of his wheelchair to stand ("Head back, George! Get back," he screams, red-faced, as a servant tries to help) to prove that nothing is impossible. Not only is the scene historically inaccurate (like other moments in the film, which is one reason the movie got such lackluster reviews), but also it abuses the notion that Roosevelt routinely went around pointing out his inability to walk as a trump card to win arguments. It's supposed to be a triumphant moment in the picture and instead is quite embarrassing to watch if one knows Roosevelt's feelings toward his physical condition.

Another angry Roosevelt, played by Henry Goodman, briefly appears in the parody film *Churchill: The Hollywood Years* (2004), written and directed by Peter Richardson. The movie was released to theaters in the United Kingdom before disappearing without even a US video release but is worth a mention for its setup by the former *Comic Strip* writer and performer. The film makes fun of typical Hollywood war movies that depict battles fought by foreign armies as being won by a small group of Americans or even a singular US patriot. In this case, the real Winston Churchill is a young American GI who single-handedly defeats Hitler before he can marry into British royalty. A similar setup for a parody film can be found in the 2012 straight-to-video release *FDR: American Badass!* with Franklin performed by Barry Bostwick (Washington in the 1984 miniseries *George Washington*). Written by Ross Patterson (who costars) and directed by Garrett Brawith, *American Badass!* immediately diverges from historical accuracy by suggesting FDR became wheelchair bound after being attacked by a Nazi werewolf in 1921. Even so, with the help of similar characters from history who have no comparable likenesses to the real people, such as Louis (Bruce McGill) and Eleanor (Lin Shaye), and with a pep talk from a pot-smoking Abraham Lincoln (Kevin Sorbo), Franklin crafts retaliation against the Axis werewolves and single-handedly wins the war. The film is a scatological mess (literally so in one scene) that on occasion comes up with a funny gag, thanks to a game cast willing to go all out. As an aside, the casting of Bruce McGill in such a low-budget presidential parody in the same year he appeared in Steven Spielberg's *Lincoln* as Edwin Stanton and as Calvin Coolidge in the movie *Outlaws* is also surprising, although he is effective in all three.

Of course, as with *Churchill: The Hollywood Years*, the joke is that the movie portrays Franklin Roosevelt and other real figures of the period in a way that obviously didn't exist, as certainly FDR did not fight werewolves during World War II. Yet even with the obvious satire, it is surprising how it portrays these real individuals in a manner that would have never seen the light of day in even the most anti-FDR material while Roosevelt was alive. What at one time would have been discarded immediately as being in bad taste, libelous, and a call for burning torches and pitchforks against the creators is now seen as permissible. Admittedly, and perhaps remarkably, *FDR: American Badass!* allows for some character development, with the relationship between Franklin and Eleanor (who are never seen as other than monogamous) blossoming in its final feel-good moments and making it rather hard to completely dislike it, even if it does overstay its welcome (both it and *Churchill: The Hollywood Years* would have played better as five- to ten-minute shorts rather than full-length features).

*Hyde Park on Hudson* (2012) is the most recent theatrical film about Roosevelt, although he is mainly a secondary character who guides the narrative, with the focus on his sixth cousin Margaret "Daisy" Suckley, who became a close friend of Franklin and the family during the 1930s and 1940s as well as helped to run Roosevelt's presidential library. While there had been some speculation about how close the two were, there has never been any evidence to suggest that they were lovers, an idea that the film's plot deeply depends on. *Hyde Park on Hudson* was originally developed by screenwriter Richard Nelson (*Chess, The Rhinebeck Panorama*) and produced in 2009 as a radio play on BBC3, with Tim Pigott-Smith as Franklin, Emma Fielding as Daisy, and Julia Swift as Eleanor. The play as well as the movie deal with Daisy's memories of her friendship with Franklin during the presidential years, leading up to a June 1939 visit by King George VI and Queen Elizabeth at Hyde Park to promote friendship at a vital time for England, with war pressing on them. As the royals try to fit in during their visit, the intimate friendship that has developed between Daisy and Franklin comes to a head when Daisy finds out that there are several women in Franklin's inner circle in similar relationships with him.

A version of the play began filming in 2011, with Roger Michell (*Notting Hill, My Cousin Rachel*) directing. The casting of Bill Murray (*Groundhog Day, Ghostbusters*) as FDR surprised some, as he remains known for comedic roles, but he had played more serious roles, such as in *Lost in Translation* (2003) and even *The Razor's Edge* (1984). Oddly, he's not very identifiable in the role as scripted, with little in his voice, looks, or actions to suggest the Franklin Roosevelt familiar to audiences beyond the standard-issue pince-nez spectacles, the cigarette holder, and his ever-present alcohol (many movies and television shows depict Franklin as a heavy drinker). He is even seen walking around on crutches and maneuvering around furniture without assistance, a feat impossible for the president to do unassisted, even in the best of health after contracting polio. The production wants to show us Franklin as laidback and ready with a quip, which suits Murray well, as that is his public persona, but without the other elements of Roosevelt's personality shining through, it feels more like President Bill Murray rather than President Roosevelt. Laura Linney, who played a presidential mistress in *Dave* (1993) and appeared in a thriller about the killing of a presidential mistress in the 1997 film *Absolute Power*, stars as Daisy Suckley and does what she can with a character scripted as childlike rather than introverted. Also in the cast are Samuel West as George VI, Olivia Colman (who plays the queen's daughter Elizabeth II in the series *The Crown*) as Elizabeth, Elizabeth Marvel as Missy LeHand, Olivia Williams as a briefly seen Eleanor, and Elizabeth Wilson as Sara.

The film was promoted in an ill-advised move as a comedy, with a movie poster putting a laughing Bill Murray front and center, with Linney as Daisy giving the camera a knowing smile, suggesting hilarious, perhaps naughty, adventures with FDR. While the film does have some humorous touches, those come mainly from the babes-in-the-woods antics of the king and queen as they arrive and attempt to bear with the Americans. Such moments quickly become more sober, as we see their concerns about this very important visit and their fears that they are being set up to be mocked. In many ways, this storyline (which some critics quickly wrote off as only there to make the king and queen foolish for the sake of comedy), along with Franklin running such a meeting in hopes of it being beneficial for all, would have made for a fascinating movie alone. For example, the scene with Franklin and George VI discussing their difficulties—Franklin's wheelchair versus Bertie's stutter—while not perhaps factual, at least has a dramatic purpose in discussing Franklin's stance that the public's need for strong leaders will allow certain human elements to be ignored as long as it is not pressed upon them.

Yet the dramatic focus of the film is on Daisy, who is invited to visit Franklin in the early 1930s, although the film does poorly in establishing

The movie poster art for *Hyde Park on Hudson* (2012), with Bill Murray as FDR. The poster makes the film out to be a wry comedy, but it is actually a drama. *Courtesy of PhotoFest.*

how long Daisy was a regular visitor to not just Franklin but also the entire Roosevelt family. The film suggests Daisy was soon under Franklin's
spell, to the willful ignorance of Eleanor and the annoyance of Missy
LeHand. Meanwhile, Franklin is also henpecked by all the women
around him except Daisy, especially his mother. (Elizabeth is also quite
snappish with the king at several moments, helping to complete a rather
unfortunate misogynistic feel to the movie.) The film ends with Daisy
coming to terms with her place as just one of many women who services the president. There's also the moment where Franklin convinces
George VI to eat a hot dog for the cameras and help push a relatable
image of the British to gain sympathy for the country, just as the German were about to start bombing a few months later in World War II.
Daisy even narrates how this moment was important to that cultivation
of friendship between the two countries, even though the real-life Daisy
admitted to reporters over the years that she never understood what the
big deal was.

As stated though, that story demonstrating Franklin's ability to put
people at ease, which helped him so well during his presidency, along
with the willingness of George VI to risk embarrassment to help bring
the countries together, takes a backseat to what the film focuses on and
the press ate up in reviews: the idea of Roosevelt as a nihilist and sexual
predator. This is made worse in that most historians agree that Daisy's
relationship may have been sometimes flirtatious, but there has been
no evidence of any type of sexual activity between the pair at any time,
even as the film attempts to brush it off as stories taken directly from her
diaries. It goes deeper than this: Researchers may still argue about how
intimate Franklin was with Lucy Mercer (who gets a brief name-check
in the film), but once that gate was opened by such fare as *Eleanor
and Franklin* and *Warm Springs*, it became easier to suggest that any
woman Roosevelt spent time with—except for Eleanor—was a potential
lover. Missy LeHand, reporter Dorothy Schiff (who later denied any affair with Roosevelt), and Daisy Suckley all have been seen as probable
mistresses of the president, although no one has ever uncovered information to prove such. Even *Atlantic Crossing* (2020), a recent eight-part
television series from Norway that deals with Franklin (a handsome Kyle
MacLachlan) assisting Princess Martha (Sofia Helin) and her husband
in the aftermath of the Nazi invasion of their country, plays up a possible

romantic pairing between FDR and the princess. This is most evident
in a scene in one episode that is nearly a frame-by-frame remake from
*Hyde Park on Hudson* of Franklin waving off security following him so
he can go off for some alone time with the woman in his car. And while
there had been some rumors even at the time about the way the two in-
teracted, including the princess being Franklin's "last great love," there
is simply no evidence anything odd occurred between the two beyond
friendship. Further, as with *Hyde Park on Hudson*, it dilutes a dramatic
story of people earning the trust of others during a time of war, simply to
suggest Franklin's motives were only to fulfill his own emotional, if not
physical, needs or—perhaps worse—that the Princess may have been
emotionally manipulating the president for political favors.

*Hyde Park on Hudson* ends with a narrative from Daisy telling the
viewers that there used to be a time in America where things could be
kept private, which is poignant in a movie that wishes to expose emotional events pertaining to Franklin Roosevelt that many researchers do
not believe even occurred. Roosevelt's reign as president was a gift in
the media for himself and the country; even Americans who opposed
FDR's programs or steering the country into World War II would admit
that he was successful in holding sway over the American public and
was beloved by many people. To give *Hyde Park on Hudson* some due,
it may not have been true dialogue from the man, but the film isn't far
off when discussing Roosevelt's belief that the people's image of our
leaders is more important than the humans behind the image. He never
shied away from the fact that he had trouble walking due to polio, but he
also avoided emphasizing the wheelchair and his difficulties in standing
or walking upright assisted. And with that spark of control of the world's
perception of him came the ability to guide the media's hand on how he
was represented, even for a time after his death.

Franklin Delano Roosevelt's presidential career came at the same
time that Americans began falling in love with talking pictures. Hollywood shook hands with the White House and gave us valentines to Roosevelt, showing him as the happy warrior, the man who would heal us,
guide us, even sing and dance. Further, through the control of the FCC
and the short-lived OWI, Roosevelt had more say over his depiction in
movies than any president before or since. It worked because the movies gave us that vision of FDR that we wanted. We didn't need to see

the wheelchair or Roosevelt's affairs or even his political mistakes; like with our Founding Fathers, we wanted the hero. Perhaps the financial disappointment of *Hyde Park on Hudson* after potential ticket buyers heard the plot shows we're still not comfortable in seeing Roosevelt any other way.

The family tried to continue protecting that stately version of Franklin after he died, but they knew the days of being able to manage that image would last only so long. By the 1970s, we had heard of John F. Kennedy and his affairs with women before and after entering the White House, and we had seen Nixon fall to scandal. The scars of reality were changing our views of the presidency, and once Eleanor's own words revealed a glimpse of the real man behind the image, the gloves were off, and Hollywood went their own way with how Roosevelt could be seen in the movies, as would be the case for those who followed him.

There no doubt will be more Franklin Delano Roosevelts in the future of cinema, perhaps even one that will challenge Ralph Bellamy and Edward Herrmann in our mind's-eye image of how FDR should look and act. Will there be more emphasis on the rumors of the times, or will the storytellers to come opt to find the facts as thrilling?

The most recent theatrical film to feature Roosevelt is the 2014 movie *The Monuments Men*, starring George Clooney, Matt Damon, and Bill Murray (but not as the president). The movie is a fact-based story about a group sanctioned by Roosevelt to locate historical art pieces and protect them from the Nazis and destruction during the final days of World War II. Franklin Roosevelt, played by Michael Dalton, is seen only briefly near the beginning of the film, as he is being given a lecture about the endangered art objects in Europe that need protection. Ironically, FDR is shown only from the back and in shadows, with only his cigarette holder clearly in view—just like the old days when we believed.

## 8

# PRESIDENT NOIR

## The President in Thrillers

Take running alongside that limousine: It'd take an antitank missile to put a dent in that damn thing. There we are, out for show, trying to make the president look more presidential.

—Frank Horrigan (Clint Eastwood) describing the job of the
Secret Service in *In the Line of Fire* (1993)

**C**hapter 2 shows the president, or an associate of the president, as a pawn to be used thanks to a coup or kidnapping attempt. There are so many films with that structure that they needed to be separated from other action thrillers or crime dramas that feature the president in some form of danger or, in some cases, the cause of danger. Still, there are plenty of other films that use the presidency in some manner to set up the plot. Further, just as the MacGuffin role of the president in previously discussed films shows the importance of a character's mission (because it's coming from the president, for gosh sakes!), then so, too, can a president propel a suspenseful movie forward to give the plot an added element of importance or a variation on a theme. For example, *My Fellow Americans* in chapter 5 features a plot that follows the structure of an action thriller, with two people on the run, trying to prove their innocence and avoid being killed. The comedy and drama come from the bonus of those two individuals being former presidents.

One of the first thrillers to center around a president outside the kidnapping format is *Suddenly* from 1954. The movie stars Frank Sinatra as John Baron, a gunman who plans to assassinate the president when his train stops in a Californian small town named Suddenly (hints of the possible Baltimore plot against Lincoln, as mentioned in chapter 4). To do so, Baron and his two partners take over a house that is in direct line of sight of the train station, holding the family of the household and the local sheriff (Sterling Hayden) hostage. The film then deals with the family and the sheriff attempting to either alert the people outside the house to what is happening or to stop Baron and his men somehow. The movie was directed by Lewis Allen and written by Richard Sales, who based it on his own short story (Sales comes up again here in a bit). It is one of the few examples of Sinatra in a villainous role, and reviews of his efforts were positive. As it turns out, the train never stops in the small town, making the efforts of the hitman pointless. Nevertheless, the needs of the family to take out Baron are still there, as he proves himself to be a psychopath who plans on killing everyone in the house once he has done his job, thus making the president's visit merely the starting point for everything that follows.

There were rumors for years that Lee Harvey Oswald saw the movie a month before arriving in Dallas on November 23, 1963, to assassinate John F. Kennedy (research shows that *Suddenly* was playing in a syndication television package at the time around the country, although the closest it played in October 1963 was El Paso, six hundred miles from Dallas, so pretty unlikely with television reception at the time). The story goes that when Frank Sinatra heard about Oswald possibly watching the movie showing him as a would-be presidential assassin, he asked that the United Artists pull the film from distribution. There's never been evidence of this, and most likely the film simply faded from view for many years and was forgotten. That is, until the 1980s, when movies on videocassette became a common sales item. With *Suddenly* out of circulation, it also went out of copyright, allowing any video company to release the movie on video without paying a studio, so the film could be seen by a much wider audience. Uwe Boll directed a made-for-television update to the film in 2013 starring Ray Liotta that diverges from the original but essentially tells the same story.

Sinatra was involved with another assassination-plot film soon after *Suddenly*, *The Manchurian Candidate* (1962), which also was rumored to have been suppressed due to the JFK assassination. Directed by John Frankenheimer (*Seven Days in May*, *Birdman of Alcatraz*, *Black Sunday*) and written by George Axelrod based a novel of the same name by Richard Condon, the movie stars Frank Sinatra as Bennett Marco,

**Frank Sinatra, as the would-be assassin, looking ready to get his shot at the president in the 1954 film *Suddenly*. Courtesy of PhotoFest.**

a man who fought in the Korean War with Raymond Shaw (Laurence Harvey), the stepson to Senator John Iselin (James Gregory), a red-baiting imbecile who is on his way to the presidency thanks to Shaw's mother, Eleanor (Angela Lansbury). Shaw returns from Korea as a war hero, but Marco and some of the other men from their unit begin having nightmares where they are being brainwashed by Chinese scientists. As Marco continues to investigate, it turns out that Shaw has been made a sleeper agent with plans for him to assassinate a presidential candidate so that the stooge Senator Iselin can be nominated and become the next president. Racing against time, Marco tries to stop Shaw from going forward with the plan, with unusual results.

*The Manchurian Candidate* is considered a classic psychological thriller and a classic film beyond that. Sinatra is good as a man starting to question his own history, although the love-interest story with Janet Leigh seems tossed in for little reason. Laurence Harvey has the role of his career as the troubled, awkward Raymond Shaw, who could so readily be a good guy if only given the chance. The film's top actor is Angela Lansbury, however, who plays the manipulative Eleanor, so ready to use even her own son in order to gain the power she needs (see *State of the Union* in chapter 5 for Lansbury as another manipulator behind the throne). Despite rumors that Sinatra had gotten the film pulled from distribution after the assassination, it simply had run its course in theaters, and there wasn't enough interest in the movie for it to be revived until the 1980s, when, once again, video helped the film reclaim its spot in many "top ten" film lists.

Yet like *Suddenly, the Manchurian Candidate* doesn't feature a president, only the idea of someone wanting to do something involving the president or presidency. It was another twenty-five years before a movie dealt with another assassination attempt involving the president, although this time it's the president himself who okays the deed. The movie is *Assassination*, released in 1987 by Cannon Films, directed by Peter Hunt, and written by Richard Sale, who had done *Suddenly*. The film stars Charles Bronson as Jay Killian, a member of the Secret Service given the job of protecting the new First Lady (Jill Ireland) instead of the president, Calvin Craig (Charles Howerton). Killian is not thrilled with the job and even less so when he discovers that the First Lady is a snob who refuses to follow his rules to help protect her. Soon enough, it appears that a group of people are out to kill her, and when Killian figures out that it is the president who wants her dead to stop her from revealing personal information about him, he knows they will have go on the run.

The film's plot isn't that unusual in itself; it reflects such earlier movies as *The Gauntlet* (1977), with Clint Eastwood as a cop who is supposed to protect a witness (Sondra Locke) and ends up on the run because of information she has, leading to others wanting them dead. However, the added touch of the target being the First Lady and the villain being the president makes for an interesting twist on the concept. *End Game* (2006), starring Cuba Gooding Jr., puts a spin on a similar story, as it begins with the president (Jack Scalia) being assassinated and Alex Thomas (Gooding) as a Secret Service agent who begins working with a reporter (Angie Harmon), when they stumble on a conspiracy about his death. After many dead ends, Thomas finally discovers that the First Lady (Anne Archer) had orchestrated the killing because the president was cheating on her. Goose meets gander between *Assassination* and *End Game*, one could say.

*The Sentinel* (2006) also features another Secret Service agent falling for the First Lady, only this time it is Michael Douglas as Pete Garrison who falls for First Lady Sarah Ballentine (Kim Basinger). The film, directed by Clark Johnson and with a script by George Nolfi, has Garrison as an older agent who was involved in protecting Ronald Reagan in the failed assassination attempt and is admired, but his affair with the First Lady troubles him. When Garrison finds out that there are plans by the KGB to have the president assassinated in Toronto (shades of *The Kidnapping of the President*), Garrison is suspected of lying, as he cannot pass a polygraph test due to his conflict over the First Lady. With the help of the First Lady coming clean about their relationship, however, Garrison finally convinces everyone about the assassination attempt and stops it in time, although he ends up having to resign his duties due to the affair.

If some of this plot sounds familiar, especially an older agent who must deal with the personal consequences of an earlier real attempt on a president's life, then one only needs to go back to the 1993 thriller *In the Line of Fire*. The movie, directed by Wolfgang Petersen (*Air Force One*) and written by Jeff Maguire, stars Clint Eastwood as near-retirement

Secret Service agent Frank Horrigan, who had been on detail with John F. Kennedy during his visit to Dallas in 1963. Evidence is collected to show that Mitch Leary (John Malkovich) is planning to assassinate the president (Jim Curley) at some point, but no one knows what he looks like or where he will strike. Leary becomes obsessed with Horrigan due to his Kennedy connection and begins contacting him to engage him on the upcoming assassination, feeling Horrigan is a kindred spirit. Horrigan has difficulty controlling his anger over the patronizing Leary, while realizing his age is catching up to him and may cause him to make mistakes that could end up costing the president his life.

Again, the president is incidental in the story, and his biggest scene is where he is rushed out after the assassination attempt. The movie is mainly about Horrigan and his regrets in his career but also deals with Leary's bizarre fan worship. As writer Jeff Maguire pointed out in 2020, the script had been pitched for an older actor to play the part, with the backstory of the JFK assassination, but at one point, Tom Cruise took interest in the script and requested that it be written out, as he would have been too young to play such a part. After he passed, as did Sean Connery, it was picked up by Clint Eastwood, leaving the narrative and historical link to the past in the film intact, which helps ground the film better than if that plot thread had been changed.

*The Sum of All Fears* (2002), the final theatrical release in the series based on the character Jack Ryan created by Tom Clancy, features an attempt on the president's life on a much deadlier scale than is typical. Enemies of both the United States and Russia try to set each against the other with attacks, including one involving a nuclear device at a stadium in Baltimore, where the president (James Cromwell) is watching a football game. Surprisingly, the film does not have a traditional "stopping the bomb at the last second" moment that would be expected in most spy thrillers. Instead, the president is hastily moved out of the stadium, and his motorcade is just outside deadly range of the bomb when it explodes (although not quite enough to avoid the blast, sending his car off the road in the blast waves, like Marine One being destroyed in a similar fashion in *Dawn's Early Light*). On one hand, the president is saved, but on the other, a stadium full of people and anyone within miles of the blast are instantly killed, leading to even further complications with

Russia and probably the most unnerving remedy seen in movies when it comes to an attempt on the president's life.

A return to more standard spy fare is *xXx: State of the Union* (2005), with Ice Cube as Darius Stone, an ex-Navy SEAL who must deal with the secretary of defense, a former boss, who has plans to kill the president (Peter Straus) and others in order to become the new president and stop the administration's aim to reduce military spending. It's a common theme of the "president is kidnapped" films, only with the emphasis on assassination. Meanwhile, two films from 2008 deal with assassination attempts that veer off to tell other types of stories, *Nothing but the Truth* and *Vantage Point*. *Nothing but the Truth* begins with the attempted assassination of the president (Scott Williamson) in Venezuela, which leads to the United States bombing the country in retaliation. After this, the president is no longer part of the story, as it focuses instead on Rachel Armstrong (Kate Beckinsale), who receives information from an accidental source that a person in the CIA had discovered the Venezuelans had nothing to do with the assassination attempt. Because of her reporting in the press on the situation, an operative's identity is revealed, and Armstrong is threatened with prison unless she reveals her source. The remainder of the movie then deals with what occurs when she refuses to do just that. Thus, once again, we have a president setting up the plot but then is jettisoned from the story when he is no longer needed.

*Vantage Point* takes a more action-oriented tact, as well as dealing with multiple viewpoints of an assassination attempt on the president. Dennis Quaid stars as Secret Service agent Thomas Barnes, who must track down who was involved in an attempt on President Ashton (William Hurt) during an outdoor speech in Salamanca, Spain. To do this, multiple people at the event are interviewed, allowing the film to rewind and reset what occurred to show the attack from different points of view, like an action-film variation of Akira Kurosawa's *Rashomon* (1950). In the end, it turns out there is a mole with the Secret Service who has been helping the attackers (and if you're this far in the book, then you're bound to suspect that the Secret Service sure seems to have problems with moles among their ranks). With the protagonist on his way to save the president, the president actively helps to stop his own kidnapping in an action-president moment to end the film.

One of the most recent presidential assassination plot thrillers occurs in 2010's *Salt*, starring Angelina Jolie as the title character, a CIA operative who turns out to be a sleeper agent assigned to kill the president (Hunt Block). The movie is directed by Phillip Noyce and written by Kurt Wimmer and features several twists and turns as Salt works out whom to believe and how to subvert her mission to stop the nuclear retaliation planned by a crazed member of the CIA that will occur with the president's death. In the director's cut of the film, the bad guy succeeds in killing the president, but the country avoids the nuclear destruction. Doing so allows for a new president to be named, who quite possibly is a sleeper agent himself, thus giving the film one final twist, with a destructive president now in office. The bad guys must win once in a while, it seems.

Surprisingly, considering how often earlier western movies have featured "real" presidents sending agents off on missions like a cowboy M to a bronco-busting James Bond, there are relatively few examples of fictional presidents doing so in films set during modern times. The main exception is in the films of Robert Rodriguez, who has used this setup in at least three films, such as *Machete Kills* (2013), where the president (Charlie Sheen) sends Mexican Federale and hero Machete to stop a man who plans to fire a nuclear missile at Washington, DC. When he succeeds in stopping the plan but sees the villain escape, the president offers another job to Machete: to find the bad guy in space, thus setting up a sequel film that unfortunately was never made. Rodriguez did so again with two of his *Spy Kids* movies, featuring Alexa Vega and Daryl Sabara as the Cortez siblings, the children of two Secret Service agents who become agents themselves. In *Spy Kids 2: The Island of Lost Dreams*, the president (Christopher McDonald) arrives to push the plot along near the end of the movie and fire the bad guy who was working under him. In *Spy Kids 3-D: Game Over*, the president (George Clooney) sends Juni Cortez to find his sister, who was lost in a mission. As is typical of the MacGuffin president in the movies, once the missions have been set, the president pretty much disappears from the films.

At least the president is trying to do the right thing in many of these cases, but like in *Assassination*, a small number of movies have been done over the years to show the president abusing power. The first of these is the 1994 Jack Ryan film *Clear and Present Danger*, starring Harrison

Ford as Ryan and directed by Phillip Noyce (*Salt*). In that movie, the president (Donald Moffat) orchestrates the destruction of a drug cartel in Colombia in order to help cover up the embezzlement from the cartel by a close friend of the president. This only leads to worse problems for those trying to stop the drug cartels as well as for Ryan, and once Ryan figures out the details, he goes public with the president's involvement. Escalating issues also occur in *Absolute Power*, a 1997 movie with Clint Eastwood as Luther Whitney, a jewel thief who, while trying to rob a house of a billionaire, witnesses the president (Gene Hackman) attack the billionaire's wife in a drunken rage. When she defends herself, the president cries out in pain, leading to Secret Service agents arriving and, assuming the woman was attacking the president, killing her. Whitney manages to escape with money and the weapon the woman had used, with determination to bring the president to justice. With his daughter in danger, Whitney must avoid those who want him silenced as he works out a way to tell the billionaire (E. G. Marshall) what occurred to his wife. The film ends with news breaking that the troubled president had killed himself with the same letter opener that the billionaire's wife had used on the president. It is implied that the billionaire had done

**Gene Hackman as the president who causes the death of a woman and tries to cover it up in *Absolute Power* (1997). *Courtesy of PhotoFest.***

the deed while visiting the president after Whitney gives the man the weapon his wife had used, which satisfies Whitney's sense of justice but avoids giving us a final showdown between our hero and the bad guy (although that probably would have simply ended with more Secret Service agents shooting Whitney, so it's probably for the best this way).

*Murder at 1600*, which came out the same year as *Absolute Power*, follows a death at the White House of a secretary. Directed by Dwight Little and written by Wayne Beach and David Hodgin, the movie has Wesley Snipes as police detective Harlan Regis, who is assigned to the case. While investigating, Regis discovers that the president (Ronny Cox, who plays the president in the 1990 *Captain America*) and his son Kyle (Tate Donovan) had both been having an affair with the woman who is now dead. Eventually, the detective discovers that the national security advisor (Alan Alda) had the secretary murdered in order to blackmail the president into resigning so that the vice president (Chris Gillett), who agrees with the advisor's military plans against North Korea, can take over. When he is exposed, the advisor tries to shoot the president, only to be killed by the Secret Service, and we are left once again with the evil-vice-president plot where shenanigans ensue to get the person into the presidency.

Finally, *An Acceptable Loss* (2018) has a national security expert, Libby Lamm (Tika Sumpter), compiling notes to expose the president, Rachel Burke (Jamie Lee Curtis), who had bombed a terrorist meeting in Syria four years previously as vice president that killed more than 150,000 civilians. The president tries to talk Lamm into giving up her notes, but ultimately Lamm refuses to do so. At that point, the president decides that perhaps the truth can come out, and the chips can fall where they may, but her chief of staff decides to kill Lamm in an explosion that is blamed on another person. As it turns out, it is too late, as one of the people working with Lamm had already transmitted the notes to the press for release, sealing the fate of the president and her staff.

Not too surprisingly, action movies do not really lend themselves to telling us much about the presidency or those in power. It's all about the action, with the president's involvement merely heightening the importance of what occurs in the movies. Yet, starting off with the discussion of seeing the president involved in action films, it feels only natural that we would end up finding the president involved in dirty dealings of some type, even if the commander in chief makes excuses for them. After all, one of the best-known political movies of the 1970s, *All the President's Men*, focuses on one of the biggest scandals in presidential history, the Watergate cover-up. It would shock the nation and show that power could be abused on a level not expected. It would also spell the downfall of one of the more popular presidents of the twentieth century, as discussed in the next chapter.

## 9

# TRUMAN AND ONWARD

Bombs, Assassination, Scandals, and the Toilet

Fame is a vapor, popularity is an accident, riches take wings, those who cheer today may curse tomorrow and only one thing endures—character.

—Harry S. Truman

The first film to feature an actor portraying Harry Truman was also the first to portray FDR with the camera showing the actor's face, *The Beginning or the End* (1947). The portrayals of both presidents in the film faced hurdles, with the story of Roosevelt's family disagreements discussed in chapter 7. The issues for Truman came when the studio making the picture, MGM, wanted an agreement with the government on the script before filming. The OWI was no longer around to review Hollywood features; Truman ended the group in September 1945, and most of their functions moved to the CIA and OSS, but that didn't mean the White House wasn't keeping an eye on how the US government was being represented in movies. To help with the film, MGM gave script approval to the director of the Manhattan Project, General Leslie R. Groves, while Harry Truman also met with the producer to discuss the movie. As detailed in Greg Mitchell's book *The Beginning or the End: How Hollywood Learned to Stop Worrying and Love the Bomb,*

Truman initially agreed with the movie being a cautionary tale about the dangers of such a weapon, going so far as to give Marx the title of the film by stating, "Tell the world that in handling the atomic bomb, we are either at the beginning or the end." He was so enthused that his advice was promoted in newspaper articles at the time production was underway.

The White House's position quickly changed as the film began production, no doubt helped by General Groves's reaction to the polished script. At a time when there were growing concerns over the Cold War developing between the United States and the Soviets, plus a mostly now-forgotten backlash over the use of the bomb on Japanese cities at the end of the war, the White House felt the script enforced a negative view of the Manhattan Project. Soon, story elements that had the scientists involved raising concerns about the ethics behind the bomb were flattened, emphasizing the then commonly held belief that the bomb had to be developed and used to "save lives" in the war. Combine a need for a Hollywood film to have romance, and the film ultimately became a forgotten forerunner of docudramas to come, with the characters all in agreement over the necessity of the bomb to lead the way into a happy "nuclear family" future.

Truman had okayed an actor portraying him in the film, although he insisted in the tradition agreed to with FDR, that the actor playing him be filmed from behind his desk and, in this case, partially in shadows. The scene shows Roman Bohnen, who had appeared in both *Edge of Darkness* and *Mission to Moscow*, as Truman, discussing the use of the bomb in Japan with Truman's secretary, Charley Ross, played by Harry Carey. In June 1946, promotion of Bohnen in the role began in various newspaper articles about Hollywood happenings, with some going so far as to say that Bohnen looked like Truman "from a distance." Bohnen, in a brief interview with Bob Thomas at the time, even went into character to demonstrate some dialogue from the original scene, with Truman describing how Roosevelt's White House refused to give him information about the bomb: "When I was a senator, I didn't know anything about the bomb. They told me the big plants were bubblegum factories."

While Truman's initial thoughts on the film were that it would be an opportunity to discuss the ramifications and dangers of such nuclear weapons, the script had swung so far into a patriotic "we can do no wrong" direction after clearance from Groves and the White House that Truman was portrayed in the scene dismissively agreeing to the bombing because it was the right thing to do. After a Washington viewing of the completed film in November 1946, it was decided that the scene had to be reshot to make Truman appear more thinking, cautious, and yet firm in his agreement to use the bomb. Perhaps another reason for the restaging of the scene, as Mitchell mentions in his book, was due to the White House learning that Roman Bohnen was a possible member of the American Communist Party, which would not have looked good in the growing embers of what would become the Red Scare of the 1950s. Thus, not only was a new scene with Truman to be filmed, delaying the film from the January 1, 1947, opening it had hoped for, but also Bohnen was out as Truman by early December 1946.

The official reason, ignoring all the earlier press, was that Truman was not satisfied with Bohnen's performance, and the White House objected to his "nonmilitary posture," even though the scene is little more than Truman filmed from behind a desk in shadows. Bohnen's response to the news that he had been replaced was to write to Truman, as he told Hollywood reporter Erskine Johnson, contemplating that if the president really wanted to do it right, then he should play the part himself: "For history's sake, I thought since he did it, he should act it." Bohnen's statement may have been laced with sarcasm, but if so, Truman didn't take the bait and instead responded to Bohnen by thanking him, stating, "I don't want to be a movie star."

The new scene was filmed with Art Baker, an actor and announcer best known for hosting the 1950s television series he created *You Asked for It*, as Truman and Edward Earle as Ross. The sequence is very much a photocopy of an early scene in the movie, with FDR discussing the formation of the Manhattan Project with his secretary, except with Truman and Ross replacing them in the reasonings for dropping the bomb. Gone is the flippant attitude suggested by the dialogue Bohnen described to the press as well as the suggested callous dialogue. Instead, the movie's Truman runs down a list of reasons he should not feel bad about dropping the bomb, while describing the nuclear research as leading to a golden age of prosperity and well-being for the world. Ross even parrots the secretary's dialogue from the FDR scene, suggesting that if the enemy had the bomb, then they would surely use it on America, so the United States had to be the first.

Truman continues by stressing he had discussed the upcoming bombing with every expert at his disposal to show he thought long and hard ("must have spent many sleepless nights over it," as Ross says in response) before stating that leaflets would be dropped for ten days over Japanese cities to advise people to get away. In real life, although it is possible that leaflets were dropped (some still dispute if it is true), it has been suggested that the leaflets were neither specific to Hiroshima and Nagasaki alone nor were written in a way to suggest that the destruction to come would be more than the firebombing that was occurring in 1944 and 1945. In trying to show Truman's conflict in deciding to drop the bomb, the scene perpetuates the common myth that the United States was not just right in dropping the bomb on the two cities but also righteous in doing so. Thus, the movie builds on the atomic fairy tale of what good comes from the bomb popular with the US government at the time instead of addressing the fears and concerns the scientists and others had and still have over nuclear weapons, which was the initial purpose of the film.

*The Beginning or the End* came and went quickly at the box office, losing more than a third of its cost for MGM and facing tepid reviews around the country, with reviewers not taken in by the propaganda element of the feature. Hazel Flynn of *The Valley Times* stated that it was obvious Marx and Taurog "were not able to cope better with the subject . . . the awful holocaust which, no matter how we try to justify ourselves, still makes us wonder whether or not we were right." *The Beginning or the End* was a wartime propaganda picture when audiences were tired of the multiyear feast of them now that the war was over. Nor did they want to share their popcorn and candy with reminders of how thousands of men, women, and children were wiped out with a bomb that could so easily be dropped on themselves.

If ticket buyers wanted war-related films, then they were looking for more serious fare, such as the same year's *The Best Years of Our Lives* (featuring Truman reject Roman Bohnen) that deals with the ramifications of soldiers returning home after the war. Our appetite for the atomic age would be candy-coated soon enough in the 1950s, with giant atomic animal and insect mutations to laugh at as a means to shake off the fear of the bomb. *The Beginning or the End* was too soon, too clearly whitewashed, and—worst of all—too bland to find an audience. As Gita Bumpass reported in her review for the *Fort Worth Star-Telegram*, "It does not entertain. It couldn't, with doom forecast on the one hand, and the beginning of a fascinating new era the alternative."

Harry S. Truman found himself involved with moviemaking at a point in his life when he had no idea he would be doing so or that he would be president, which was understandable, as many others didn't expect to see him there either, including FDR. As mentioned in chapter 7, in the 1995 HBO movie *Truman*, starring Gary Sinise as Truman and based on David McCullough's biography, there is only one brief exchange between Truman and Roosevelt (Lee Richardson). This may seem like an afterthought, but it represents in filmic shorthand how the pair rarely had a chance to talk during the election or in the few weeks that Truman became Roosevelt's vice president. In fact, Roosevelt had been spending so much time in the Little White House in Georgia that he did not even inform Truman about the Manhattan Project (thus going back to Truman's joke in *The Beginning or the End* of being told about a bubblegum factory), and the new president received details only after being sworn in. It was a big step for a man who had not even seen himself being in politics until he was thirty years old.

Truman (1984–1972), the first president in fifty years who had not gone to college, was born and raised in Missouri (hence the nickname as the "Man from Missouri") where he handled a series of jobs before running his grandmother's six-hundred-acre farm until the age of thirty-three. He dabbled in politics by working as a road overseer and then the postmaster of Grandview, Missouri, before entering World War I in 1917 and becoming the commander of a division in the Second Battalion of the 129th. After returning from the war with the rank of major, he married his childhood sweetheart, Elizabeth "Bess" Wallace, and in 1922, he was elected county court judge in Jackson County, Missouri. A clash with the Ku Klux Klan, who thought Truman was part Jewish due to his grandfather being named Solomon Young, led to Truman not being reelected, but he returned in 1926 and set up public works projects before becoming a senator for the state in 1934.

Truman achieved these goals thanks to the help of party boss Tom Pendergast, and when Pendergast was sent to prison on bribery changes, there was an assumption that Truman would not be reelected due to their association. But even with the possibility of scandal following him, Truman refused to distance himself from Pendergast, and there was no evidence that Pendergast ever tried to make a deal with Truman, leading to his reelection. Truman made a name for himself as senator for going after war profiteers, with an estimated $15 billion saved from the investigations his committee was involved in, and it was through this effort that Truman ended up being thrown into the presidential race of 1944 as Roosevelt's vice president. With Roosevelt's win, Truman was sworn in on January 20, 1944. Seven weeks later, he took the oath of president after the death of Roosevelt in Georgia.

The world was rapidly changing. Germany surrendered less than a month after Truman took office, leading to the end of aggression in Europe, while Japan surrendered in August after the bombing of Hiroshima and Nagasaki (as well as the threat of invasion from Russia). Truman's stance on allowing the bombs to be dropped never wavered. He stated more than once that given the information he had and the argument that it would save more lives than lose in conventional warfare, he would not hesitate to do so again. It is an argument ongoing today, although with more distance, the less popular stance is Truman's.

With the war ending, so, too, ended the love affair with the Roosevelt ideology of the previous twelve years. Truman tried to carry on with the liberal leanings of the New Deal and at first kept much of Roosevelt's cabinet, but the fatherly Roosevelt had been replaced with a hard-nosed stepdad, and Truman's brisk attitude and coarse language skills would find a cold shoulder with the media. The war had also pushed off domestic concerns that now came back into focus, including dealing with segregation, inflation, and union strikes, while foreign concerns showed that Russia was looking to eat up parts of Europe and that China was rapidly retooling itself into a major communist power looking for recognition. Truman struggled with a Congress that had turned Republican and Southern Democrat, looking to loosen tax laws for the rich and restrict the progressive projects Truman wanted to pass. In July 1948, two years after being the first president to address the NAACP, Truman signed executive order 9981 to eliminate segregation in the armed forces and federal agencies, an act that was thought to destroy his chances with Southern voters. He also recognized Israel, an action strongly advised against by his cabinet as causing issues with other countries in the Middle East. Many thought he would not get reelected in 1948, but a stunning landslide against Thomas Dewey resulted in the famous photo of Truman holding up the *Chicago Tribune* with the incorrect headline, "Dewey Defeats Truman."

Truman went on to help create the North Atlantic Treaty Organization (NATO) and to help structure the United Nations while also working to form the US Air Force, the Central Intelligence Agency (CIA), and the National Security Agency (NSA). There were dwindling returns from Congress on his other prepared plans for the country, however, and the growing success of Senator Joseph McCarthy, Representative Richard Nixon, and the House Un-American Activities Committee (HUAC) were seeding discourse in Congress that stalled progress. The invasion of South Korea by North Korea in 1950 created another headache for Truman, who agreed to help with UN forces to battle the invasion, only to run into trouble with its commander, the World War II hero General Douglas MacArthur. The Battle of Inchon helped pushed the North Koreans back, and there was hope for a cease-fire, but MacArthur's public insistence that the war needed to push into China went against Truman's orders and drew the Chinese into the war in defense of the North Koreans. After firing the war hero MacArthur, as well as a rebuke over the White House reference to the war as a "police action," Truman's reputation was damaged, which was a goldmine for Republicans looking to the presidency in 1952.

As it was, the Twenty-Second Amendment, passed by a mostly Republican Congress in retaliation for Roosevelt's four terms, made it so a president could serve no more than two terms or one additional term, if they had served less than two years of a previous term if another president's term was cut short. However, the amendment had a loophole for Truman, where it only became active after the amendment had been passed; therefore Truman could have run again if he wanted (he would even tease a run after retiring from politics, saying he planned to run again when he was ninety). Even so, Truman saw the writing on the wall and looked to Dwight Eisenhower to run for the Democratic nomination. Eisenhower declined, only to be talked into doing so instead for the Republicans. Against Adlai Stevenson, Eisenhower won the election in 1952 to become the thirty-fourth president of the United States.

Truman retired, although he was always ready to tell people his thoughts if asked. He continued to press McCarthy and Nixon, going so far as famously saying, "Richard Nixon is a no-good lying bastard. He can lie out of both sides of his mouth at the same time, and if he ever caught himself telling the truth, he'd lie just to keep his hand in." Although seen as a bit of a joke during and after his presidential run, by the 1970s, the public's perception of him reversed, and he was seen as a politician not afraid to talk from the gut and who appeared to be in sync with more liberal times (albeit Truman's attitude on the civil rights movement of the 1960s showed he had little patience for the demonstrations done in support), making him one of the better presidents of the twentieth century in various opinion polls.

*The Beginning or the End* was the only time Truman would take a full hand in how he was presented in the movies, mainly as there wasn't much call for him to be seen in films until the 1970s, when interest had reemerged. Both Truman (Jerry Kaliszewski) and Roosevelt (Innokenty Smoktunovsky) are represented in the Russian two-part film from 1974 *Take Aim* but simply to fill out the atmosphere of a story dealing with the Manhattan Project and the Soviets' response of getting their hands on the weapon. The ABC television network in 1974 did a one-hour film in their *Portrait* series on Truman, starring Robert Vaughn (*The Man from U.N.C.L.E.*) as the president. "The Man from Independence," however, deals only with a dramatic representation of Truman's confrontation with the Ku Klux Klan while working as a county judge and nothing more. Vaughn, who at times looks more like Lyndon Johnson instead of Truman, is fine in the role, although the story is slight and has nothing to do with the presidency. (One suspects Vaughn probably grimaced at the show's title, trying to play off his old series, as well.)

The next appearance of Truman takes a page from FDR, with a stage play written about Truman that was performed around the country first before being committed to celluloid. The difference this time is how it was presented on the screen. The project was *Give 'Em Hell, Harry!*—a phrase shouted to the Republicans during a speech on the 1948 campaign trail in Bremerton, Washington. Truman's response, which commonly does not get reported, was, "I don't give them hell. I just tell the truth about them, and they think it's hell." The play was put together by producer-writer Samuel Gallu using quotes from Truman's various

**James Whitmore recreating the famous picture of Harry Truman with the dubious *Chicago Daily Tribune* headline in *Give 'Em Hell, Harry!* (1975). Official press still, author's collection, © 1975 by Avco Embassy Pictures.**

speeches, interviews, and letters from over the years. The stage production was directed by Peter Hunt (*1776*), with Steve Binder (*Elvis Presley's '68 Comeback Special, The Star Wars Holiday Special*) directing the cameras for the film version. Playing Truman was James Whitmore, who became well known in his one-man show *Will Rogers' USA*, which he starred in 1970. Although appearing in many movies over the years, Whitmore is probably best remembered today as Brooks Hatlen, the old librarian in *The Shawshank Redemption* (1994).

This, too, was a one-man show, with Whitmore interacting either with the audience or with individuals simply not seen onstage with him. The sets were minimal, with only a few desks, the back of a train's caboose, and a couple props. The focus mainly was on Whitmore, who doesn't overdo the makeup to play the role—simply glasses and straight, short hair—but he comes across well in the fast clip of a voice that Truman was remembered for. The play begins with Truman in office as president, with act 1 looking at his younger days, including talking back to the Ku Klux Klan, his relationship with Pendergast, his early days struggling in business, and World War I. Act 2 follows his second term, including winning against the odds in his reelection and the famous *Chicago Tribune*, dropping the bombs, MacArthur, his feelings on Richard Nixon, and disappointment in Eisenhower not taking on McCarthy when he could. Truman even gets a turn at the piano, a favorite instrument he was known to play at parties, in order to play Thomas Dewey's unused victory song.

The play had the cooperation of Truman's daughter Margaret, who appeared for opening night on March 19, 1975, in Hershey, Pennsylvania, whereupon it went on an eleven-city tour. President Gerald Ford saw the play at Ford's Theatre in April 1975, being the first president to see a play there since Lincoln. Two performances were then recorded with eight to nine cameras at the Moore Theatre in Seattle, Washington (the final stop of the tour). The filming of the show was done with TheatroVision, a system created by Bill Sargent that involved a method of video recording that could be transferred to 16mm and 35mm film (*Richard Pryor Live in Concert* from 1979 was another TheatroVision production and probably Sargent's biggest success using the filming method). The show itself was filmed as is, with brief blackouts in the film to cover slight edits of shots used between scenes. Whitmore is very energetic, with his rapid-fire responses as Truman, including a somewhat off-putting wheeze that was actually a common trait in Truman's speech pattern. With it being a one-man show, there is a slight oddness as Whitmore as Truman interacts with people who aren't there, but after a short time, you get used to it. Whitmore is excellent in the role and comes across as friendly and relaxed, as one would wish Truman would have been in a proper frame of mind to talk about himself. It is little wonder that he was nominated for Best Actor for the Academy Awards and won a Grammy for Best Spoken Word Recording with the release of the soundtrack that year.

The film was sent to theaters in September 1975 as a special three-day run that was expanded in several cities after strong ticket sales, allowing the movie to make back forty-four times the cost of production. While that was going on, the play continued to be performed around this country but with a new performer in the role, Ed Flanders. Flanders is discussed in chapter 7 as playing Louis Howe in the *Eleanor and Franklin* miniseries. He played Truman in several productions in the next few years, particularly in television. His first was in *Harry S. Truman: Plain Speaking*, which is based on a book by Merle Miller that purports to be an oral biography by Truman (some have contested that, such as Francis Heller in a 1995 article for *American Heritage*, which reviews the tapes in comparison to what was used in the book). The hour-long special, with Flanders as an older, more sedate Truman talking to the camera about his life, ran on PBS in March 1976.

Flanders then moved to the big screen to play Truman in the 1977 film *MacArthur*, with Gregory Peck as Douglas MacArthur between 1942 and 1952. The movie was directed by Joseph Sargent (*The Man*) and written by Hal Barwood and Matthew Robbins. Dan O'Herlihy briefly appears as FDR, but Flanders as Truman gets a bit more to do. However, because this is a movie playing up MacArthur, it mainly makes Truman out to be a bad guy who spoils MacArthur's plans in Korea, which isn't necessarily the truth. Truman gets little to do in *Inchon* (1981), another love letter to MacArthur that reduces Truman to a stumbling voice-over on the telephone, with a grumpy MacArthur played by Laurence Olivier.

Ed Flanders makes one final appearance as a president in a television film, and it includes Truman but not with Ed Flanders in the role. That would be the television miniseries *Backstairs at the White House*, which aired as four episodes on the NBC television network in early 1979. Flanders plays Calvin Coolidge in the miniseries, while Harry Morgan plays Truman. The series follows the career of Lillian Rogers Parks, who worked as a seamstress and wrote a book with Frances Spatz Leighton called *My Thirty Years Backstairs at the White House*, covering her years in the White House from Taft (Victor Buono) to Eisenhower (Andrew Duggan) and the interactions she had and incidents she saw while there.

A similar plot is featured in *The Butler* (2013), a theatrical film starring Forest Whitaker as Cecil Gaines, a butler who worked at the White House for thirty-four years, from Dwight Eisenhower (Robin Williams, looking much more like Truman than Eisenhower) through Ronald Reagan (Alan Rickman, looking like Alan Rickman with an allergic reaction to a bee sting). In both cases, the emphasis is on the heavily dramatized stories of the domestic workers dealing with class and racial issues while sometimes crossing over with the various presidents they work for. Because the stories weigh more on the protagonists' personal stories instead of on the presidents, there's not much for the actors playing the presidents to do in either the miniseries or the film beyond occasionally pushing the narrative along, such as Lillian feeling forced out by the coldness of the Eisenhowers, while Cecil cannot reconcile working for Ronald Reagan after Reagan refuses to do anything about Apartheid (some historians have argued that the film does not represent Reagan in a correct context).

As mentioned, Gary Sinise plays a very sedate Truman in the HBO movie *Truman* (1995), who has more in common with Paul Giamatti's John Adams from the HBO miniseries than the Truman most people recognize. Truman also pops up in *Flags of Our Fathers* (2006, with David Patrick Kelly); *The Hundred-Year-Old Man Who Climbed out a Window and Disappeared* (2013, Kerry Shale); and finally in 2014 for *The Monuments Men*, discussed chapter 7. Christian Rodska appears at the very end of the movie in silhouette, as has been the tradition from the 1940s when showing presidents in movies, but it was not done for his first appearance in *The Beginning or the End*. And it took only seventy years to show Truman with the same respect as earlier presidents.

*The Long Gray Line* (1955), directed by John Ford, is a movie about Martin Maher Jr., who worked at West Point for fifty years and wrote an autobiography entitled *Bringing Up the Brass: My 55 Years at West Point*. The film starts with Elbert Steele as Eisenhower, filmed from behind as he sits at a dinner table with various military representatives and Maher to hear his story. Eisenhower is also shown as a young cadet played by Harry Carey Jr. The film concludes back at the White House, before showing Maher at a parade in his honor at West Point. Eisenhower is nothing but a messenger here, setting up the story and then helping to resolve a minor crisis at the end, and his appearance is namely to set up a running joke about Maher trying to convince Eisenhower to do something about his balding head.

Eisenhower gets a handful of other presidential appearances in movies but again as a messenger or a praeses ex machina. Robert Beer shows up as Eisenhower for a few minutes in two movies to deal with space stuff. He kicks off the main plot by first initiating test pilots to be used for the space mission in *The Right Stuff* (1983) and scuttles an alien spacecraft found in 1957 in *My Science Project* (1985). Oddly enough,

Beer appeared as David Eisenhower, grandson of Dwight Eisenhower, in *Americathon* (1979) just four years before playing the president. Keene Curtis plays Eisenhower in the 1994 romantic comedy, *I.Q.*, where the president turns up just long enough to create some additional misunderstandings for the man and woman at the heart of the movie, before becoming their praeses ex machina willingly going along with a ruse to save their relationship and their necks from going to prison. Beyond these, a brief appearance by David A. Cooper as Ike in *J. Edgar* (2011) and the aforementioned *The Butler* appearance by Robin Williams, where they both look worried about some things for a couple of minutes before disappearing, there's relatively little seen of the two-term president in movies, even in World War II movies, where it would make more sense to see Eisenhower because it is what propelled him to the presidency.

Dwight Eisenhower (1890–1969) was raised in Kansas and went to West Point, graduating as a second lieutenant in 1915. He married Mamie Geneva Doud in 1916 and then became the commander of tank training at Camp Colt in Pennsylvania during World War I. After the war, he did various military assignments, and then in 1926, he was sent to the Army General Staff School to learn how to become a commander and graduated first in his class. He served under Douglas MacArthur in the Philippines for four years before returning to the United States in 1940.

In December 1941, after the bombing of Pearl Harbor, Eisenhower worked in Washington primarily to nail down plans for fighting in the Pacific, thanks to his experience in the Philippines. In 1942, he was named Supreme Commander Allied Expeditionary Force of the North African Theater of Operations, which was a fancy way of saying that he was to organize and command the successful invasion of French North Africa in 1942 and then Sicily and Italy in 1943. His success led to Roosevelt making him the Supreme Commander of all Allied forces in Europe, where he had to navigate the various egos and resources of other military commanders in order to see out the successful invasion of Normandy (D-Day), which established the turning point in the war in favor of the Allies. The war ended with Eisenhower as a war hero to most Americans, and he helped set up the Department of Defense with Truman in 1947.

Eisenhower had never made public his position in politics, with no designation for being either a Republican or Democrat. He was just the "war hero." That was enough for both parties to fight for him in the 1952 presidential election. As mentioned earlier, Truman sought him out but could not convince him to run as a Democrat. Meanwhile, the Republicans were falling over themselves to convince him to run. The issue was that Eisenhower was not particularly thrilled with the idea of being president. Republicans felt he was their last hope before being stuck with Senator Robert Taft of Ohio, who was too far to the right ("always to the right," as they say in 1776), had fought the US entry into World War II, and was an isolationist who was running on the idea of pulling troops immediately from the Korean War if elected. Taft spelled disaster for the Republicans, and they saw Eisenhower as their only possibility for relief. Eisenhower reciprocated and allowed himself to be added to the nomination, although he was disheartened to be saddled with Richard Nixon. (Eisenhower, in August 1960, before the election between Nixon and Kennedy, was asked what contributions Nixon made to his administration, and Eisenhower buried Nixon by replying, "If you give me a week, I might think of one." Kennedy used Eisenhower's words against Nixon, helping to win the election.)

Eisenhower showed himself to be what today is termed a liberal Republican. He supported many ideas crafted by Roosevelt and Truman before him, which dented the plans of Conservatives, who thought they would be able to dismantle Social Security and labor laws under a man hired because of his military record and not for his political skills. Eisenhower invested heavily in the nation's infrastructure with the creation of the Interstate Highway System Bill in 1956 and also saw waste in the military, so he pulled money back to fund other governmental projects. The *Brown vs. Board of Education* decision in 1954 while Eisenhower was in office ended segregation in schools, and Eisenhower brought out the National Guard in Arkansas to escort Black students to school in Little Rock in 1957. He also appointed five Supreme Court justices in his time in office, some more liberal than others.

Things were not completely rosy during Eisenhower's run, however. He was slow to criticize Joseph McCarthy's anticommunist campaign, ostracizing J. Robert Oppenehimer, one of the country's leading nuclear scientists, among many others. Eisenhower in 1953 also issued executive order 10450, which barred gays and those suspected of being so from working in the federal government (which may explain why previously discussed movies such as *The Best Man* and *Advise and Consent* made same-sex affairs a subplot). He pushed moving soldiers into Vietnam and strongly suggested to Kennedy that he do more there, a strategy that turned out to be a poor one for the country. Eisenhower was also seen as too dependent on those working under him to resolve issues, making him seem a bit ineffectual at times, although some of that came from having to deal with a Democratic Congress in his second term as well as a heart attack in 1955 and a mild stroke in 1957 that kept him off the campaign trail for Nixon in 1960. His health issues also led to considerations on what to do in the event that the president could no longer perform his duties, thus helping form the Twenty-Fifth Amendment, discussed so often in these chapters.

Yet Eisenhower's lasting movie memories are theatrical films like *The Longest Day* (1962, with Henry Grace as Eisenhower) and *Churchill* (2017, with John Slattery) and television movies, such as *Ike* (1979, with Robert Duvall); *Countdown to D-Day* (2004, with Tom Selleck); and *Last Days of Patton* (1986, with Richard Dysart). The common theme is World War II, with Eisenhower as a military leader and winning the day rather than sitting behind a desk with middling results.

Eisenhower had a good run as president, with two full terms, but it was his successor who became the most iconic president of the second half of the twentieth century (and, in fact, the first president to be born in that century): John F. Kennedy (1917–1963). Kennedy was the second son of Joseph Kennedy, a rich businessman who dabbled in politics, including being the ambassador to the United Kingdom during FDR's presidency and the first chairman of the Securities and Exchange Commission (SEC). Joe groomed his sons to be involved with politics, which saw success for three of them, John (typically referred to as Jack), Robert (1925–1968), and Ted (1932–2009). When his oldest son, Joseph Kennedy Jr. (1915–1944), died in a mission during World War II, he pressed his efforts on Jack instead. Jack was not seen as a promising politician growing up, having suffered through various illnesses and with little aptitude, living more the life of a playboy than someone looking for serious pursuit. That changed in 1940, when he began to apply himself at Harvard and passed with honors after writing a thesis that became the book *Why England Slept*, which deals with the ramifications of the Munich Agreement that allowed Germany to begin their conquest of Europe and why England agreed to it (and, by extension, how easily other countries could fall into the same trap).

In 1941, John Kennedy joined the navy, and although suffering from severe back pain due to various illnesses in his youth, he requested to do more than office work. In March 1943, he arrived in the South Pacific to command a PT (patrol torpedo) boat, the PT-109. The PT boats were common in the South Pacific during World War II in hopes of creating a fleet of small, speedy boats that could easily maneuver and launch torpedoes at the enemy in a manner that larger ships could not. They also tended to be cheap wooden boats (the commonly seen gray paint of the boats in movies mistakenly suggests steel, but that was not the case) that were hard to navigate. Many of those alongside Kennedy's were missing equipment, including radar. In early August 1943, Kennedy and his crew were sent out with more than a dozen other PT boats to stop Japanese destroyers coming through the area with supplies. To stay hidden from the destroyers, the boats were advised against using their radios or their lights, and without radar, there was nothing more that could be done beyond simply hoping to spot a Japanese ship before they spotted you. In fact, some boats had already turned back to port, with no way of informing the others, leaving several, like the PT-109, to drift for a time. Kennedy's crew did finally spot a Japanese destroyer coming straight at them, but they could not maneuver out of the way, and the PT-109 was sliced in two by the ship, killing two members of Kennedy's crew and leaving the rest, including one badly injured, holding onto debris in the water.

Kennedy managed to motivate the surviving members to work together and, dragging the injured crewmember, swam with them to a nearby island. Once there, although having suffered a back injury in the accident, Kennedy then swam out two miles to see if he could spot a PT boat to pick them up. The following night saw the crew swim to another larger island. Kennedy later surveyed another island and found some supplies left by the Japanese and a canoe. Soon after, they were located by two natives of the area who were sent out to search for them, leading to the crew's rescue a week after their boat sank. The press was mixed about the rescue, with a lingering assumption that the "rich man's son" managed to get two men killed because he did not know what he was doing, but all accounts suggest that the collision was not his fault, and his ability to keep his crew together and safe even while suffering from other injuries made him a hero.

Kennedy returned to the United States and began his climb in Congress, first in the House of Representatives and then in the Senate. During that time, Kennedy married Jacqueline Lee Bouvier in September 1953 and wrote a book, *Profiles in Courage*, in 1956 that won the Pulitzer Prize. He ran for the presidency in 1960 with an emphasis on his liberal leanings while a senator. Being Roman Catholic was thought to be detrimental for Kennedy, as there was a strong anti-Catholic bias in the country at the time, but he aggressively worked for the nomination, and his addition of Lyndon Johnson as his vice-presidential pick helped with Southern voters who were apprehensive about the Northern-born and Catholic Kennedy. A series of television debates against Richard Nixon, the first for any presidential race, had Nixon looking nervous and unprepared in comparison to the photogenic and calm Kennedy, helping to cement the voting for Kennedy in 1960.

Kennedy's presidency is well remembered for his New Frontier policy, with such forward thinking as creating the Peace Corps, working for civil rights, and pushing for the space program to land a man on the moon before the end of the 1960s. With a beautiful family in a somewhat peaceful era for the country, there was a tendency to look back at Kennedy's White House as if it was a fantasy, like Camelot of the musical of the same name that hit Broadway the year Kennedy became president. It is that perfect image that has been tarnished over time as more behind-the-scenes details of Kennedy's presidency have emerged. We were fed this image of the perfect young man leading us by virtue, only to later discover that he was just as human as the rest of us, with an addiction to painkillers stemming from his back problems and various liaisons with women before and during his presidency. Early missteps in foreign policy also hurt Kennedy, with an attempt to overthrow Fidel Castro in 1961, leading to the failed Bay of Pigs invasion, and a conference with Soviet prime minister Khrushchev about Germany, which ended with the Russians beginning to build the Berlin Wall.

The biggest crisis for Kennedy came in October 1962, when Soviet missiles that could contain nuclear warheads were installed in Cuba in what is remembered as the Cuban missile crisis. Many in the National Security Council wanted to immediately attack the bomb sites before they could go any further, but Kennedy and others in his cabinet felt that there had to be more proof that the missiles were there to show the world they were not about to "Pearl Harbor" Cuba if they had to attack. Kennedy and his advisors also felt the necessity to give the Soviets some type of out so that there would be no chance of an escalation leading to World War III. Khrushchev, who assumed Kennedy to be weak on foreign policy, believed the president would passively allow the missiles. Instead, Kennedy blockaded Cuba and threatened to go forward with a bombing of the sites if the missiles were not removed and the sites dismantled. Eventually, negotiations were worked out to secretly withdraw US missiles in Turkey and Italy in exchange for the withdrawal. Publicly, the United States stated they would not invade Cuba in return for the Soviets dismantling the missile sites, thus giving everyone a win, especially Kennedy at a time when he really needed one.

On November 22, 1963, Kennedy was in a motorcade with Jackie and the governor of Texas, John Connally, through the main streets of Dallas, when he was assassinated by Lee Harvey Oswald from a building along the route. The death shocked the nation, and ever since, there has been speculation that more was involved in Kennedy's death than just Oswald working alone. While other presidents since have had attempts made on them, John Kennedy was the last president to be killed while in office.

Much like Eisenhower, Kennedy also saw his career divided in Hollywood, with just two theatrical films dealing specifically with him: *PT 109* (1963) and *Thirteen Days* (2000). However, he is a minor character in a large number of other films. The problem is that while Eisenhower's minor roles are mainly as a commander in World War II and at least breathe life into him as a person, most of Kennedy's roles are not as a human being but rather as a moment in time—his assassination. *Executive Action* (1973) and *JFK* (1991) both deal with conspiracy theories about his death from the point of view of a conspiracy so well hidden that it seems to be all that we've talked about since it occurred. But let's humor the movies for the moment. *Executive Action* was directed by David Miller and written by Dalton Trumbo (*The Remarkable Andrew*) and stars Burt Lancaster as James Farrington, a man organizing the assassination of Kennedy with a group of businessmen and others. Their reasoning is Kennedy's liberal leanings, including a supposed inclination to leave Vietnam (a common link for assassination conspirators about why Kennedy would be killed by the government). The film then plays out the assassination and follows the group as they make sure there is no way they will be discovered. The film did not do well, probably because it was not only a controversial topic in the early 1970s, but also the movie is pretty much a series of scenes with people sitting in one room after another, talking about what is to come or has happened, thus ultimately dull stuff to watch while eating popcorn.

*JFK* (1991) is the more remembered of the two, with an all-star cast, writer-director Oliver Stone's involvement, and a kinetic visual style that keeps the film rolling along. Stone, who had been riding high in Hollywood after the success of *Platoon* (1986) and *Wall Street* (1987), dived into bringing to the screen an adaptation of the book *On the Trail of the Assassins* by Jim Garrison. Garrison had begun an investigation into the assassination in 1966 and came to believe that the CIA was involved in the president's death and framed Lee Harvey Oswald as the assassin. (Jim Marrs's book *Crossfire: The Plot That Killed Kennedy* was also used as a source for the movie.) Garrison is played in the film by Kevin Costner, and the film follows his investigation, with avenues heading off in many odd directions and an assortment of witnesses and other resources that both contest and confirm his theory that Oswald's involvement was not singular. As Garrison continues his investigation, he begins to believe that the assassination of other men, such as Martin Luther King Jr. and Robert Kennedy, were connected to JFK's death, as well. The film climaxes with the trial against Clay Shaw (Tommy Lee Jones), a businessman who supposedly was involved with the assassination, and Garrison's evidence suggesting many others beyond Oswald were involved in the death of Kennedy. The movie ends with the jury finding Shaw not guilty within an hour of deliberation, although the film purports that many members admitted to being convinced that something had happened but that Garrison had not proved his case against Shaw.

The film was met with a strict division in reactions when it was released. Some saw it as a brilliant movie that told its tale in an exhilarating way and tried to show how the conspiracy could have worked. The flip side of the debate was that Stone took so many liberties with the truth in order to tell the story the way he saw it that the film ended up not really saying anything to either prove or disprove the conspiracy. Even Stone himself seems to suggest that something is not right with his narrative; he has other characters who are helping in the investigation finally turn on Garrison for turning it into a vendetta rather than looking for the truth (as some critics would say of Stone after the film's release). The various types of film (color, black-and-white, odd angles) also seems to challenge our perception as viewers to question what is real when we see it on the screen. (Stone frequently returned to this style of filmmaking in the future, including in *Nixon* and *W.*)

In the end, *JFK* isn't so much about the death of Kennedy or a whodunnit but rather the death of reason in American culture. Nothing is what it appears to be, so everything is questionable. We leave the film with Garrison supposedly off to pursue his investigation and a title telling us that the jurists believe him. We want to believe in that statement because if we just spent more than two hours (three hours in the special edition) watching this all play out in a movie with no resolution, then what was the point? Yet we are here many years later with most of the information finally released about the assassination and can still only come to one real-life conclusion: Lee Harvey Oswald killed John F. Kennedy. No great revelations, no villains to expose, no resolution to our grief—just a madman killing the nation's leader.

That doesn't quite sit well with us. A lone gunman managed to alter the country's future—the world's future—with just a rifle one day in Dallas in 1963? We believed it when it happened to Lincoln, Garfield, and McKinley because it was "old times" or security wasn't that great or who thought someone would kill the president? But this was our time and our Camelot. To have something so brutally simple occur in our technologically advanced world where we are in control of so many things made no sense. Hollywood has told us that bad guys will be found out and stopped and that the good guys will win. Nothing like that happened here. Oswald won and in death got to keep whatever secrets he had to himself. That isn't how it is supposed to work.

We turn to the media for help to understand, hoping another angle or source or perhaps through fantasyland thinking, we will find answers that tell us something satisfactory. *JFK* helped by trying to tell us that, yes, it had to be the bad guys in Washington, along with the mob and other insidious individuals, and that worked for many viewers. We can sleep at night if it was a big government conspiracy, after all. That appeals to the status quo of us hopelessly against the machinery of the government, where things can be changed in the blink of an eye because they have all the power. To have it come down to a single person who changes everything is frightening and means anyone at any time could alter the world on us. Best to stick with the movies and hope for relief in the darkness than go down that path. A handful, like *Executive Action*, *JFK*, and to a lesser extent *The Private Files of J. Edgar Hoover* and *An American Affair* (2008), try to suggest that there has been a cover-up and that multiple people were involved in Kennedy's death. That provides relief, as does seeing the various films that deal with the aftermath of the assassination and how those directly involved reacted. What's interesting is how often these movies, like in the two previously mentioned, show us so very little of John F. Kennedy in order to concentrate more on the aftereffects of his violent death.

*The Greek Tycoon* (1978) tries to do so in such a vague way that the entire film seems like a mistake from the start. Directed by J. Lee Thompson and written by Morton S. Fine, the movie stars Jacqueline Bisset as Liz Cassidy, a person who is very much like Jackie Kennedy. It shows her with her husband, James Cassidy (James Franciscus), a senator from Massachusetts who becomes president (wink, wink), only for Cassidy to be shot on a beach. The film then moves to focus on Liz's growing relationship with a Greek tycoon named Theo (Anthony Quinn), who (gosh, what a coincidence) is very much like Jackie's second husband, Aristotle Onassis. Although the film tries to deal with how Liz and Theo would get together in the first place and Liz working through the trauma of her first husband's death, the movie takes such a smarmy position to pass off the actors as representing the people without saying who they are that the film falls flat and doesn't make much of a point at all. Franciscus at least has a bit of screen time as the president before dying in the surf, which is more than can be said in some other films mentioned here.

The immediate ramifications of Kennedy's death are better felt in other films, although we see less of Kennedy in them. The first is a television movie from Fox about Robert Kennedy, *RFK*, released in

2002 and with Martin Donovan as Jack Kennedy seen right before his death, allowing the film to focus on how his brother Robert deals with the situation and his own rise in power until his own death at the hands of a gunman in 1968. The next theatrical film dealing with the assassination is *Parkland* (2013), written and directed by Peter Landesman, who based it on the book *Four Days in November: The Assassination of President John F. Kennedy.* Brett Stimely appears as Kennedy but only to be shown in death. Instead, the film is about how eyewitnesses, people at the hospital where Kennedy was sent, others immediately investigating the crime, and even Oswald's family deal with the ramifications. Stimely appeared three other times as President Kennedy over the years, sometimes with a little more to do, although two of them are fantasy films. He is shown being assassinated by the Comedian in the superhero movie *The Watchmen* (2009) and deciding to send men to the moon in *Transformers: Dark of the Moon* (2011). His final appearance is in the 2013 movie *Kill the Dictator*, where Kennedy is seen multiple times looking into the politics of the Dominican Republic and the dictatorship of Rafael Trujillo, who was assassinated in 1961.

Another take on the assassination comes in the 2016 film *Jackie*, directed by Pablo Larrain and written by Noah Oppenheim. The film stars Natalie Portman as Jackie Kennedy and deals with her immediate reaction to the death of her husband, including flashbacks to the shooting in Dallas. The film's take is on a woman who has little chance to mentally deal with the death of her husband but must present this calm image of herself to the public to show she is handling it well (hence the setup of her being closely guarded during an interview that is the wrap-around of the film and ends with her stating she will control what is printed about her). The film certainly gives audiences a more human side to Jackie Kennedy than seen in *The Greek Tycoon*, although Portman ends up having to play most of the film as a person in a daze who is having trouble focusing on events around her (Larrain's 2021 film about Princess Diana, *Spencer*, also deals with a media-observed woman in a stupor looking for release for most of the picture). John Carroll Lynch is given the unfortunate role of playing Lyndon B. Johnson as a mild villain in the film who is determined to get his oath done as quickly as possible after Kennedy's death, but there's the suggestion that this may not be quite as devious as intended and he later is shown concerned about Jackie. Caspar Phillipson as Kennedy has not much to do besides the assassination scene and a momentary glance of him dancing with Jackie in a flashback at the end of the film, however.

The movie *LBJ* (2016) deals with the assassination from Lyndon Johnson's perspective, along with the acknowledgment that his position as vice president had more to do with whipping up votes for Kennedy than anything Johnson could bring to the administration. In providing that narrative, *LBJ*, which was directed by Rob Reiner and written by Joey Hartstone, shows us the image of a vice president as we have suspected all along and going back to the days when John Adams found himself doing nothing in the role: The Kennedy administration ignores the vice president once the election is over. Jeffrey Donovan, who plays Robert Kennedy in *J. Edgar*, plays John Kennedy in *LBJ* as a manipulator who sees keeping Johnson close as a means to shut Johnson down. Johnson, played by Woody Harrelson in makeup that is somewhat distracting, struggles to hold onto what little power is available to him as vice president, only to then be stunned to find himself with all the power once Kennedy dies. Johnson is seen making the best of the transition and continuing to move forward with work involving civil rights (leading ultimately to the Civil Rights Act of 1964), leaving the film on a somewhat positive note.

Manipulation is the key when it comes to Jack Kennedy and his brother Robert in both *The Private Files of J. Edgar Hoover* (1977, with William Jordan as Jack) and *Prince Jack* (1985, with Robert J. Hogan as Jack), and the Kennedy boys come off as mafia men looking to rough up the country rather than the politicians usually seen in movies. Having actors who do not look anything like the Kennedys in cheap locations that appear to be hotel rooms or someone's small cabin in the woods doesn't help much either. A less aggressive Jack pops up in other films to push the narrative along, such as a simulated appearance by the real Jack Kennedy in *Forrest Gump* (1994); Chriss Anglin as Jack in *An American Carol* (2008, discussed in chapter 1); and Rick Kelly as Kennedy promoting *Spartacus* in *Trumbo* (2015).

The first movie to really focus solely on Kennedy is the 1963 film *PT 109*, with Cliff Robertson as Jack Kennedy. The movie, directed by Leslie Martinson and Lewis Milestone and written by Richard Breen, naturally enough covers Kennedy's command of the PT-109 in the

South Pacific and concentrates on the destruction of the boat and the eventual rescue of Kennedy and his crew. Although FDR, Truman, and Eisenhower were portrayed in minor roles for a few movies while they were still in office, *PT 109* was the first time a movie solely told a story about someone who was still president at the time of its release (June 1963). Based on a book about the PT-109 incident by Robert J.

# In response to countless inquiries and requests, this theatre is honored to announce a special engagement of PT 109

The true story of young John F. Kennedy and his actual wartime adventure in the South Pacific. A remarkable insight into the qualities inherent in this man that were to later make him a legend in his own time.

**Poster artwork for *PT 109* (1963), starring Cliff Robertson as JFK. The use of an actual image of JFK in the poster art is a rare case of a current president okaying their image being used as such. *Official press still, author's collection,* © 1963 by *Warner Brothers.***

Donovan, *John F. Kennedy in World War II*, the movie shows Kennedy arriving to take over the crew of the PT-109 and then their eventual collision with the destroyer that led to their trying to survive on an island while avoiding the Japanese soldiers in the area as they wait for rescue. Kennedy requested and got the right to pick the actor who was to play him in the film as well as made sure the film stayed accurate and that profits from the film went to the other men from PT-109. Robertson got the nod from Kennedy and met with him before filming began.

Most of the film sticks with the story as known by the public, but there are two standout moments that were changed. The first is an earlier story that shows Kennedy and his crew saving a group of marines on an island while being attacked. This did occur but after the PT-109 incident, when Kennedy and many of his crewmates were given the PT-59 (outfitted as a gunboat rather than the torpedo boat previously used). The other discrepancy is about the two natives who find the crew, as the film makes it look as if they discovered the crew by accident, when the pair, Biuku Gasa and Eroni Kumana, were actively searching for them. As to the carved coconut with information about the crew to be handed off by the natives, there are claims on both sides that it was one of the natives who suggested the idea or one of the crewmembers who did so. Either way, the results were the same. Robertson makes for a likable Jack Kennedy, and an incident showing the boat ramming the dock by accident appearing early in the movie allows us to see a fallible side to Kennedy that is not commonly expected in a movie such as this. Nevertheless, the film is overlong at two and a half hours (even Kennedy, upon seeing the movie, thought the length was too much for what could be seen as a minor incident), and there's little character development for Kennedy in the movie beyond keeping his men together as they wait to be rescued. Thus, it is somewhat understandable why it tends to be forgotten when looking for films about JFK.

The other major film with Kennedy is *Thirteen Days* (2000), based on the book *The Kennedy Tapes: Inside the White House during the Cuban Missile Crisis* by Ernest R. May and Philip D. Zelikow, although there are obvious parallels with Robert Kennedy's book from 1969, *Thirteen Days: A Memoir of the Cuban Missile Crisis*. The material from that book is the basis of a famous television production called *The Missiles of October*, which ran on the ABC television network on December 18,

1974. The 150-minute program, with limited commercial breaks, had William Devane as John F. Kennedy, Martin Sheen as Robert Kennedy, and Howard Da Silva (Ben Franklin in *1776* and FDR in *The Private Files of J. Edgar Hoover*) as Nikita Khrushchev, along with a few other famous faces who had played presidents in other films (Ralph Bellamy, Keene Curtis, and Andrew Duggan). Missing from the program is Lyndon B. Johnson, who attended most of the meetings but simply isn't there for the movie (he has a similar fate in *Thirteen Days*).

The television program has limited sets and actions, with nearly all of it taking place in two rooms. Kennedy talks with his advisors about the crisis, and Khrushchev struggles to understand how they got to this point and is frustrated with the bureaucracy he faces in trying to resolve his side of the issue. With those limitations in place, the emphasis is on the acting, with Devane and Da Silva having the bulk of the dialogue and both in excellent form in their roles. The story follows the known

**William Devane as JFK and Martin Sheen as Robert Kennedy in the TV film *The Missiles of October* (1974), which details the Cuban missile crisis of 1962 that is also the basis for the film *Thirteen Days* (2000). *Official press still, author's collection, © 1974 by American Broadcasting Company.***

events of the crisis, with the bonus of allowing some suggested insight into what Khrushchev was dealing with on his side of the issue, a factor completely lost in *Thirteen Days* twenty-six years later. The theatrical film from 2000 instead focuses solely on reactions within the White House as seen through the eyes of Kenny O'Donnell (Kevin Costner, making this his second movie featuring Kennedy), one of several advisors for Kennedy and an old friend. Bruce Greenwood plays Jack Kennedy, with Steven Culp as Robert Kennedy, and the movie emphasizes a partnership between O'Donnell and the Kennedy brothers that suggests O'Donnell was not only present during most of the negotiations but also had an active hand in deciding what needed to be done. This was not the case in reality but was seen as a necessity in order to keep the audience's viewpoint with one character rather than many. The main addition to the plot from that of *The Missiles of October* is the negotiations over the missiles in Turkey, a factor that was not disclosed until 1989. Because that condition remained secret, Khrushchev was seen as having the Soviets back off without gaining much beyond a promise from the United States not to invade Cuba, making him look weak (and some consider a reason he was ousted from office two years later). Such a development was a missed opportunity for the film to show Khrushchev's side of the story like in *The Missiles of October*, which instead spends time showing O'Donnell's family life to demonstrate how the general public was reacting to the ongoing crisis. The film received mixed reviews, praising the look of the film and the acting but feeling that something seemed missing in the storytelling, while others contested using O'Donnell to depict how America was responding rather than Kennedy. The movie performed weakly at the box office, not making back what it cost, and was the last film to concentrate on Kennedy for the big screen.

Lyndon B. Johnson (1908–1973) was a powerful senator from Texas who had control as the majority whip for many years. His Southern heritage had people assuming he would return to the more conservative and racial-oriented tactics of some of his colleagues when he became president, but he surprised many by being aggressive in liberal policy for domestic issues. He helped create many programs still in use today, including Medicare, Medicaid, the Civil Rights Acts of 1964 and 1968, the Voting Rights Act of 1965, immigration policies, and public broadcasting. Born in Stonewall, Texas, he went through a variety of jobs that typically involved helping those less fortunate before becoming a secretary to Representative Richard Kleberg in 1932, leading to his interest in politics. He became a representative himself in 1937 and stayed in the role until 1949, when moved over to the role of senator for the state of Texas. He worked on acts for civil rights in 1957 and 1960 while a senator, while also actively pushing for money to be given to the space program after the launch of the Russian satellite Sputnik in 1957.

Johnson competed with Jack Kennedy for the Democratic nomination in 1960, with Johnson controlling many delegates in Southern and Western states, leading Kennedy to ask Johnson to take on the vice president slot in the nomination and combine their delegates. Johnson contributed to the administration in his role, with frequent trips overseas and work in various committees, but the vice presidency was still seen as a "runner-up" role that offered little in actual authority. Johnson also had a boorishness about him that, along with his heritage of being from Texas, was often ridiculed in public and among some of the White House staff, including Robert Kennedy.

Johnson continued Kennedy's work when he became president on November 22, 1963, less than a year before the next election. He was sworn in on Air Force One just a little over two hours after Kennedy was assassinated, which some saw as being too quick and helped stoke the flames of some conspiracies about Kennedy's death for years to come. Concerns about how Johnson would go forward were eased with his "Let Us Continue" speech in a special joint session of Congress the day after Thanksgiving in 1963. His policies became part of the Great Society program, and Johnson saw an impressive landslide win in 1964 for the presidential election. Issues for him came mainly from the growing concerns about the Vietnam War, which had expanded under Kennedy and much more so with Johnson. Going with consensus of his cabinet, Johnson's response to what was increasingly looking like a lost cause was to throw more soldiers at it, leading to protests by younger Americans who felt the war was ineffective at best and some type of power play by Johnson at worst. Because the Twenty-Second Amendment allowed him to run for a third term, John considered doing so but decided that due to the dwindling power he felt he had in the role and health issues, he would not run. Richard Nixon was elected in 1968, throwing the country into the Republican arena for the next several years. Johnson retired with scorn from some, even as his policies still resonate today.

The buffoon image of LBJ was a common sight in television during the late 1960s and early 1970s (*Laugh-In* commonly showed LBJ only from the back, with his cowboy hat seen above the chair he sat on, talking like a hick and making what amounted to variations of redneck jokes). That image would continue in one of the earliest portrayals of Johnson in theatrical movies, with Donald Moffat as LBJ in *The Right Stuff* (1983). Ignoring Johnson's interest in getting the Apollo program going, the film shows Johnson having a tantrum in his limo when one of the astronaut wives refuses to be seen with him. Johnson ends up with little to do in *The Private Files of J. Edgar Hoover* (1977, with Andrew Duggan) and *JFK* (1991, with Tom Howard), although *JFK* insinuates that Johnson was as much a part of the conspiracy as others in the government. LBJ is also seen in films already discussed, such as *Parkland* (Sean McGraw), *Jackie* (John Carroll Lynch), and *Forrest Gump* (altered footage of the real Johnson).

The first film to solely concentrate on Johnson is an NBC movie from February 1987 called *LBJ: The Early Years*, directed by Peter Wierner and starring Randy Quaid as Johnson. The movie focuses on his career between becoming a representative and president, including the feelings of being shut out of the Kennedy administration. The movie did not do well in the ratings (and concentrates a bit much on Johnson's possible affairs), but Quaid's performance is considered one of the better portrayals of Johnson over the years and gives us a good slice of the animosity between Robert Kennedy (James Kelly) and Johnson, with Jack Kennedy (Charles Frank) taking a bit of a backseat to the action for once.

Television continued to be the main place to find Johnson, with Michael Gambon playing LBJ in the John Frankenheimer movie for HBO *Path to War* (2002). The movie focuses on his time in office after being elected in 1964 and his decision to not run again in 1968, with an emphasis on decisions made about the Vietnam War. Gambon is fine acting the role, although his attempt at the Texas accent comes off as a bit thicker than needed, and the movie does a good job filling in the actions of the administration of the time. *Path to War* is also the first movie to depict a story often told about Johnson—his willingness to talk to people while in the bathroom with the door open as he sat on the toilet. It's a common story that has crept into many biographies about the man, with some believing it to be base crudeness, while others have insisted it was a power move to put people on the defensive. Johnson was also known to have aides talk to him as he showered and dressed, but it is the toilet story that is often referred to and pops up in several movies with Johnson, including *Path to War*; *The Butler* (2013, with Liev Schreiber as Johnson); *LBJ* (2016); and *All the Way* (2016). *All the Way* was even promoted by HBO with a toiletry bag with the name of the film on it as a publicity item, although HBO tried to insist it was not trying to make such a connection.

Tom Wilkinson plays LBJ in the movie *Selma* (2014), directed by Ava DuVernay and written by Paul Webb. The film is about the 1965 march from Selma to Montgomery in Alabama in support of voting rights. LBJ is shown in the movie working against Martin Luther King Jr. and the movement, having the FBI watch King and trying to ignore the move-

**So many films have documented Lyndon Johnson's habit of having meetings while on the toilet that HBO sent out toiletry bags as promotional gifts to promote their 2016 film *All the Way*. Photo by author, author's collection.**

ment in getting civil rights passed. But this is counter to history records, along with his generally good relationship with King, and the accounts by those who lived through the events (as well as the surveillance of King coming from Robert Kennedy and not Johnson). It also makes the ending of the film, with Johnson requesting Congress to pass a bill on voting rights in 1965, seem more "out of the blue" after nearly two hours of LBJ fighting such talk. Turning LBJ into just another villain is an unfortunate detrimental element in an otherwise brilliant movie that deals with the drive of those involved with the march.

The relationship between King and Johnson are better examined in the HBO movie *All the Way*, featuring Bryan Cranston as Johnson, based on the Broadway play also starring Cranston, and written by Robert Schenkkan. The movie starts with Johnson becoming president and his work with Martin Luther King Jr. on the Civil Rights Act of 1964. The film then continues with Johnson running for president in 1964 and his eventual win over a mudslinging campaign against Republican nominee Barry Goldwater. The movie has Johnson on an upswing, but issues with civil rights, the war, and other pressures from a Congress turning against him creep in as the movie ends. Cranston, having portrayed Johnson for a time onstage as others had before him with Roosevelt and Truman, is excellent in the role and with minimal makeup, showing Johnson's willingness to do whatever it takes to get his agenda moved along, even at the expense of his political future. It would come out the same year as Rob Reiner's *LBJ*, which was the only movie about Johnson to actively see a theatrical release, although it did poorly at the box office.

There is no doubt that the public perception of the presidency was changing in the late 1960s. Earlier presidents had been made fun of in the media, but the venom became sharper. Kennedy had the luxury of quaint parodies like Vaughn Meader's *The First Family* comedy album, even though off the record, he wasn't happy with the ridicule, no matter how gentle it was. There were joke songs about Truman, Roosevelt, and plenty of others before that, going back to Washington being parodied in the press. LBJ stood to stronger jabs, with jokes about his appearance, his accent, and his policies. Even that, however, could not compare to what Richard M. Nixon would go through.

Richard Nixon (1913–1994) was born in southern California to a Quaker family. He went to Duke University to study law and had hopes of joining the FBI before beginning to work as an attorney in business cases. In 1940, he married Pat Ryan and was stationed in the South Pacific during World War II. He joined the House of Representatives in 1947 and became a member of the House Un-American Activities Committee (HUAC), which led him to an association with Senator Joseph McCarthy when Nixon became a senator in 1950. In 1952, Nixon was picked to run with Eisenhower for the presidency. When it was leaked that Nixon had possibly used a political fund for personal expenses, there was talk of removing him from the ticket. Nixon went on national television in September 1952 to explain himself, saying the only gift that he could not return was that of a dog named Checkers that his daughter, Tricia, loved. The famous "Checkers" speech cemented his spot on the ticket, allowing him to become vice president in 1953. When Eisenhower had his heart attack in 1955, Nixon took his place in cabinet meetings while he recovered. Nixon also was the chairman of the president's Committee on Government Contracts and was directly involved with a short subject filmed in 1960 with Gail Fisher (later of *Mannix* fame) called *The New Girl*, which deals with the nondiscrimination clause that is supposed to make sure people receive the same benefits for their jobs.

As previously discussed, Nixon ran for president in 1960, only to be beaten by Jack Kennedy, with the television presidential debates and a tossed-off comment by Eisenhower helping to lose him the election. He ran for governor of California in 1962 and did so poorly that he conceded by infamously telling the press, "You won't have Nixon to kick around anymore because, gentlemen, this is my last press conference." He returned in 1968 to run for president again, fighting off Nelson Rockefeller and Ronald Reagan, among others, for the nomination and then winning against the weak vice president Hubert Humphrey, who faced issues after protests outside the Democratic convention in Chicago turned violent.

Nixon found some success in office, including in foreign policy, by going to China to help broker a better relationship between that country and the United States, and his work with the Soviets proved agreeable, as well. He slowly began to phase out troops in Vietnam, although he encouraged the bombing of Cambodia in the early 1970s to disrupt supply lines, killing possibly hundreds of thousands of people. He helped create the Environmental Protection Agency (EPA) and the Occupational Safety and Health Administration (OSHA) and pushed for additional health insurance outlets, such as HMOs. Although war protests continued, Nixon was well on his way to winning the next election in 1972.

Then the bubble burst. Concerned that his Democratic opponent, George McGovern, might pull ahead in the election, members of the Committee for the Re-Election of the President (formally known as CRP but comically referred to in the press as CREEP) broke into the Democratic National Committee's headquarters at the Watergate Hotel in Washington, DC, to copy paperwork and set up wiretapping devices. The crew did such a poor job breaking in that they were immediately arrested and booked, and slowly the event spread to other incidents where members of Nixon's team had possibly done illegal things to help the president. Nixon's response was to deny any connection with the break-in or any cover-up pertaining to it.

Investigations by the media, especially the *Washington Post*'s Bob Woodward and Carl Bernstein and the *New York Times*, found Nixon's direct involvement in the cover-up. Meanwhile, Nixon's vice president, Spiro Agnew, had to resign due to bribery charges (covered in chapter 2). The scandal escalated into an impeachment trial in 1974, and with the writing on the wall, Nixon decided to resign the presidency on August 9, 1974. It was the first and only time a president resigned from office. Nixon left office and retired from politics. He occasionally popped up on television to talk about his time in office but always in defense of what he did, including a series of interviews with David Frost that came the closest to getting Nixon to admitting that he did something wrong. The years were kinder to Nixon than some would have expected, with his early success in foreign policy and some of his programs, such as the EPA and the Endangered Species Act, seen as positives, although results were mixed with the scandals of Cambodia and Watergate.

The Nixon of the media changed as we grew to know what he did in the 1970s. The first theatrical image of Nixon is a joke that has more to do with the media than Nixon, the comedy *Cold Turkey* (1971). In the film, written and directed by Norman Lear, a small town is trying to win $25 million from a tobacco company if everyone in the town can stop smoking for thirty days. The comedy shows the people suffering through withdrawal, while the tobacco company attempts to get them smoking again before the thirty days are up. In the final scene, as the town has just received the money for making it thirty days, a limo arrives with President Nixon. The joke is that the cameras of all the networks are situated in such a manner that they cannot get a shot of his face and can see only an occasional arm and the top of his head (a glimpse of the extra playing the president suggests someone wearing a mask as Nixon because we're never actually supposed to see his face anyway). Nixon then announces that the town will become the location of a new missile plant, which is seen at the end of the movie belching smoke into the air and turning the entire town gray.

The film is a comedy classic but did not do well at the time. It at least did better than the next comedy appearance of Nixon, which was in the Bob Einstein comedy *Another Fine Mess* from 1972. The comedy stars Rich Little as Oliver Hardy as Richard Nixon and Herb Voland as Stan Laurel as Spiro Agnew doing presidential duties. The movie is just a little over an hour long and is best remembered today for the first appearance of Steve Martin in a small role. It isn't so much a parody of Nixon and Agnew as simply several sight gags in the tradition of Laurel and Hardy and loosely at that (although Voland as Agnew makes for a rather good Laurel).

The CBS miniseries *Blind Ambition* aired in 1979 and is based on John Dean's memoir on his time in the White House, with Martin Sheen as John Dean and Rip Torn for once not in a military uniform and instead playing Richard Nixon. The series also includes William Daniels (John Adams from *1776*) as G. Gordon Liddy and Ed Flanders (Truman in *MacArthur* and several television shows). This was followed by the Robert Altman film *Secret Honor* from 1984, where Philip Baker Hall plays Nixon in a one-man performance. The film starts with a disclaimer, stating that it is strictly a work of fiction using the image of Nixon to tell its story and is not a historical document. This is understandable, as the film pivots from Nixon talking into a microphone for a recording about simple moments in his life to rants about others. Nixon then decides it needs to be wiped from the tape and ultimately admits to being part of a vast worldwide conspiracy. The movie ends with Nixon breaking down and admitting that he was being pushed to continue the Vietnam

War by a group of powerful people above even the president and that he orchestrated the Watergate scandal to get out from under them. It's an interesting theatrical production, much in the spirit of something like *Give 'Em Hell, Harry!* or as a nightmarish revelation of someone quickly having a mental break from reality (and fits readily in the era of Robert Altman's productions dealing more with the theater than film).

Next came the ABC movie *The Final Days*, with Lane Smith as Richard Nixon and based on the book by Bob Woodward and Carl Bernstein that covers the last days of Nixon in office. Many moments in the movie are reflected in the next theatrical film about the president, *Nixon* (1995). Oliver Stone directed the film, with Anthony Hopkins as Nixon and Joan Allen as Pat Nixon, and it starts with the Watergate break-in, leading into the cover-up and Nixon reflecting on his life and

**Anthony Hopkins as Richard Nixon in Oliver Stone's *Nixon* (1995).**
*Original lobby card, author's collection, © 1995 by Hollywood Pictures.*

his struggles. Hopkins takes a departure from his usual understated acting to portray Nixon as paranoid and confused but ultimately wanting to do the right thing to prove himself to the world and his mother. It's a common thread in many of Stone's movies, including *JFK* (although Garrison is trying to prove himself to the nonbelievers) and especially in *W.*, with George W. Bush trying to prove himself to his father. The movie also continues Stone's fascination with using different camera elements together to tell a disjointed story, using Nixon's medicine and alcohol use to explain the effects, and makes some late accusations that Nixon had a minor link to Kennedy's assassination. Oddly, the film in trying to make Nixon sympathetic has him whining too often about how others are against him, and one grows cold to the narrative after a while, leaving it not as effective as perhaps a calmer presentation with the same cast could have made it.

Two movies have been made about a meeting between Nixon and musician Elvis Presley at the White House. The first is a Canadian movie called *Elvis Meets Nixon* (1997), with Bob Gunton (the warden in *The Shawshank Redemption*) as Nixon and Rick Peters as Elvis. The film follows the course of the real event, with Elvis, a collector of state and federal badges, wanting to get one from the Bureau of Narcotics and Dangerous Drugs and meeting with Nixon to request one. Nixon and Elvis talk for a bit and pose for a picture, and Elvis gets his badge. The weirdness of such a meeting, especially considering Elvis's eventual death due to an overdose, makes the story one worth telling, although it's strictly for laughs here, as it is in the 2016 film by Liza Johnson called *Elvis and Nixon*. That movie has Michael Shannon as Elvis and Kevin Spacey as Nixon and tells pretty much the same story, although for a slightly more dramatic effect.

Comedy occurs again in *Dick* from 1999. Written and directed by Andrew Fleming, the movie involves two teenaged girls (played by Kirsten Dunst and Michelle Williams) who are caught up in the Watergate cover-up by accident and end up becoming Deep Throat, the informant who helped Woodward and Bernstein uncover the plot and cause the downfall of Nixon (Dan Hedaya). It was followed by *Frost/Nixon* in 2008, written by Peter Morgan and with Frank Langella as Nixon and Michael Sheen as interviewer David Frost. The movie was based on a play that opened in London in 2006 and then moved to Broadway, with Sheen and Langella in the roles, before being turned into a movie directed by Ron Howard. The film deals with the negotiations and then the filming of the multiple interviews David Frost did with Richard Nixon that were then shown on television in the late 1970s. The movie presents each individual with his own quirks and reasons for doing the interview: Frost is spending his own money in hopes of elevating his name, while Nixon wants to do it to clear his own. As time goes on, the interviews become more of a cat-and-mouse game, with Nixon outmaneuvering the too cautious Frost, who slowly begins to agree with his researchers that Nixon needs to come clean about doing something illegal. It's an excellent film, with both actors in fine form, as could be expected for actors who played the roles for a time onstage before filming. Langella, who is not a name that instantly jumps to mind when thinking of someone to play Nixon, is convincing, as is Sheen's chameleon work in the role of Frost. The depiction of the interview is not quite accurate, however, and leans a bit too much into looking as if Nixon confesses to crimes, when the actual interview is a bit more along the lines of Nixon admitting that he set himself up for people to accuse him of crimes and allowed his own downfall, but overall the film makes for a diverting and ultimately sympathetic look at Nixon in the years after his presidency.

We return to comedy in the next film, *Black Dynamite* (2009). The movie is directed by Scott Sanders and written by Michael Jai White, Sanders, and Byron Minns. White stars in a parody of Blaxploitation movies of the early 1970s as Black Dynamite, a former CIA operative who works the streets to clean them up. Black Dynamite and his friends discover that there is a government project to emasculate Black men with a tainted malt liquor named Anaconda. Black Dynamite discovers that Nixon (James McManus) is behind the operation, and they have a kung-fu battle, with Nixon ready to win, only for the ghost of Abraham Lincoln (Pete Antico) to stop him, leading Black Dynamite to victory and Pat Nixon (Nicole Sullivan) falling in love with him. It's a savagely funny movie but hardly one that can be said to treat Nixon with any respect.

After that, the appearances of Nixon are less about understanding the man and more about setting up a timeline by showing us a famous president from the period. Robert Wisden appears as Nixon in *Watchmen* (2009), where he gets a third term in the corrupt world of superheroes (he is heard getting a fifth term in *Back to the Future II*), while John H. Tobin decides to keep the location of "the Ark" secret when the crew of Apollo 11 find it on the Moon in *Transformers: Dark of the Moon* (2011). Mark Camacho plays Nixon in the 2014 movie *X-Men: Days of Future Past*, where it is 1973, and Nixon is announcing the Sentinels, giant robots created to capture mutants in a world where Magneto assassinated John F. Kennedy. On a more serious side, John Cusack appears in *The Butler* (2013) for a few minutes as Nixon, although there is little done to suggest that he is Nixon. Finally, there is a jokey moment where the protagonist helps set up Nixon (Darrell Duffey) meeting Leonid Brezhnev in *The 101-Year-Old Man Who Skipped Out on the Bill and Disappeared* (2016).

But the lasting impression of Nixon is one that comes from a movie not showing anyone playing Nixon at all—*All the President's Men*. A 1974 book with the same title by Bernstein and Woodward details their investigation into the Watergate scandal. Robert Redford, who had been out promoting *The Candidate* in 1972 (covered in chapter 2), became interested in the investigation and bought the film rights to the book in 1974. William Goldman (*The Princess Bride, Good Will Hunting, Absolute Power*) wrote the script, with Alan J. Pakula directing. The focus of the movie details more about the Watergate break-in than covered in the book, up through Nixon accepting his second term and the story breaking. Robert Redford plays Bob Woodward, and Dustin Hoffman plays Carl Bernstein, and the movie follows their investigation, which involves interviews with several people who provide information to help or deter Woodward and Bernstein's work (much like how *JFK* is structured several years later) and a sense of growing paranoia as they close in on the story.

The movie was a blockbuster at the theaters and won two Academy Awards. As a critical success, it is listed in multiple "top 100" lists with the American Film Institute and also set up a renaissance in movies dealing with newspaper investigations that were so popular in the 1930s as well as the premise for the popular *Lou Grant* series of the late 1970s and early 1980s. Nixon is nowhere to be found in the movie, besides some archival footage, but the movie has everything to do with our growing dissatisfaction with government and how it can corrupt.

The major takeaway from Nixon's run as president in the movies is that the most powerful person in the country uses his position for his own personal satisfaction. Nixon, of course, rationalized (as he is seen doing in *Frost/Nixon*) that it was done for the betterment of the country, but incidents like Watergate had no better benefactors than himself, his campaign, and his cronies. The heroes of the 1970s were not Nixon or the presidents that followed but the press members who discovered the story, like Bob Woodward and Carl Bernstein, at least at the time. By the time we get to *Dick* in 1999, Woodward and Bernstein were considered as much of a joke as Nixon (and portrayed that way), along with pretty much everything else we hold dear. The presidents before Nixon could have been shown as wrong, weak, and even temperamental, but now we had one who was willing to do something wrong for his own self-interest. It was personal. It was human. And it would change our perception of the presidency forever after that.

Gerald Ford (1913–2006) became the thirty-eighth president of the United States on August 9, 1974, after the resignation of Richard Nixon. Ford had been Nixon's vice president for less than a year, when Spiro Agnew resigned due to the bribery charges he was facing at the time. His ascent to the presidency happened so quickly that he never got a chance to live in the house used for the vice president. Ford had served in the navy and then was in the House of Representatives from 1949 to 1973 and even served on the Warren Commission that investigated the Kennedy assassination. Ford became known as pro-choice when it came to abortion (although he saw it as a state rather than a federal issue), and he was in favor of the Equal Rights Amendment. He also allowed amnesty for American draft dodgers of the Vietnam War, with conditions. He tried to promote restrictions on spending by the public with a campaign called WIN (Whip Inflation Now) to help stop inflation of the 1970s. He was also known for once tripping while exiting Air Force One, leading to comedian Chevy Chase spoofing him on *Saturday Night Live* as an incredibly clumsy man. Yet he is most remembered for his first action in office, which was to pardon Nixon of any crimes he may have committed. Ford's take was that the country has been through enough with the Watergate scandal, and to drag it out any further with additional criminal proceedings against Nixon would hurt the nation. It was not a notion that many agreed with, as Ford's action said it was okay for someone like the president to get away with a criminal act without ramification. As likable as President Ford seemed to be, he damaged the reputation of the presidency by doing this. In other words, he was remembered as the man who saved Nixon instead of us.

Jimmy Carter was born in Plains, Georgia, in 1924 and served in the US Navy until 1953, when he came back to take care of his father's peanut business. From 1963 through 1967, he was a state senator and then became governor of Georgia from 1971 through 1975. He was elected the thirty-ninth president in 1976, defeating Gerald Ford and immediately pardoning all Vietnam War draft evaders. Carter dealt with inflation and other forms of economic turmoil, along with a fuel crisis that saw many gas stations able to sell gas only on alternating days of the week. Carter turned to the public to ask them to conserve and do things to help the nation. The Iran hostage crisis occurred during his time in office, as well, with American hostages being held in Iran after the shah left the country for the installation of the radical Ayatollah Khomeini as a leader. An attempt to save the hostages failed when a helicopter crashed early in the mission. Carter was an honest man who called it straight by maintaining that we needed to help ourselves as a nation and protect the planet. We needed to be adults. And we took that advice and told him to get lost by removing him from office in 1980. We wanted a savior, not a lecture.

Considered a great humanitarian, if not a good president, Jimmy Carter has managed to avoid being seen in theatrical movies beyond a brief gag in the film *An American Carol* (2008). In that movie, Fred Travelena plays Carter in a gross parody of the man who looks and sounds nothing like him. He is depicted as weak in a "future America" where he is willing to surrender the country to pretty much anyone who asks (counter to the man who authorized an attempt to save hostages and worked to bring peace in the Middle East). That one film is more than earned by Gerald Ford, however, who has yet to appear as a character in any theatrical film (although he pops up as himself in an episode of *Dynasty* in 1983).

Ronald Reagan (1911–2004) moved to California in his midtwenties to become a movie star and ended up getting minor roles in many films, along with a few starring roles, thanks to work in such movies as *Knute Rockne, All American* (1940) and *Kings Row* (1942). Reagan, as the president of the Screen Actors Guild, also went in front of the HUAC to discuss communism in Hollywood, although he was tepid in giving names or suggesting that anyone claiming to be a communist should be restricted by the government. His career as an actor with a limited range (which he acknowledged himself) could be hit or miss, and for every *Santa Fe Trail*, there would be a *Bedtime for Bonzo* soon enough. Reagan found additional work in television in the 1950s, hosting the *General Electric Theater*, which lasted for ten seasons on the networks.

He became interested in politics in 1964 after campaigning for Barry Goldwater and then ran for governor of California in 1966 and remained there until 1975. He then ran for president in 1980 with the platform of "Make America Great Again" and moved away from Carter's concerns about responsibility. He looked to cut taxes as part of a "trickle-down economics" theory that years later was determined to be ineffectual and cut government programs in what he saw as waste. Reagan pushed for a War on Drugs that spent a lot of money with questionable results, while his detractors found him slow to take up the issue of AIDS in America as well as Apartheid. The Iran-Contra deal, which set up selling arms to Iran to secretly finance rebels in Nicaragua (funding that Congress had forbidden), for which Reagan would plead ignorance, did little to help his reputation.

Even though he was seen as a movie star, Reagan's legacy has had little spotlight beyond a television miniseries from 2003, *The Reagans*, with James Brolin as Reagan, and a movie from 2001 with Richard Crenna as Reagan depicting John Hinckley Jr.'s attempt to assassinate him in 1981. A theatrical movie about Reagan, entitled *Reagan* and starring Dennis Quaid as the former president has been filmed, although it is still not released as of 2022. It will focus on his work to dismantle the Soviet Union, but many historians claim that the Soviet Union was well on its way even without Reagan's involvement.

George H. W. Bush (1924–2018) had a bigger success in the movies than Ford, Carter, and even Reagan over the years, being seen in three movies, although not always in the most flattering light. Bush was born in Greenwich, Connecticut, and served in the US Navy during World War II. He worked in oil in Texas until 1967, when he joined the House of Representatives, until 1971, when he was named ambassador to the United Nations by Richard Nixon. Bush moved to be a liaison to the

People's Republic of China and then the director of the CIA under Gerald Ford. When Reagan ran for the presidency in 1980, he named Bush his vice president, and Bush remained in that role until winning the 1988 election for the presidency himself.

Bush's time in office mainly focused on the Gulf War, which was started when Iraqi leader Saddam Hussein invaded Kuwait. Bush worked with the United Nations to push Hussein's forces out and in-state a ceasefire. The war was over seven months later. Bush helped set up the North American Free Trade Agreement (NAFTA) with Canada and Mexico and introduced the Americans with Disabilities Act of 1990 that set up requirements for employers to help employees needing assistance due to various disabilities. While seen as having a successful run as president, some felt he was a bit out of touch and was sometimes pushed to more conservative views by members of his cabinet than by his own analysis of issues. After he left office in 1992, he became a bit more outspoken with the press and with his fellow Republicans.

His son George W. Bush (born 1946) had a variety of jobs, including co-owning the Texas Rangers baseball team, when he was elected governor of Texas in 1990. His election in 2000 for the presidency was problematic due to an issue over the voting cards used in Florida, which led to questions about who really won in the state that would decide the presidency. A Supreme Court decision stopped a recount in Florida and gave the results to Bush, allowing him to win, even though he had fewer total votes than his opponent, Al Gore. Bush served two terms and initiated wars in Iraq and Afghanistan that would prove to be counterproductive to the nation and resulted in false accusations of Iraq having "weapons of mass destruction" to force the war. The country went into a recession during his time, and he left office in 2009, seen as being ineffectual and commonly referring to his vice president, Dick Cheney, to implement work for him.

Bush Sr. first popped up as a character while he was still president in the comedy *The Naked Gun 2½: The Smell of Fear*, directed and written by David Zucker of *Airplane!* fame and *An American Carol*. Bush (John Roarke) is seen twice, along with the First Lady, Barbara (Margery Ross). The first time is at the beginning of the film, when the protagonist, Frank Drebin (Leslie Nielsen), is being given an award by the president, but Drebin keeps absentmindedly doing things that end up hurting Barbara Bush, including sending her flying. The end of the movie has Drebin once again being commended by President Bush, with Drebin accidentally kissing Barbara Bush while giving a speech and then knocking her off a balcony and ripping off her dress in trying to save her. Although there's some roughhousing with Barbara, she is not actually hurt, and it is certainly an innocent use of the Bushes in the film.

The next appearance is in one movie featuring a characterization of Bush's son and later president, George W. Bush, in the Oliver Stone movie *W.* (2008). James Cromwell (*The Sum of All Fears*) plays George H. W. Bush to Josh Brolin's George W. Bush. The movie follows George W. Bush's career leading up to his becoming governor of Texas in 1995 and then president in 2000. Looking to take up where he feels his father left off with Saddam Hussein, George W. Bush invades Iraq and appears with the "Mission Accomplished" sign (discussed in chapter 2), but events soon play out with Iraq not having "weapons of mass destruction" and a war that some saw as not needed and hurting America's reputation just so Bush would deal with his daddy issues (it's an Oliver Stone movie, after all). George W. Bush is presented as a man way out of his league but trying hard to do what is right, while George H. W. Bush is seen as a man who has little hope for his son, even after he becomes president.

Bush's final appearance in films came with the 2018 movie *Vice*, written and directed by Adam McKay (*Don't Look Up*). The movie deals with the career of Dick Cheney (Christian Bale), the vice president under George W. Bush (Sam Rockwell), and stars John Hillner as George H. W. Bush. The film suggests that George W. Bush essentially handed over power to Cheney, allowing him to run the country while he did little but look presidential. If *W.* is not seen as overly sentimental about Bush, then *Vice* expresses clear anger over the Bushes and what occurred during their time in office.

Between the two Bushes was the presidency of Bill Clinton (born 1946), who has been discussed in chapter 2, about the film *Primary Colors*. Born in Hope, Arkansas, Bill met John F. Kennedy when he was a teenager in 1963, which inspired him to consider politics later in his career. He met Hillary Rodham in the Yale Law Library in 1971, and they married in 1975. He became the attorney general of Arkansas in 1976 and then governor of the state in 1979 through 1981 and again in 1983 through 1992. Although facing scandal in 1992 over rumors of an affair with Gennifer Flowers, Clinton ended up being elected to the presidency that year, becoming the forty-second president of the United States. He saw a decline in the abortion rate and a decrease in the deficit, worked to fight global warming, and presided over a mostly harmonious eight years for the country, although his attempt to pass health care did not occur. His time was rocked by an impeachment trial that mainly had to do with his insistence that he did not have sexual relations with an intern during defense of a sexual harassment lawsuit filed against him by a woman named Paula Jones. When he admitted to lying about the relationship, Congress commenced with an impeachment trial for perjury. It ultimately failed.

Clinton left office in 2000 with a divisive history among voters, who either see his work as progressive and helpful to the country or do not (which, honestly, is hardly different from most other presidents over the years). Beyond *Primary Colors*, which is only a flimsy representation of the Clintons, there isn't much of Clinton in the movies beyond manipulated footage of him meeting aliens in the 1997 movie *Contact*.

After George W. Bush, film appearances by the three remaining presidents are slim, as there simply has not been enough time since their elections for Hollywood to want to do anything with them as characters. Barack Obama (born 1961) was an attorney who taught constitutional law at the University of Chicago while also representing the thirteenth district in Illinois until 2004, when he ran for the US Senate. He achieved national visibility when he spoke at the Democratic National Convention in 2004, which arguably led to him winning the nomination in 2008. He beat John McCain in a race that saw McCain add Sarah Palin as his vice-presidential pick, which many saw as detrimental to his run (and is covered in the HBO film *Game Change* from 2012). Obama got the Affordable Care Act (ACA) passed while in office, had mixed results with LGBTQ rights, and saw a drop in unemployment and a better economy during his eight years in office. Two movies have been made about Obama, both in 2016 and both with a young Obama dealing with relationship issues. The first is *Southside with You*, written and directed by Richard Tanne and starring Parker Sawyers as Barack. It includes his meeting Michelle Robinson (Tika Sumpter) and their growing relationship that would eventually lead to their marriage. The other movie is *Barry*, starring Devon Terrell as Obama, written by Adam Mansbach, and directed by Vikram Gandhi. The movie deals with Obama as a college student struggling to find his place in the world. Both are minor movies that sweetly cover events from Obama's life, but ultimately they could be about anyone's life and really do not represent stories defined as only Obama's.

The forty-fifth president was Donald Trump (born 1946), a businessman who had enough media exposure through television (like his reality show series *The Apprentice*) that he eventually decided to run for office in 2016. Surprising many, he was elected and remained president for four years, although he faced two impeachments and many scandals while withdrawing the United States from a series of foreign policies and dealing with COVID-19 pandemic. Trump's media past makes for a small number of movies where he has appeared, such as *Zoolander* and *Home Alone 2*, almost always as himself. Yet for dramatic films that portray Trump as a character, whether as president or otherwise, there has been little interest so far.

Joe Biden (born 1942), the forty-sixth president, was elected in 2020, after having served eight years as vice president for Barak Obama. Initially a liberal Republican, Biden eventually became an independent before finally becoming a Democrat in 1969. From being one of the youngest senators ever elected at the age of twenty-nine in 1972, he became the oldest person ever elected to the presidency at the age of seventy-seven. Biden's presidency also broke a couple of other barriers, with his vice-presidential pick of Kamala Harris, making her the first woman and first person of color to be elected to the position. Biden has had a personal and professional life that could easily transfer to the silver screen, but as with Trump, it simply hasn't happened.

But give him and Trump time. For better or worse, there are bound to be stories yet to be told that will make them of interest to Hollywood in the future, as it has for nearly all those presidents who have come before them.

And speaking of the future . . .

# GABRIEL OVER THE WHITE HOUSE

## The Once and Future President

Men live by pride, and the predominantly White population of this country is mortified by the fact that their beautiful land and their beautiful lives are being run by a person who is—they have been brought up to believe—so shockingly their inferior, by a person whom one and all think they are superior to, and whom consequently they cannot respect, and whom they cannot have pride in before each other and the world at large.

—Nat Abrahams in *The Man* (1964)

It's sometime in the future. The Japanese have invaded the United States, and George Primrose, a recent graduate of West Point, is sent to fight the enemy and given a dispatch to deliver to his brother, who is now president of the United States. Losing his horse in the Everglades and wounded in battle with the Japanese, George is happened upon by a classmate from West Point who despises him. The man, Denison, steals the dispatch and delivers it, claiming George deserted. When George's fiancée discovers a bloody thumbprint on the dispatch that matches George's, she races to the Capitol to tell the president. President Primrose, in proper praeses ex machina fashion, stops George's execution just in time.

That's the plot of a movie from 1913, *The Sons of a Soldier*. It's possibly the earliest film to feature a fictional president of the country as well as a small moment with Fred Truesdale as Woodrow Wilson. It's also a tale set in the future (as much of the future as could be expected from a movie filmed in 1913), with thoughts of invasion from another country and America fighting to be free. As we grew more accustomed to elements of fantasy and science fiction in the movies, most of our invasion movies would be based on aliens from other worlds, but *The Sons of a Soldier* was there first with an invasion from another country. And even in that world where we have been invaded but still use horses for transportation, we saw a president who would save us.

We still expected it in 1996, when the Roland Emmerich film *Independence Day* was released (another of his films with the White House being destroyed; see also *The Day after Tomorrow*, *2012*, and *White House Down*). In the movie, President Thomas Whitmore (Bill Pullman), a former fighter pilot (allowing him to take an active part in saving the planet, carrying on in the tradition of the classic action president), rallies the nations against the aliens attacking with a speech about how we will take back the Earth. He is cool and reassuring, even after the death of the First Lady (Mary McDonnell), and leads a squadron of planes against one of the main alien ships set to destroy everyone. In the film, the squadron and everyone else is saved by a deranged pilot played by Randy Quaid (*LBJ: The Early Years*), claiming to be abducted by aliens years before, who sobers up and rams his jet into the ship's main weapon, allowing the others to destroy the aliens and giving them all a means to win the war. And although the crazed man sacrifices himself to win the war, we still look to President Whitmore as the man who inspired everyone to turn the tide and beat the aliens.

*Gabriel over the White House* is commonly seen as the first movie to feature a fictional president, although we know for sure that was not the case, thanks to *The Sons of a Soldier*. The film, discussed in some detail in chapter 7, has Walter Huston as President Judd Hammond, a self-indulgent do-nothing who, after a car crash, is transformed into a new, serious individual who works to change the nation for the better, as if guided by a heavenly hand. With the help of the nation behind him, Hammond transforms the country and brings about world peace but at a price: He eliminates Congress and creates a dictatorship for the country, with firing squad set up to immediately deal with those who oppose him. Nevertheless, the film was an inspiration for many, including Frankling Delano Roosevelt, as we looked for any salvation from the Depression of the early 1930s and hoped to find someone to guide us, like Hammond. After his turn in *Gabriel over the White House*, it was no surprise to see Walter Huston return as another hero president of the United States in the 1935 movie *The Tunnel* (also known as *The Trans-Atlantic Tunnel*). Although he does little beyond looking at maps and nodding, Huston's president oversees the development of a fantastic tunnel under the ocean between Britain and the United States.

At least Huston's presidents saw the world with positive progress. The year 1964 saw two movies dealing with nuclear annihilation and a president trying to calmly deal with the crisis: *Dr. Strangelove or: How I Learned to Stop Worrying and Love the Bomb* and *Fail Safe*. In *Dr. Strangelove*, General Jack D. Ripper (Sterling Hayden) deliberately

**A heavenly glow engulfs President Hammond (Walter Huston) in *Gabriel over the White House* (1933). *Official press still, author's collection, © 1933 by MGM Studios.***

sends jets to drop nuclear bombs on Moscow on orders that cannot be countermanded by anyone once he has sent the planes off. President Merkin Muffley (Peter Sellers, looking like a cross between Adlai Stevenson and Dwight Eisenhower) is amazed at the complicated plans that had been hidden from him, including the Soviets' secret doomsday device that will be activated once the bombs drop, killing everyone on the planet. Even with all that, he perseveres in trying to figure out a way to stop the jets and then talks to the Soviet leader by phone calmly, even as the Soviet leader goes into hysterics. Muffley may be a bit too sedate, but his actions do speak as if he is trying to do the sane thing in a very insane situation. He may ultimately be ineffectual, but at least he's trying the best anyone could under the circumstances.

Henry Fonda also plays a calm president in *Fail Safe*, where jets with the bombs are accidentally sent to nuke Moscow, and many try to do what they can to stop them. The president is pressured to go ahead with a full attack because the bombs will probably not be stopped, but

**Peter Sellers as President Merkin Muffley, one of the few voices of reason in Stanley Kubrick's *Dr. Strangelove or: How I Learned to Stop Worrying and Love the Bomb* (1964). *Courtesy of PhotoFest.***

**The president (Henry Fonda) tries to make a deal at a desperate moment in** Fail Safe **(1964).** *Official press still, author's collection, © 1964 by Columbia Pictures.*

he realizes that it will only escalate into an all-out war that no one will survive. Instead, he makes the decision that if the bomb does drop, then he will have a plane drop an equivalent bomb on New York as the one hitting Moscow. It's a terrible decision to make, killing millions, but one that must be done to stop retaliation that will end the world. And as mentioned in the introduction to this book, we accept it, as we see Fonda's president as the voice of reason in an unreasonable situation.

Nuclear war is also discussed in the 2000 film *Deterrent*, with Kevin Pollak as President Walter Emerson. The movie has the president stuck in a diner during a snowstorm, when he is presented with news that Iraq has invaded Kuwait. From the diner, the president demands Iraq withdrawal from Kuwait, or he will have Baghdad hit with a nuclear weapon. Iraq threatens to retaliate against the United States with their own black-market nuclear weapons. The film thus sets up debate between the people in the diner over using nuclear weapons to resolve issues but then entirely backs off the consequences of such a dilemma when it is revealed that the president knew all along that Iraq's weapons are duds. It's the type of last-minute cheat that allows for all the debate brought up by the film to be ignored thanks to a "magic reset button" allowing the "good guys" to win and working against the movie (and undoubtedly many innocent dead in another country because of the president's actions, but we're not really supposed to focus on that part).

Future presidents kicking off wrong decisions began popping up in movies by the late 1960s. Case in point: *Wild in the Streets* (1968) stars Hal Holbrook as Johnny Fergus, a senator running for president who agrees to have a rock band work with him to win the presidency. Their efforts help, but it leads to members of the band becoming part of Congress and their leader, Max Frost (Christopher Jones), becoming the new president instead. Due to this, the voting age is lowered to fourteen, and everyone over the age of thirty is forced to retire, while those over thirty-five are sent to concentration camps, where they are drugged to keep them pacified. This advances to a worldwide revolution, and Frost seems to be in a powerful position, but soon, kids under ten are looking at Max at the age of twenty-four as being too old, and a new revolution is around the corner. It's a silly movie, but it does show how power put into the wrong hands, even for possible good reasons, can have even worse consequences down the road.

Such as in *Escape from the Planet of the Apes* (1971). The movie was the third in the five-film series about a future Earth where apes rule over a subservient human race. The second movie, *Beneath the Planet of the Apes* (1970), ends with the world blown up by a doomsday device triggered by a human. However, before the world ends, three chimpanzees from the future, Cornelius (Roddy McDowall), Zira (Kim Hunter), and Dr. Milo (Sal Mineo), manage to repair a human spaceship left behind and find themselves via time warp back on Earth in 1973. The chimpanzees are at first seen as an oddity who create a media blitz, but when it turns out that Zira is pregnant and that their stories of a future war between intelligent apes and humans leading to mass destruction are feasible, the president (William Windom) is advised to have Zira abort her baby and have the pair sterilized to negate the history to come. Finding out what is to occur, Cornelius and Zira try to escape, only to be killed, but not before Zira gives birth, and their child escapes with a circus, starting the war that comes in the fourth film of the series, *Conquest of the Planet of the Apes* (1972), and leading to the very future the humans were trying to avoid.

At least the president in *Escape from the Planet of the Apes* is trying to do what is right, even though it triggers events that will ultimately doom humankind. That's better than in the comedy *The Werewolf of Washington* (1973), written and directed by Milton Moses Ginsberg and featuring Dean Stockwell as the press secretary for the president (Biff McGuire). The press secretary is bitten by a werewolf and becomes one himself, attacking political enemies of the president. The president, however, remains woefully ignorant of the attacks, even when he can see that something is wrong with the secretary. Eventually, the secretary turns on a plane in front of the president and the Chinese prime minister. The movie ends with the secretary being killed after attacking the president, and as per werewolf legend, the president can be heard giving a speech to the nation over the ending credit, only to slowly turn into a werewolf as he speaks, and finally howling. In a way, the president gets what he deserves for ignoring the dangers around him (and thus perhaps we do as a nation, as well).

*Death Race 2000* (1975) has the American government setting up a televised cross-country motor race that involves the drivers hitting pedestrians for points and trying to eliminate each other in the process.

The best known of the drivers is Frankenstein (David Carradine), who supposedly has been in so many accidents that his body is made up of parts. It turns out that several men have been trained to play Franken- stein, and if one is killed, they are merely replaced. There are rebels trying to stop the race, but Frankenstein wants to win so he will be awarded by the president and thus get close enough to assassinate him. By the end of the film, Frankenstein fulfills his dream by ramming the stage and killing the president with his car, allowing him to become the new president of the United States and declare an end to the totalitarian society and the violence. He allows himself to hit one more pedestrian, though, before it is all over. Still, even as a homicidal race-car driver, the president is looking out for us.

By 1979 (after Nixon, Ford, and Carter), our perception of the presi- dent begins to change. In *Americathon* (1979), directed by Neal Israel and written by him with Phil Proctor, Peter Bergman, Michael Mislove, and Monica Johnson, the country is out of money and desperate to pay back loans given to the government by a Native American billionaire (it also mentions the country lynching Jimmy Carter after he announced that people needed to cut back on fuel to help save the country). The president in the future is Chet Roosevelt (John Ritter), a chipper, soft- spoken young guy who is a combination of Ford and Carter but without the brains of either. Even though not very intelligent and easily con- fused, the president agrees to the idea of a telethon to cover the money, leading to a series of skits that play out in the film as part of the telethon, which ends up saving the country. The movies may have been starting to readjust their attitude about the presidency, but even a dull-witted president can still save the day.

The president soon shows his limits in the movies as we get into the 1980s. E. G. Marshall plays the president in *Superman II*, where he finds himself at the mercy of General Zod and his cronies from the Phantom Zone. He surrenders the planet, leaving Clark Kent, who had given up his powers, to find a way to return as Superman and save the world. Glenn Ford, as the president, stops a nuclear device from be- ing detonated against the enemy as long as he survives in the Japanese horror-action film *Virus* (1980). After his death from the virus, a de- ranged general (Henry Silva) activates the device, showing the limits of the president. It is then up to a group of survivors of the plague to reach the device and try to stop it in time. Meanwhile, *The Dead Zone* (1983) has Christopher Walken's character realize that a candidate for Senate, Greg Stillson (Martin Sheen), is a madman who will eventually destroy the planet in his paranoia once he becomes president.

In *Whoops Apocalypse* (1986), Loretta Swit plays Barbara Adams, the first female president, who is trying to stop World War III starting in several other countries. She's not very good at her job, and her husband helps start the whole thing so he can sell weapons. This is still more presidential than the television miniseries of *Whoops Apocalypse* (1982), where President Cyclops (Barry Morse, as a variation of Reagan) accidentally ends up starting World War III through product placement.

The 1984 movie *Dreamscape* has the president (Eddie Albert) dealing with recurring nightmares of a nuclear holocaust, which the villain (Christopher Plummer) sees as a weakness for a president and decides to have him killed. To do this, the villain finds a way for psychics to enter dreams and kill the people in their sleep (a Freddy Kruger move before there was a Freddy Kruger). Dennis Quaid plays a psychic who sets out to enter the president's dream to protect him, although the president actually saves himself in the process, making him an action president in the end.

In *The Puppet Masters* (1994), the president (Tom Mason) is also saved by agents from aliens who take over the body of people. The president (Jack Nicholson) isn't so lucky in *Mars Attacks* (1996), however, as the Martians finally meet up with him in the bunkers of the White House. At least the president gets to berate them for a time, although he is suckered into shaking hands with the head Martian, thus trapping the president into being killed by a fake hand that turns into a flagpole for the Martians' flag, which skewers him. Yet there is no other resolution for the president in *Mars Attacks*, who shows himself to be completely ineffectual and with a staff who readily allow the aliens to waltz into the White House.

*Deep Impact* has the return of Morgan Freeman as the president, only this time all he can do is try to alert the world about a comet that will crash into the Earth. President Beck, however, is forward thinking and with other leaders starts working on trying to destroy the comet in the year they have left before impact sends hundreds of thousands of people into underground shelters. Through the actions of the president and other leaders, the planet is saved, and only a small portion of the comet hits, leading to destruction and multiple deaths but nothing like the mass extinction promised when the comet was discovered.

The Earth faces similar destruction in Roland Emmerich's *2012*, with Danny Glover as the president. In this case, an issue with the Earth's core is rapidly changing the crust, leading to mass destruction, but the president and others have arks built to hold hundreds of thousands of people. The film then plays out as a group tries to make their way to the arks in time, while the president stays at the White House to help those left behind. The White House is again destroyed, albeit this time in a natural event. At least in the 1979 movie *Meteor*, which features Henry Fonda as the president (whose time is spent mainly listening to reports and negotiating with the Soviets to try to stop a meteor from destroying the world), it's just New York that gets wiped out instead of most of the world.

Horror creeps into the story of the presidents as the movies move into the 2000s, with two of them dealing with the end times as suggested by Revelation in the Bible. In the case of *Megiddo: The Omega Code 2*, the antichrist persuades the president (R. Lee Ermey) to join in the one-world government that is supposed to be part of the coming apocalypse. When the president gets too wise to the situation, the antichrist kills him and replaces him with the vice president (Michael Biehn), who spends the rest of the film fighting off the antichrist until the arrival of Jesus and the defeat of Satan. In a way, one could say it's an example of the accidental president once again doing the right thing when the time comes. In *Left Behind: World at War* (2005), the president (Louis Gossett Jr.) and the vice president (Charles Martin Smith) are aware of the antichrist's plans, but the vice president is killed before they can do anything. In the end, the president becomes a Christian before he destroys himself and a base for the Antichrist, ending what was supposed to be a continuing film series. That at least allows the president to be on the side of the angels, unlike the president seen in *The Omen* (1976 and its 2006 remake), where it appears he will be directly involved with the raising of the antichrist at the end of the film.

Odder horror comes in *Bubba Ho-Tep* (2002), directed and written by Don Coscarelli. The movie deals with a man who may or may not be Elvis Presley (Bruce Campbell) living in a nursing home. The man has a friend who may or may not be John F. Kennedy (Ossie Davis), who survived the assassination attempt, only to be given Black skin and left in the home by Lyndon Johnson years before. The pair work together when an Egyptian mummy is reanimated and begins stealing the souls of other residents of the home, while also dealing with the struggles of the lives they left behind before they gave up and started living in the home.

If Kennedy can live to find ancient mummies, then Lincoln can certainly fight vampires, which he does in the 2012 movie *Abraham Lincoln: Vampire Hunter*. Directed by Timur Bekmambetov and written by Seth Grahame-Smith (who wrote the book on which it is based), the movie has Benjamin Walker as Lincoln, who not only has his political career and deals with the Civil War but fights vampires, as well. It's a silly idea, but there's heart behind the concept and an attempt to make it work while still allowing us a president set to do the right thing. It certainly works better than the Asylum film, *Abraham Lincoln vs. Zombies* (2012), with Bill Oberst Jr. as Lincoln in what is a second-tier version of the *Vampire Hunter* movie that came out the same year.

The president becomes dimmer but goes on the attack in a handful of invasion films, with Stephen Colbert as the president in the animated film *Monsters vs. Aliens* (2009), Kevin James as an obnoxious president in *Pixels* (2015), and Mark Cuban as the president fighting flying sharks in *Sharknado 3: Oh Hell No!* (2015). Ironically, as reported by the *Hollywood Reporter*, Donald Trump was set to play the president in *Sharknado 3* but delayed his answer until the producers went with Mark Cuban. Then Trump threatened to sue when he lost the job.

The president not only becomes less mentally sharp but also begins to show diminishing returns over time. In *Iron Sky* (2012), a Sarah Palin–like president (Stephanie Paul) refuses to deal with Nazis from the moon, and in *Don't Look Up* (2021), Janie Orlean, a Sarah Palin–like president (Meryl Streep), refuses to deal with a comet threatening to destroy all life on Earth, exactly like in *Deep Impact* (only everyone dies instead). It wasn't really that funny of a joke the first time around. The HBO film *Superintelligence* (2020) also has a rather dimwitted female president (not to suggest that a female president would be dumb, but these films ended up with such a character). In the movie, an artificial intelligence plans to wipe out the human race, and the government works to deal with the threat by eliminating all electronics that the AI can enter as they discuss their plans. As it turns out, the president (Jean Smart) still has her Blackberry running, assuming no one uses one anymore, so she should be safe. Fortunately for her, the only person who can talk to the AI, Carol (Melissa McCarthy), has calmed the AI down by that point, and the danger is stopped.

And then there is *Idiocracy* (2006). Made by Mike Judge and cowritten by him and Elan Cohen, the movie deals with a man from the twenty-first century, Joe (Luke Wilson), with average intelligence, waking up in the twenty-sixth century to find that the world has become so dumbed down that he and another survivor from the twenty-first century, Rita (Maya Rudolph), are the smartest people on Earth. Everything is based on a commercial product, and spelling is all phonetic in nature. When an IQ test shows that Joe is the smartest person on Earth, he is taken to the White House, where he meets President Dwayne Elizondo Mountain Dew Herbert Camacho (Terry Crews), a pumped-up wrestler-style idiot who demands Joe figure out why crops are no longer growing and destroying the economy. Joe discovers that people are using what is essentially cola on the crops, which kills the vegetation.

**Future president Comacho (Terry Crews) and future-future president Not Sure (Luke Wilson) from *Idiocracy* (2006). *Courtesy of PhotoFest.***

He uses water instead, which of course shows no immediate results and send sales of the cola plummeting, hurting the economy even more. Figuring that Joe has destroyed everything, the president sends Joe out to be killed in a monster truck demolition. Fortunately for Joe, Rita can prove the water solution to be correct, as crops begin sprouting, saving everyone. The president realizes his mistake and gives Joe a pardon. Joe eventually is elected president and begins running things as best he can, while the world continues to get dumber anyway.

The movie has a depressing message that the world will continue to get dumber as the dimmest of us continue to breed, just creating more of the same. But there's still a nobility in the human spirit to be found in *Idiocracy*. President Camacho is an idiot, but when shown he is wrong, he changes his way and admits it, allowing Joe to live and even eventually to see Joe becoming president himself. The president will ultimately do the right thing for us and will guide us, even in this stupid world of *Idiocracy*.

Then 2016 brought *Independence Day: Resurgence*. The sequel to the earlier invasion movie has the world progressing and working together as one, and reverse-engineering of the alien materials left behind has led to advancements in technology. Yet the aliens are not far away, and twenty years after their first attack, they return. Meanwhile former president Whitmore (Bill Pullman again) is having episodes due to a link with the aliens, which he gained in the first movie. Through no intentions of his own, he becomes a wreck and nearly a shell of his former self. The confident president of the first movie in 1996 is now the crazed pilot who Randy Quaid was in the first movie. And in keeping with that, Whitmore ends up sacrificing himself in the second movie to help save humanity, just as the crazy pilot in the first movie did. It took twenty years, but we changed the president from hero to lunatic, and we accept it. He still saves us, but he's damaged at the same time. And for some reason, we're not surprised he is damaged. With the dents caused to our image of the presidency over the past few presidents, we expect the same or worse for those in our movies these days.

**With the world in danger, it needs an action president, and President Thomas Whitmore (Bill Pullman) is the man to do it in** *Independence Day* **(1996).** *Original lobby card, author's collection,* © *1996 by Twentieth Century-Fox Film Corp.*

There's an image of Walter Huston from *Gabriel over the White House* that is often used when describing the film. He sits with his arms folded on a desk and his head up, his face staring up into the light as if receiving divine guidance to help us. It's a powerful photo that speaks to us. We want that image for our president, that strong person who understands us and can be our parent (our Founding Father), like the men Henry Fonda plays in the films discussed, be it Lincoln, the president in *Fail Safe*, or the senator in *The Best Man*. This book examines various cinematic presidents over the years, whether they are action presidents, accidental presidents, messengers, MacGuffins, or the praeses ex machina. Many were real, and plenty are not, but we look to them as if to say, "Here is our voice. He or she will speak for us." We want that person to do us right. We expect that in the movies.

We expect that in real life and perhaps we expect too much in looking for that righteousness. We rejoice when we elect someone to office whom we see as having potential, but then a mistake is made or a crisis unearthed that damages their reputation. It shakes us because we've too often believed stories of these men as perfect beings, which goes back to our preconceived notions of those past presidents since the beginning of the country. Thomas Jefferson told us that "all men are created equal," which we can't reconcile with the man who owned slaves. Andrew Jackson was considered a hero to many after the Battle of New Orleans and a legend for his actions for the "common man," but we can't escape his approval of slavery and his actions against Indigenous people on the Trail of Tears. Lincoln wrote the Emancipation Proclamation, but we have to remember he allowed border states to keep slavery in order to not lose them to the Confederacy. Nixon created the EPA but tangled the government in paranoid crimes like Watergate that hurt the nation. These were all heroes at one time, and some we even still see as such, but we see the wrongs they did, and their images are chipped away. We compare it to what the movies and our limited view of history have taught us to expect, and we cry out, "Where is our Henry Fonda?"

Yet knowing more of our history shows us that if we recognized those presidents as being human rather than gods, then maybe the ones in office now who will sometimes stumble are not really the bad guys either. This chapter starts with a quote from Irving Wallace's book *The Man*, discussed in chapter 2. It is spoken by a character to the first Black president, Douglass Dilman, to explain why people cannot find it in themselves to accept him as president because he doesn't represent what they expect the president to be. One could have easily heard the same misguided sentiment when Barack Obama came into office because of the color of his skin. Yet if one looks past the word *White* in that sentence, then could the same comment not be made about other presidents? Even someone like Donald Trump or Richard Nixon or Bill Clinton, whom so many consider themselves superior to?

The movies are a window into seeing presidents through history and fables. They give us courageous fighters and masterminds as well as our share of villains and damaged souls. We want to believe in them and that they will ultimately do the right thing, and we want to transfer that loftier ideal to our current leaders, as well. But not everyone is Henry Fonda or rather the image of the man we see Fonda play in the movies. And even if we find someone like that, we cannot have him forever.

History has shown us that the presidents have, for the most part, tried to do the right thing for the country, even if sometimes the results did not turn out as hoped or only prolonged issues because those individuals have only the foresight given them at the time. Yet we tend to take the best of them, put that on the silver screen, and make them larger than life, and we fall under the spell that it is how it should be, forgetting the mistakes made along the way. We want to wish the bad things away, like the studios can in a movie, leading us to paint a rosier picture of our present that makes us lash out when critics point out the flaws. After all, we are still facing many of the same problems that Washington, Jefferson, and Adams faced when they first forged the country—we still struggle with how to handle race; federal versus state rights; the economy; and many other issues, just in evolved form. We haven't really changed that much, no matter how much smarter we think we are.

But we've always been a country of make-believe; of hope and renewal. And overall, the movies' mirror of our country and our presidents remain a positive reflection because we as a country *want* to believe. It's even in our Preamble of the Constitution. It doesn't say we formed a perfect union, but rather we will "form a more perfect union." We never said, "okay, one fix and we're done." We knew there would be mistakes along the way—we wrote it right into our most famous document; and we knew it would be a never-ending process to make our union "more perfect." Hollywood, at times, gives us a fun-house reflection of how we are, skewing our self-image at times, but rightly or wrongly, they help us reflect on ourselves. Every so often, by way of all those action, comedy, drama, and even horror films, things can come into focus through that camera lens and tells us something we need to know about our past and our future. We just need to make sure we do not let the gods of Hollywood presidency overtake our understanding of real human spirit of those individuals who led our country. No matter how much we sometimes tearfully wish that fantasy celluloid were true. In doing so and working to create a "more perfect union," we may end up with people to look up to as much as we do our Henry Fondas.

# BIBLIOGRAPHY

Abramovitch, Seth. "How *Sharknado* Casts Its C-Listers and Nearly Landed Trump as President." *Hollywood Reporter*, August 2, 2017. https://www .hollywoodreporter.com/tv/tv-features/how-sharknado-casts-c-listers-landed -trump-as-president-1025676/.

Bumpass, Gita. "Truman Supplied Title for Picture on Atom." *Fort Worth Star-Telegram*, March 14, 1947.

Burstein, Andrew. *The Passions of Andrew Jackson*. New York: Alfred A. Knopf, 2003.

Butler, Robert W. "Was the City of Lights Ever Really This Tedious?" *Kansas City Star*, April 21, 1995.

Byron, Stuart. "I Can't Get Jimmy Carter to See My Movie!" *Film Comment*, March/April 1977.

Cameron, Kate. "*Sunrise* Tells of FDR Battle to Beat Polio." *Daily News* [New York], September 29, 1960.

Collins, Eliza, and Nick Gass. "Trump: Cruz Stole My Policies, Michael Douglas' Line." Politico. March 23, 2016. https://www.politico.com/blogs/2016-gop -primary-live-updates-and-results/2016/03/ted-cruz-wife-trump-221141.

Connolly, Mike. "Gisele Fiddles with Gift from Jack." *Evening Eagle* [Wichita], October 14, 1957.

Considine, Bob. "Cold Weather Forced Russians to Practice Music to Keep Warm." *Knoxville Journal*, February 21, 1947.

Crockett, Davy & Dumas, Alex J. *Col. Crockett's Exploits and Adventures in Texas*. London: R. Kennett, 1837.

Dallek, Robert. *An Unfinished Life: John F. Kennedy*. New York: Bay Back Books, 2003.

Donald, Aida D. *Lion in the White House*. New York: Basic Books, 2007.

Donald, David H. *Lincoln*. London: Simon and Schuster, 1995.

Ebert, Roger. "*Jefferson in Paris* (1995)." RogerEbert.com. April 7, 1995. https://www.rogerebert.com/reviews/jefferson-in-paris-1995.

Ellis, Joseph J. *Founding Brothers: The Revolutionary Generation*. New York: Vintage Books, 2000.

"Escapism Orgy." *Des Moines Tribune*, October 29, 1940.

Fehrman, Craig. "The Mystery Buffs in the White House." *New York Times*, May 23, 2018.

Feller, Daniel. "Andrew Jackson's Shifting Legacy." Gilder Lehrman Institute of American History: AP US History Study Guide. 2014. https://ap.gilderlehrman.org/essay/andrew-jackson%27s-shifting-legacy.

Filsinger, Amy Lynn. "George Washington and the First Mass Military Inoculation." Science Reference Services, Library of Congress. February 12, 2009. https://www.loc.gov/rr/scitech/GW&smallpoxinoculation.html.

Fleming, Thomas. "Andrew Jackson: Leading the Battle of New Orleans." Historynet. Winter 2001. https://www.historynet.com/andrew-jackson-leading-the-battle-of-new-orleans.htm.

Flexner, James Thomas. *Washington: The Indispensable Man*. Boston: Little, Brown, 1969.

Flynn, Hazel. "Terrific Cast Teams with Great Results." *Valley Times* [North Hollywood], March 8, 1947.

Gardner, Eriq. "Australian Political Leader Caught Plagiarizing *The American President*." *Hollywood Reporter*, January 27, 2012. https://www.hollywoodreporter.com/business/business-news/anthony-albanese-austrialia-plagiarism-the-american-president-285277/.

Garner, Jack. "*Jefferson in Paris* Is Big Disappointment." *El Paso Times*, April 21, 1995.

George Washington's Mount Vernon. "Depictions of George Washington On-Screen." 2022. https://www.mountvernon.org/george-washington/pop-culture/#-.

Heath, Roderick, "*Unconquered* (1947)," *This Island Rod*, September 4, 2010, https://thisislandrod.blogspot.com/2010/09/unconquered-1947.html.

Hopper, Hedda. "Hollywood." *Daily News* [New York], February 18, 1946.

———. "Wallace's *The Man* Will Star Poitier." *Los Angeles Times*, March 1, 1965.

Hunt, Kristin. "The Sinatra Movie Some Blamed for JFK's Death." JSTOR Daily. February 27, 2020. https://daily.jstor.org/the-sinatra-movie-some -blamed-for-jfks-death/.

Janik, Erika. "Ask Civics 101: What Is the 25th Amendment?" New Hampshire Public Radio. January 7, 2021. https://www.nhpr.org/politics/2021-01-07/ask -civics-101-what-is-the-25th-amendment?gclid=EAIaIQobChMItcXD877u 9AIVgRvUAR2tDQ7hEAAYASAAEgLZp_D_BwE#stream/0.

Johnson, Erskine. "Criticism of Posture Brings Muscle Mail." *Marshfield News-Herald*, April 11, 1947.

Jordan-Smith, Paul. "New Deal Mystery." *Los Angeles Times*, January 5, 1936.

"Kalem's Achievements as Pioneer." *Moving Picture World* 31, no. 10 (March 10, 1917): 1504–5.

Knebel, Fletcher, and Charles W. Bailey. "Register Men Elated by Movie of Novel." *Des Moines Register*, August 18, 1963.

Kuest, Frank. "Holly Takes OWI Censor Advice as Helpful Gesture." *Poughkeepsie Journal*, March 12, 1943.

"Life of Abraham Lincoln." *Moving Picture World* 3 (July–December 1908): 298.

Lyons, Leonard. "The Lyons Den." *Montgomery Advertiser*, March 25, 1943.

Mallon, Thomas. "*Advise and Consent* at 50." *New York Times*, June 25, 2009. https://www.nytimes.com/2009/06/28/books/review/Mallon2-t.html.

Mankoff, Robert. "Lincoln's Smile." *New Yorker*, November 28, 2012. https:// www.newyorker.com/cartoons/bob-mankoff/lincolns-smile.

Matthews, Chris. *Jack Kennedy: Elusive Hero*. New York: Simon and Schuster, 2011.

McCullough, David. *John Adams*. New York: Simon and Schuster, 2001.

Meacham, Jon. *Thomas Jefferson: The Art of Power*. New York: Random House, 2012.

Mitchell, Greg. *The Beginning or the End*. New York: New Press, 2020.

Monk, Herbert L. "Movie Reviews." *St. Louis Globe-Democrat*, December 19, 1936.

Nugent, Frank S. "A Melodrama of Purpose Is *The President's Mystery* at the Globe–*Cain and Mabel*, at the Stand." *New York Times*, October 19, 1936.

"O.W.I. Suggests Remake to Metro." *Gazette* [Montreal], September 25, 1942.

Parker, Ryan. "Glenn Close Refused *Air Force One* Scene That Made Her Vice President Character Look Weak." *Hollywood Reporter*, November 25, 2020. https://www.hollywoodreporter.com/movies/movie-news/glenn-close -refused-air-force-one-scene-that-made-her-vice-president-character-look -weak-4097539/.

Parker, T. H. "Play about FDR Opens at Shubert." *Harford Courant*, December 27, 1957.

Parson, Louella. "Walter Wanger Collects Actors for His Picture *The President Vanishes*." *San Francisco Examiner*, August 14, 1934.

"Pictures on View This Week." *Indianapolis Star*, December 19, 1926.

Ramsay, Jack C., Jr. *Jean Laffite: Price of Pirates*. Austin, TX: Eakin Press, 1996.

Robb, Inez. "Roosevelts Plan No Action about Book." *News Press* [Fort Myers], September 2, 1968.

Schallert, Edwin. "Schary Obtains Rights to Roosevelt Life Story." *Los Angeles Times*, April 10, 1957.

Shepherd, Jack. *The Adams Chronicles*. Boston: Little, Brown, 1975.

"Shirl Going Straight; Seek Fonda as F.D.R." *Daily News* [New York], July 5, 1957.

Smith, Jean Edward. *FDR*. New York: Random House, 2007.

Soanes, Wood. "Curtin Calls: 'Jimmy' Starts on FDR Biography." *Oakland Tribune*, February 26, 1947.

Soward, F. H. "Week's Assize Find Three Worth More Investigation." *Province* [Vancouver], February 1, 1936.

Stuart, William L. "The Radio Reporter." *Nashville Banner Sun*, November 15, 1936.

Sullivan, Ed. "Little Old New York: Med and Maids, and Stuff." *Daily News* [New York], February 29, 1960.

Sutherland, Henry. "Crying Time Near in Hollywood as Taxes Approach." *Nevada State Journal*, January 21, 1937.

Thirer, Irene. "Sing Sing Wired for Talkies; Deforest System for Prison." *New York Daily News*, August 15, 1929.

Thomas, Bob. "Closeup of FDR, Eleanor Sunday." *Pittsburgh Post-Gazette*, January 6, 1976.

Thomas, Bob. "Movie Truman Earning More than Real One." *Denton Record-Chronicle*, June 21, 1946.

Thomas, Evan. *Being Nixon: A Man Divided*. New York: Random House, 2005.

Trussell, Robert C. "*Kidnapping of President* Is Nail-Biter." *Kansas City Star*, August 24, 1980.

Updegrove, Mark K. *Indomitable Will: LBJ in the Presidency*. New York: Crown, 2012.

"Vitagraph Company: *Washington under the British Flag*." *Moving Picture World* 4, no. 26 (June 26, 1909): 884.

"Washington at Valley Forge." *Star-Gazette* [Elmira], March 12, 1908.

Weinraud, Bernard. "With *Line of Fire*, Writer Discovers Ending for Hollywood-Failure Story." *New York Times*, July 20, 1993.

Whitney, David C. *The American Presidents*. New York: Doubleday, 1967.

Wilson, John M. "Matt Salinger Plays the Waiting Game." *Los Angeles Times*, October 28, 1990.

Wister, Emery. "Show'Nuf, Kathy and Cathy C. Two Different Girls." *Charlotte News*, February 19, 1959.

Zibart, Eve. *"Jefferson in Paris." Washington Post*, April 7, 1995.

# INDEX

Page references for figures are italicized.